# FINANCIAL RECKONING DAY

# FINANCIAL RECKONING DAY

*Memes, Manias, Booms & Busts
Investing in the 21st Century*

3rd Edition

ADDISON WIGGIN

WILEY

Published by John Wiley & Sons, Inc., Hoboken, New Jersey.
Published simultaneously in Canada.

For general information on our other products and services or for technical support, please contact our Customer Care Department within the United States at (800) 762-2974, outside the United States at (317) 572-3993 or fax (317) 572-4002.

Wiley also publishes its books in a variety of electronic formats. Some content that appears in print may not be available in electronic formats. For more information about Wiley products, visit our web site at www.wiley.com.

*Library of Congress Cataloging-in-Publication Data*

Names: Wiggin, Addison, author. | Bonner, William, 1948- Financial reckoning day fallout.
Title: Financial reckoning day : memes, manias, booms & busts ... investing in the 21st century / Addison Wiggin.
Description: Third Edition. | Hoboken, New Jersey : Wiley, [2024] | Revised edition of Financial reckoning day fallout, c2009. | Includes bibliographical references and index.
Identifiers: LCCN 2023032806 (print) | LCCN 2023032807 (ebook) | ISBN 9781394174669 (cloth) | ISBN 9781394201945 (adobe pdf) | ISBN 9781394201952 (epub)
Subjects: LCSH: Financial crises—United States. | Stocks—United States. | Business cycles—United States.
Classification: LCC HB3722 .W54 2024 (print) | LCC HB3722 (ebook) | DDC 330.973—dc23/eng/20230807
LC record available at https://lccn.loc.gov/2023032806
LC ebook record available at https://lccn.loc.gov/2023032807

Cover design: Mark O'Dell
Cover Image: © tomwachs Getty Images

SKY100546880_090723

"Just as in the realm of pugilism, a few years of soft living will make a Dempsey easy prey for a Tunney, so a period of prosperity contains the seeds of its own destruction."

—Philip Carret

# CONTENTS

# FOREWORD

Some people want to buy baseball teams or chase women, but I'm told the number one dream that comes to mind when young people are asked is: "I want to see the world."

I've been around the world twice now: Once on a motorcycle. Once in a Mercedes. So I guess that means I'm crazier than most people.

The reason that I love doing it, other than the sense of adventure, and I certainly love the adventure, is that it's the only way I can figure out what's going on in the world. I don't trust the newspapers, TV stations, or government pronouncements. That's what everyone else knows. I want to see it for myself, close to the ground.

You learn much more about a society by crossing a remote border, finding the black market, and changing money or talking to the local madam than by talking to bureaucrats or economists at the IMF and the World Bank . . . or by watching CNBC.

By the time I cross the border in the jungle, I know 25% to 30% of what I need to know about a country. I know the bureaucracy. I know the infrastructure. I know the corruption. I know the status of the economy and its currency. And I know whether I stand to make money investing there or not.

The only other way to know what's going on is to study history. When I teach or speak at universities, young people always ask me: "I want to be successful and travel around the world; what should I study?"

I always tell them the same thing: "Study history."

And they always look at me very perplexed and say, "What are you talking about . . . what about economics, what about marketing?"

"If you want to be successful," I always say, "you've got to understand history. You'll see how the world is always changing. You'll see how a lot of the things we see today have happened before. Believe it or not, the stock market didn't begin the day you graduated from school. The stock market's been around for centuries. All markets have. These things have happened before. And will happen again."

Alan Greenspan went on record before he left his post at the Federal Reserve saying he had never seen a bubble before. I know in his lifetime, in his adult lifetime, there have been several bubbles. There was a bubble in the late 1960s in the U.S. stock market. There was the oil bubble. The gold bubble. The bubble in Kuwait. The bubble in Japan. The bubble in real estate in Texas. So what is he talking about? Had he not seen those things, he could have at least read some histories . . . all these things and others have been written about repeatedly.

Alan Greenspan continues to embody the economic mindset of today's policy makers. They have the lunatic idea that a nation can consume its way to prosperity although it has never been done in history.

In the United States, if you have a job, you pay taxes. If you save some money, you pay taxes on the interest. If you buy a stock and you get a dividend, you pay taxes. If you have a capital gain, you pay taxes again. And when you die, your estate pays taxes. If you live long enough to get Social Security, they tax your Social Security income. Remember: You paid taxes on all this money when you earned it originally yet they tax it again and again.

These policies are not very conducive to encouraging saving or investing. They promote consumption.

By contrast, the countries that have been doing well the last 30 or 40 years are the countries that encourage saving and investing. Singapore is one of the most astonishing cities in the whole world. Forty years ago it was a slum. Now, in terms of per capita reserves, it's one of the richest countries in the world.

One of the reasons Singapore was so successful is that its dictator, Lee Kwan Yu, insisted that everyone save and invest a large part of their income. There are many other dictators or politicians you can condemn, but they have nothing to show for it, and, in fact, they've been worse. Whatever Lee's policies toward personal freedom, at least he forced people to save and invest.

History shows that people who save and invest grow and prosper, and the others deteriorate and collapse.

As the book you hold in your hands demonstrates, artificially low interest rates and rapid credit creation policies set by Alan Greenspan and the Federal Reserve caused the bubble in U.S. stocks of the late 1990s. Policies then pursued at the Fed made the bubble worse. They changed it from a stock market bubble to a consumption and housing bubble.

And when that bubble burst, it was far worse than the stock market bubble, because there are many more people who are involved in consumption and housing. Millions of people found out the hard way that house prices don't go up forever. Now there are a lot of angry people.

No one, of course, wanted to hear it when the original edition of this book was published. They wanted the quick fix. They still want to buy a stock and watch it go up 25% because that's what happened a few years ago, and that's what they say on TV. They want yet another interest rate cut, because they've heard that that's what will make the economy boom.

Bill Bonner and Addison Wiggin wrote me early on to tell me that "a lot of the stuff you write about in *Adventure Capitalist* (Random House) is in our book—except for the travel in the international countries."

I'd go a step further and say it's almost as though they wrote parts of my book and I wrote some of theirs—approaching the same subject from two completely different angles . . . and arriving at the same place. From the lack of government policies encouraging saving and investing to the dramatic effect demography will have on the global economy in the twenty-first century, I kept coming across things in this book that I had seen in my travels. He discovered them by reading history books and studying economics. I saw them up close, on the ground.

"Needless to say, your ideas are genius," I wrote back, "You think like I do, which means we're going to go broke together."

JIM ROGERS

# PREFACE TO THE 2009 EDITION: CONFESSIONS OF A NEWSLETTER MAN

We begin with a question: Was ever there a fairer métier than ours?

The poor carpenter risks cutting his fingers or banging his knee. The used car salesman's hearing goes bad as soon as he takes up his job: "No, I don't hear any rattle," says he. The foot-soldier gets sent to a Godforsaken hole like Afghanistan, where the women are covered up and the liquor stashed away.

But in our trade as newsletter publishers, hardly a day passes without a good laugh. Our only occupational hazard is a rupture of the midriff.

Most people, after all, read the news pages for information. They lack the proper training and perspective to fully enjoy them. The consequence is that they are always in danger of taking the humbug seriously, or worse, finding the people who populate the headlines important.

If you really want to appreciate the media you have to get close enough to see how it works—like a prairie dog peering into a hay bailer—but not so close that you get caught up in it yourself. The investment newsletter business is perfect; it is part of the media, but it wouldn't be mistaken for a reputable part.

More than 30 years ago, we began our career publishing newsletters. Those were the days! They were even more fun than today. Years of television, heavy-handed regulation, and waiting in line for airport security have taken much of the lightheartedness out of American life. In its place, a kind of earnest timidity has settled over the 50 states. Everything is forbidden, or else it is compulsory—especially in the financial markets. You can barely talk about an honest investment without some ambitious prosecutor wanting to make a federal case out of it.

But back in the 1970s, the folks you met in the newsletter trade were even wilder and more disreputable than those who are in it today. At one investment conference, we remember an investment advisor from East Germany. He had escaped the Soviets' grip by stealing a small plane and flying to the west. This alone made him a bit of a hero back in the 1970s. But his talk to investors endeared him further. He gave the following discourse:

"Take a look a zis chart," he would begin, pointing to the bottom of what appeared to be a wave pattern. "Investing is reeelly very simple. You just buy at zee bottom. Heere! Zen, ven ze stock goes up, vat do ve do? Ve sell. Heere! [Pointing to the top of the wave pattern.] It is reeelly verrry simple."

"Well, what if the stock doesn't go up," asked an investor, fresh off the Great Plains and not prepared for patterns or people that weren't perfectly straight.

"Ya . . . ve just keep our eyes on ze chart. If it doesn't go up, ve don't buy it."

We don't recall the man's name. It was something like Dr. Friederich Hasselbauer. We were always a bit suspicious of financial advisors who used the "Dr." title, though many did. Especially when they spoke with thick German accents. We imagined that they had been conducting experiments on Jews before they entered the financial markets.

And then there was the Quack man. His name was "Red Robin." As near as we could figure, he liked ducks. So he called his financial analysis "The Quack Report." He had once made his money paving airport runways. Then, in his fifties or sixties, he decided to devote himself to financial analysis and to save the world from a small group of criminal conspirators known as the Bilderburgers, who were in cahoots with the English government. Once, flying on the Concorde across the Atlantic, Ol' "Red" saw the U.K. Chancellor of the Exchequer, it must have been Lord Barber, on the same flight. He told us that he decided to confront his lordship right then and there, when he had the chance.

"I just went up to him and I said, 'I'm on to you . . . ol' buddy . . . '"

It must have been quite a scene. Red Robin was a funny-looking fellow with a paunchy stomach who always dressed in orange coveralls, which made him look a little like a red-breasted sapsucker. Why he wore orange overalls, we don't know; perhaps they were a holdover from his days working on airport runways when he didn't want the cement trucks to run him down.

Red also had funny ideas about publishing investment advice. He offered readers a Lifetime Guarantee—they could have their money back anytime. But then, he added a caveat: "My life, not yours." As it turned out, the guarantee was less valuable than readers imagined—or Red himself had hoped. He was gunned down on a beach in Costa Rica, we were told.

But that was the strange milieu in which we decided to make our career. What was delightful about it were the nuts and kooks, the charlatans and dreamers, the brazen hucksters and earnest geniuses who made up the industry. Here were thinkers whose thoughts were untainted by any trace of advanced doctrinaire theory, let alone rudimentary training of any sort. Here were mountebanks and scalawags galore . . . along with a few saints . . . dispensing market wisdom, stock recommendations, and macro-analysis so far reaching you needed a Hubble telescope to see where it came from.

And here, too, were the sort of men whom rich widows were warned about. And the sort of theorists who made you wonder about the limits of human reason itself.

Our friend, Gary North, somewhat of a legend in the business, began studying the possible consequences of the Y2K computer problem in the late 1990s. The more closely he looked, the more alarmed he became. He began writing about the subject, and the more he explored it . . . the more he thought about it . . . the more convinced he became that it would lead to a complete meltdown of modern society. He looked and he saw commerce coming to a stop. He saw trains that couldn't run without electronic instruction. He saw cash machines frozen up. He saw power plants idled by their computer brains. And what would happen to all that electronic information—bank accounts, trading records, inventories—on which the whole financial world depended? He saw millions of people with no money . . . and then no food. He saw riots in the streets . . . and worse.

Then, he looked around and saw that he and his family were as exposed to the menace as everyone else. He decided to take precautions, moving his family to an isolated rural area where they would be safe from the apocalypse he saw coming.

Maybe he would be wrong, he reasoned. But what if he were right? The cost of being right—and failing to protect himself—could be catastrophic. He moved to a mountain hollow, buried provisions, and began the countdown to the year 2000.

Of course, when the big day came . . . nothing happened. The clocks worked. The trains ran. The power was still on. Apparently, not a single cash machine failed.

People pointed and laughed. But was he wrong? What if the odds of a meltdown had been only 1 in 100 or 1 in a 1,000? Was he not right to give a warning in the strongest possible terms? And wasn't it partly because of him and others like him that billions were spent to correct the problem before January 2000?

Colorful eccentrics, careful analysts, cheerful con men, and self-assured delusionals trying to figure out how things are put together—this is the world of investment gurus.

But guess what? The gurus are often right. True, some financial gurus have gone broke following their own advice. But many have gotten rich.

In the late 1970s, we undertook a study—with Mark Hulbert, who is still at it—of how well these financial gurus actually perform. We wouldn't presume to summarize Mark Hulbert's nearly 30 years of work; we will just tell you what we took from it: There is no right way to invest.

Investment gurus are an original bunch. They come up with all sorts of systems, ideas, and approaches. Almost all of them are successful—sometimes. There are a lot of different ways to invest and to make money. And often one that works spectacularly well in one period may collapse completely when the market changes course. So, too, an approach that often works poorly under certain market conditions will work poorly in other conditions.

But, generally, an investment advisor who works hard to develop and refine a system and who sticks with it can do reasonably well, sometimes. He can be a technical analyst, a chartist, a Graham and Dodd follower, even an astrologer. Almost any disciplined approach, pursued intelligently and steadily, can pay off.

We have a theory that explains why this is so. Investing is, when you get down to the basement of it, a competitive undertaking. If you do what everyone else does, you will get the same returns as everyone else. In order to get better returns, you have to do things differently.

Investment gurus seem to be favored, in this regard, by their own originality and quirky self-reliance.

"Sometimes right, sometimes wrong," they say. "But never in doubt."

Taken together, they are probably the most independent and contrary professional class in the world. And this contrariness, alone, seems to put them at odds with the great mass of *lumpen* investors, allowing them to make more—or, often less—than the common results.

By contrast, what seems to doom the average investor is the same mushy quality that seems to be ruining the whole country. He will wait in line—without a word of protest—while guards frisk girl scouts and old ladies for dangerous weapons. If the mob is large enough, he can't wait to be a part of it and fears being isolated from it. And he will believe any line of guff—no matter how fantastic—as long as everyone else falls for it, too. Dow 36,000? House prices always go up? Interest-only negative amortization mortgage?

A man who follows a newsletter guru has no guarantee of making money . . . but a man who follows the great mass of conventional wisdom is practically guaranteed that he will not.

The trouble with the modern world is that there isn't enough trouble in it. Back when we began in the business, people had real trouble and they really appreciated it. Now, they just toss it off. They're not worried about it because they don't know what it really is.

When we were young, we fully expected that we would never be old. Nuclear war was a very real threat. "We will bury you," said the leader of the Soviet Union, while addressing Western ambassadors at a reception at the Polish embassy in Moscow on November 18, 1956. We thought he meant it. And during the Cuban Missile Crisis, the world was probably only an upset stomach away from annihilation. If either Kennedy or Khrushchev had been in a bad mood, we might never have lived long enough to enjoy the greatest economic boom in human history.

There was also the danger of too many people; India could never feed herself, the experts said. Food production worldwide couldn't keep up with population growth. Hundreds of millions would starve; it was only a matter of time.

As to financial matters, the average family was only a paycheck or two from total disaster. Losing a job could be catastrophic. No one had credit cards. There was no EZ mortgage finance available. Besides, adults back in the 1950s and 1960s were deeply suspicious of debt. It was the lesson they had learned during the Great Depression. That generation knew trouble . . . real trouble.

In the 1930s, one out of every four U.S. workers lost his job— with no unemployment insurance and no welfare system to fall back on. The elder Mr. Bonner had a knack for being in the wrong place at the wrong time. He tried to escape the poverty of his family by joining the army . . . in 1939. Then, he thought he had gotten extremely lucky when he drew the best assignment in the army; they sent him to Hawaii. He said he was recovering from a hangover on the base when Japanese airplanes appeared overhead in December, 1941. They tried to kill him for the next three years.

But Americans had it easy during the war, compared to others. Britain was bombed for months. France was occupied. Italy and France were both battlefields. There were severe financial shocks, too. Britain went broke. France had to form two new governments and replace its currency twice.

But, imagine the time your parents and grandparents would have had, had they lived in Russia, China, India, Germany, Argentina, or

Japan: War. Hyperinflation. Starvation. Police repression. Mass arrests. Occupation. Bolshevism. You name it; they lived it.

As long as the generation that had lived through the Depression and WWII were in charge of things, the United States was in pretty good shape. The United States emerged the world's biggest, strongest, most innovative and dynamic economy after WWII.

But, in the 1980s, a new generation took over. It was "morning again in America." During that period, three key events caused trouble—as we had known it—to take a holiday.

First, there was the Crash of 1987. Stocks fell hard. But then, they got right back up again, as though nothing ever happened. As a result, people began to think that crashes were no trouble. Even if stocks fell, they'd soon be on an upswing again. Books began to appear such as *Stocks for the Long Run*. People began to believe you couldn't go wrong in stocks, no matter how much you paid for them.

Second, in 1989, the Berlin Wall was dismantled. Suddenly, we no longer had any enemy worthy of the name. We weren't going to be exterminated in a nuclear war after all. From here on, it would be clear sailing.

Third, the neocons transformed the Republican Party. "Deficits don't matter," said Dick Cheney. They never seemed to matter to Democrats. Now they no longer matter to Republicans either. After the 1980s there was no longer any organized political party in favor of fiscal and monetary conservatism.

Like their federal government, Americans borrowed. And so, their debt increased. Having been the world's leading creditors in the 1950s and 1960s, they became the world's leading debtors in the 1980s and 1990s. Gradually, the consumer economy required more and more debt to produce an extra unit of output. Debtors had to borrow not only to buy . . . but also to pay back, or pay the interest on, previous borrowings. The financial sector boomed by supplying the credit.

America's most profitable businesses shifted from making things to shuffling little pieces of paper back and forth. That's why GM created GMAC and why GE staked its future on GE Finance. And it's why the center of U.S. economic power moved from the manufacturing hinterlands of Detroit and Cleveland to the financial centers on the coast . . . notably the big one in Lower Manhattan.

By the late 1990s and early twenty-first century, the American economy had entered the bubble epoque. The financial industry— aided and abetted by the Federal Reserve—was providing so much "liquidity" it was causing asset prices to bubble up everywhere. Since then, every warning turned out to be a false alarm. The dot-coms busted and it didn't really matter. The recession of 2001–2002 was so mild few people even noticed. Even terrorists disappeared from North America after the stunning attack in 2001.

Of course, bubbles always blow up—without exception. And when the dot-com bubble exploded in 2000, at first we thought that was the end of the bubble era. But the biggest bubbles were still to come. The bubbles in housing, art, emerging markets, oil, and commodities—all blew up. Then the biggest bubble of all—the bubble in credit—blew up, too, bringing the bubble epoque to a close.

We are now in the post-bubble era. The financial industry has been bombed out. It can no longer create bubbles. Governments all over the world are propping up the walls and shoring up the foundations.

Toward the end of last year, the days were getting shorter and shorter. Darkness covered the land—especially in Iceland, where even in the best of times, late December offers barely enough daylight to smoke a cigarette.

The authorities have gone back to their usual antics. They've bailed out some companies, lowered interest rates to zero, and shored up the financial sector—which just happened to have good representation in the government and its central bank—and saved the bondholders from getting what they had coming.

They've made sacrifices to the market gods, too. Unable to find any virgins in the financial sector, they threw the taxpayers down the well. And then they went after the savers (admittedly, there weren't many of them) and the next generation, too.

At first, it seemed as if the "stimulus" had failed. Then, gradually, the light increased and the days grew longer. As we write this preface in the spring of 2009, after nine weeks of rising prices, people are beginning to see the world differently, again. To simplify: It doesn't seem nearly as bad a place as it did a few months ago. Even house prices—ground zero of the financial crisis—although not actually rising, they're not falling as fast as they were before. And although people are still losing their jobs, not as many of them are losing their jobs each month as did earlier in the year. This has led many commentators to believe that government's expensive bailout/stimulus efforts are finally working.

And now, the mob screams: "The worst is over!" "We've seen the bottom." "Hoorah for the feds!"

But it is not likely to be so. The bubble epoque cannot be revived. So what should you do?

After nearly three decades in the business and writing our daily chronicle of the stock market and economy, *The Daily Reckoning*, for 10 years, we have distilled our advice down to four dicta, a few basic truths to guide you as you navigate your way through the financial news:

**Dictum Number 1: People do not get what they want or what they expect from the markets; they get what they deserve.**

Of course, people would like the downturn to be over. Many are counting on it. But the market doesn't give a hoot. He's got a "Capitalism at Work" T-shirt on and a sledgehammer in his hand.

What's he up to? He's demolishing a quarter century's worth of mistakes. There are always mistakes made. Investments go bad. Businesses go under. People go broke. When many mistakes are corrected at once, it's called a "recession." And when an entire economic model goes bad, it's called a "depression."

The economic model of the last quarter century caused more mistakes than usual. It encouraged people to spend, borrow, and speculate. And each time the market tried to make some corrections, the authorities came along with more money and easier credit. Businesses that should have gone under years ago kept digging themselves in deeper. Homeowners kept running up more debt. Speculators kept taking bigger and bigger gambles.

Fish gotta swim, birds gotta fly, and bubbles gotta blow. The bubble in the financial sector—including subprime debt, housing prices, bonuses on Wall Street, and derivatives—hit the fan in 2007. And what a mess!

And why shouldn't it be?

Which brings us to the second of our dicta:

**Dictum Number 2: The force of a correction is equal and opposite to the deception that preceded it.**

The delusions and absurdities of the bubble epoque were monstrous. Naturally, the correction must be huge, too. World stock markets were nearly cut in half. Property prices, too, have been knocked down almost everywhere. The total loss of nominal wealth has been estimated as high as $50 trillion.

In the first quarter of 2009, Warren Buffett's company, Berkshire Hathaway, booked its first loss since 2001. Fifty-nine banks have been shut down over the past 18 months. The United States' leading banks say they need another $75 billion to keep their doors open. And Fannie Mae said it lost $23 billion; it will need $19 billion more to continue jiving the housing market.

Could these losses have been prevented?

Certainly many of them could. If the U.S. Congress had never created Fannie Mae, for example, it never would have distorted the mortgage market as much as it did. And if the feds hadn't created the Federal Reserve Bank, it couldn't have provided so much ready money for so many speculators and borrowers. And if the Fed under Alan Greenspan had done what it was supposed to do—that is, to "take away the punch bowl" before the party got out of control—the bubble in the financial sector probably would have been much more modest.

Of course, people drew all the wrong conclusions. They thought "capitalism failed." They saw the car drive off the cliff . . . but didn't notice how government had twisted the road signs. Instead of warning investors of the dangerous curve ahead, the Fed's low lending rates said: "Step on the gas!" Congress, despite their recent collective cry of disbelief, helped push down the pedal.

**Dictum Number 3: Capitalism doesn't always take an economy where it wants to go; but it always takes an economy where it ought to be.**

Whoever was responsible for the mistakes, capitalism went about correcting them with its customary élan. It hit imprudent investors with trillions in losses. It knocked down mismanaged corporations. It whacked homeowners . . . and pounded housing-based derivatives to dust.

Capitalism operates by a process that the great economist Joseph Schumpeter called "creative destruction." It destroys mistakes to make room for new innovations and new businesses. Unfortunately, this puts it at odds with government and what most people want. When people make mistakes, they maintain that they are blameless. "Who could have seen this crisis coming?" they ask. "And," they say, "someone else should pay for the loss."

So today the feds, who mismanaged their regulatory responsibilities during the bubble epoque are bailing out mismanaged corporations to protect lenders who mismanaged their money. They are determined to prevent capitalism from making major changes—in the worst possible way.

What's the worst possible way? Simple. Leave the mismanagers in place. Keep the brain-dead companies alive—along with the zombie banks. Let the government take ownership of major sectors of the economy. And stick a debt-ridden society with even more debt!

The federal government is expected to borrow $2 trillion this year alone. From whom? And who will repay it?

**Dictum Number 4**: **The severity of a depression is inversely correlated with government's efforts to stop it.**

The more the feds try to delay and distract the process of creative destruction, the longer it takes to get the job done. And the higher the eventual bill.

There are only two fairly clear examples in modern history. After the crash of 1929, the Hoover and Roosevelt administrations tried desperately to stop the correction. They could not make bad debts disappear, or turn bad decisions into good ones. All they could do was to retard the necessary corrections—and cause new mistakes! It wasn't until after WWII, 15 years later, when the New Deal was largely forgotten, that the United States got back to work.

Similarly, when Japan was confronted with a major correction in 1990, its politicians followed the Hoover/Roosevelt model. Over the years, an amount equivalent to almost an entire year's output was applied to recovery efforts. But all they did was to prevent and forestall the needed changes. Now, 19 years later, the Japanese economy is still in corrective mode . . . still fighting deflation.

Is that the end of the story? Not at all. The feds' efforts to stop the progress of capitalism will have some spectacular consequences. The fireworks will start when the bond market cracks sending yields through the roof, for a nation addicted to debt cannot sustain a credit crisis for long. And that is where today's story begins . . .

WILLIAM BONNER

JUNE 2009

# ACKNOWLEDGMENTS

A special note regarding the third edition of *Financial Reckoning Day:*

In revising and adapting the third edition of this book, I was struck by how accurate and recurring our themes have been through two decades of financial analysis and economic forecasting. While studying economic history can seem like a fool's errand—and does it!—we find that some trends persist and repeat. The trick is to identify which trends have staying power and are worth putting your money behind.

We couldn't do any of this work without William Bonner. While the scope and structure of this third edition are vastly different than the previous two, Bill's fingerprints are all over it. Many of the catchphrases he wrote in the first edition remain. The character of our study and what we call "literary economics" is a constant, a testament, to the many years Bill and I wrote together.

ENJOY,
ADDISON

# INTRODUCTION: HELL IN A BUCKET

"Everything seemed so logical," we wrote to begin the first edition of this book, "so obvious and agreeable at the end of the twentieth century."

"Stocks went up year after year. The Cold War had been won. The new Information Age was making everything and everybody so much smarter—and richer. The world was a happy place and Americans were its happiest people. US consumer capitalism was the envy of all mankind. The United States guaranteed the peace and freedom of the entire species, if not with goodness, intelligence, and foresight—at least with its military arsenal, which could blow any adversary to kingdom come. People believed that Francis Fukuyama's *The End of History and the Last Man* had indeed arrived, for it scarcely seemed possible that there could be any major improvement."

These words ring as true as ever as we revise, update, and adapt the themes to our current situation at the dawn of the third decade of the new millennium.

"It's a funny old world," as Margaret Thatcher remarked nearly 50 years ago. She might have meant "funny" in the sense that it is amusing; more likely, she meant that it is peculiar. In both senses, she was right. What makes the world funny is that it refuses to cooperate; it seldom does what people want or expect it to do. In fact, it often does the exact opposite.

People do not always act as they should. Other people seem irrational to us—especially those with whom we disagree. Nor do we always follow a logical and reasonable course of action. Instead, we are all swayed by tides of emotion . . . and occasionally swamped by them.

This book was written to underline the point that the world is more peculiar than you think. And the more you think about it, the more entertaining it gets. Close inspection reveals the ironies, contradictions, and confusions that make life interesting, but also frustrating. A rational person could do rational things all day long, but then how boring life would be. Fortunately, real people are only rational about things that do not matter.

People of action despise thinking of any sort, and rightly so, because the more they think, the more their actions are beset by doubts and arrière-pensées. The more man thinks, the slower he moves. Thought uncovers the limitations of his plans. Exploring the possibilities, he sees yet more potential outcomes, a greater number of problems . . . and he increasingly recognizes how little he actually knows. If he keeps thinking long and hard enough, he is practically paralyzed . . . a person of action no more.

Will the stock market rise?

"I don't know," replies the thinking fund manager.

Can we win the war?

"It depends on what you mean by 'win'," answers the thoughtful general.

Will house values continue to go up?

"Your guess is as good as mine," responds the honest real estate broker.

This book has been written in a spirit of runaway modesty. The more we think, the more we realize how little we know. We are, frankly, in far too much awe of the world, and too deeply entertained by it, to think that we can understand it today or foretell tomorrow.

Life's most attractive components—love and money—are far too complex for reliable soothsaying. Still, we can't resist taking a guess.

We may not know how the world works, but we are immodest enough to think we can know how it does not work. The stock market is not, for example, a simple mechanism like an ATM machine, where you merely tap in the right numbers to get cash out when you need it. Instead, the investment markets—like life itself—are always complicated, often perverse, and occasionally absurd. But that does not mean that they are completely random; though unexpected, life's surprises may not always be undeserved. Delusions have consequences. And sooner or later, the reckoning day comes, and the bills must be paid.

In this sense, the investment markets are not mechanistic at all, but judgmental. As we will see, they reward virtue and punish sin.

Our approach in this book is a little different from that of the typical economics tome or investment advisory. Instead, it is an exercise in what is known, derisively, as "literary economics." Although you will find statistics and facts, the metaphors and the principles that we provide are more important. Facts have a way of yielding to nuance like a jury to a trial lawyer. Under the right influence, they will go along with anything. But the metaphors remain . . . and continue to give useful service long after the facts have changed.

What's more, metaphors help people understand the world and its workings. As Norman Mailer put it, "There is much more truth in a metaphor than in a fact." But the trouble with metaphors is that no matter how true they may be when they are fresh and clever, when the multitudes pick them up, they almost immediately become worn out and false. For the whole truth is always complex to the point of being unknowable, even to the world's greatest geniuses.

The world never works the way people think it does. That is not to say that every idea about how the world works is wrong, but that often particular ideas about how it works will prove to be wrong if they are held in common. For only simple ideas can be held by large groups of people. Commonly held ideas are almost always dumbed down until they are practically lies . . . and often dangerous ones. Once vast numbers of people have come to believe the lie, they adjust their own behavior to bring themselves into sync with it, and thereby change the world itself. The world, then, no longer resembles the one that gave rise to the original insight. Soon, a person's situation is so at odds with the world as it really is that a crisis develops, and he or she must seek a new metaphor for explanation and guidance.

Thus, we cannot help but notice an insidious and entertaining dynamic . . . a dialectic of the heart, where greed and fear, confidence and desperation confront each other with the subtle elegance of women mud wrestlers.

In the financial markets, this pattern is well known and frequently described.

In the late 1990s, those who were sure that stocks would always go up, despite having already reached absurd levels, gave countless explanations for their belief, but the main reason was simply that it was just the way the world worked. But after investors had moved their money into stocks, to take advantage of the insight, few buyers were left, and prices had risen so high that neither profits nor growth could support them.

Investors were deeply disappointed in the early 2000s when stocks fell 3 years in a row. How could this be, they asked themselves? What is going on, they wanted to know?

The answer eluded us when we wrote the first edition of this book in the summer of 2003. And as we wrote the second edition of this book in the spring of 2009, we still did not know. And even mainstream economists found it difficult to come up with an answer. Paul Samuelson, popularizer of the economic profession for *Newsweek*, admitted that he and his colleagues do not even have words to describe the "baffling economy." Boy would things change from there. Now into its third edition, rare for these kinds of books, we grappled with the after effects of the bailouts following the Financial Panic of 2008, including a decade of quantitative easing (QE) and zero interest rate policy (ZIRP), as well as the advent of blockchain and social media. Samuelson died in 2009, so he missed all the fun. What would he have made of the pandemic lockdowns, direct "stimmie" checks to US citizens, a generational bout with inflation, the rise and fall (and rise and fall) of cryptocurrencies?

As we've noted since the first edition, those who should know the answers to these challenges have not been much help. In the late summer of 2002, the most celebrated economist in the world addressed an audience in Jackson Hole, Wyoming. Alan Greenspan explained that he did not know what had gone wrong. He would not know a bubble if it blew up right in front of him; he would have to wait, he told his fellow economists and check the mirror for bruise marks—for only after the event could a bubble be detected.

Almost 7 years later, Ben Bernanke and the Obama administration still didn't understand where bubbles come from, and what difference would it make anyway? The United States' favorite bureaucrat had explained while occupying the chair at the Federal Reserve that it made none: "Even if he [Greenspan] had known where bubbles come from, he said, he could not have done anything about them." As chairman of the Federal Reserve, Janet Yellen (now Treasury Secretary) trooped on with the Greenspan-Bernanke policies. It's as if she asked herself, "What if we cut interest rates to zero whenever there's a crisis? Why not just keep them low?" During her tenure at the Fed, she maintained interest rates at near zero until 2017 when she started to "get serious" about raising rates in anticipation of a coming inflation. By the time she'd left the Fed in 2018, rates were all the way up to 1.5%! Of course, we all know the rest. First the pandemic, then a rapid onset of inflation. Yellen's successor, Jerome Powell, inherited quite a mess when he began his own stretch at the helm of the nation's bank.

We did not write and update this book to carp or complain. Instead, as always, we offer it in the spirit of constructive criticism, or at least in the spirit of "benign mischief" as my coauthor Bill Bonner would have called it. We don't know any better than Alan Greenspan or Ben Bernanke or Janet Yellen or Joe Biden what the future holds. We only guess that even today, we are living through one of history's epic crisis points—one of its long drawn out reckoning days—where the metaphors of yesterday no longer seem to describe the way the world works today. The financial markets are not the congenial ATM machines of investors' fantasies, after all. Neither are the houses we live in. Nor is the political world as safe and as comfortable as people had come to believe. No sooner had we scurried out of Afghanistan, Russian invaded Ukraine. The United States and its NATO allies entered a proxy war with Russia over what used to be known as "the" Ukraine—an agricultural region of land between Europe to the west and Russia to the east.

That is another aspect of our book that readers may find unusual. We dip into military history and market history as if passing from a hot tub to a pool. Both illustrate the lively influence of group dynamics; the currents of mass sentiment are similar. Readers will note, however, that political episodes tend to have tragic endings . . . whereas markets typically end in farce. Readers may also be curious as to our focus on European history. We make no excuses or apologies for it. Our office in Paris, when we began, is surrounded by reminders of Europe's past. Can we not help but learn from it?

Many things have changed, too, since the first edition of this book was published in 2003. Although sales were decent, the book having reached #1 on the New York Times Business Bestseller list, we were still considered "mavericks" for pointing out what seemed to us to be painfully obvious: You cannot live beyond your means forever. Policy makers did their best to postpone the inevitable, even driving the stock market to its all-time high in the fall of 2007. Then again, and again, from 2013 to its new all-time high in 2021. We maintain it was a phony prosperity and unsustainable, that much is clear to many who were skeptical in the years between our first publication date and today.

None of these editions have been easy to get a handle on.

The reckoning is still underway as we write. While updating the second edition, General Motors, the bellwether of American manufacturing, finally declared bankruptcy; California, the trendsetter state, misread revenues derived from the housing bubble and came up more than $42 billion short; David Walker, the former comptroller general of the country and the protagonist of our film and book, *I.O.U.S.A.*, warned that the United States was in danger of having its Treasury bonds downgraded from AAA status, which did, in fact, happen in 2011. We point to these events because during the final edits of this third edition we've just endured another bout of political theater as Congress debated the nation's debt ceiling yet again.[1] And we've witnessed the collapse of three banks whose combined assets under management totaled more than all 25 banks that collapsed in 2008. Of course, we've done our best to stay on top of things, but the story continues . . . wildness lies in wait.

We have not included the typical formulas or recommendations of an investment book or the detailed expositions of a book on economics.

Instead, we hope to entertain and enlighten and offer a few simple ideas readers may well find helpful in the years ahead.

Fair warning, the tale we tell is one of fraud and deception, hokum and whimsy. At one point in our lives, we entertained the idea of writing fiction. Then . . . not through any design of our own . . . it turned out we couldn't make up the stories you'll read in this book. These stories are more fantastic than our imagination, more absurd than a reality TV show, and less interesting than any LSD trip the band members of the Grateful Dead would ever cop to. With some careful consideration, you'll learn something about how the financial markets and the global economy work.

For the most part, what you'll read happened in our lifetimes. Occasionally, we dip into history to show what's hokum now has always been hokum. There are hundreds of years of modern history, of factual data, to show what a mess politics and the financial markets have been. Booms and busts are the result, for the most part, of fraud.

That said, when we first told some of these stories they were headline news. Now a lot of the names, places, and events have been forgotten. What remains are the patterns and trends that make up what we collectively call "the economy": how we make our money and finance our lives, what stories we tell our children, and what, ultimately, gets passed down to our grandchildren.

In the "here and now" we hope to recognize the primary trends that help us to forecast what's coming next. Obviously, that's a wide-sweeping statement, so let's get back to the details.

We've learned enough in the past 25 years to know all we can do is describe events. We've given up trying to understand or explain them. It's more like we're sitting in an old Caddy at Bengie's Drive-In Theatre in Middle River, Maryland, eating popcorn and watching a scratchy rendition of *Back to the Future*. We know what the plot is going to be because we've seen the movie before. But we also know Michael J. Fox has a debilitating condition called Parkinson's disease, which also took the life of my own grandfather. May he rest in peace. Not only does life imitate art, but it slavishly tries to model itself on science too.

Fair warning on tone: We write in the vernacular of our chosen field. As such, you'll read dramatic phrases and words like "reckoning," "boom and bust," "panic," and "mania." You'll likely find that a lot of our opinions sound jaded, skeptical. But they are not. The snarkiness is intentional and necessary because they give some color as we describe the events we're living through. Without them the study of economics is, well, just boring. We enjoy the spectacle of it all. We're going to hell in a bucket, baby, but at least we're enjoying the ride.

Readers who wish to keep up with our progress following the trends of our time are welcome to join us at the *Wiggin Sessions* or get our most recent commentary by going to www.JoinTheSessions .com and signing up for free.

# PART ONE

# WILDNESS LIES IN WAIT

*Life is not an illogicality; yet it is a trap for logicians. It looks just a little more mathematical and regular than it is; its exactitude is obvious, but its inexactitude is hidden; its wildness lies in wait.*

—G.K. Chesterton

# CHAPTER 1

## THE OLD "NEW ECONOMY"

When we began to tell this story, we were writing on an old Compaq laptop with a cracked screen and a faulty battery the size of your forearm. Our internet was "dial-up" and totally unreliable. We were living and working in Paris, France. The entire country only had one T1 line. Our email address was @compuserve.com. Some readers may not even know what a compuserve is.

Our story was intertwined with Gary Winnick, chairman of the then $47 billion enterprise Global Crossing, which was engaged in laying fiber-optic cable across the Atlantic Ocean from the East Coast to Europe. Nobody knows him anymore. His story is important, however, to the problems presented in this book.

At the time, Winnick did something unusual. He decided to take time off from touring art galleries with David Rockefeller, playing golf with Bill Clinton, and enjoying the Malibu beach to learn a little about the business he was in. He bought a video describing how undersea cable was laid. The video was all Winnick needed to know about laying fiber-optic cable. He understood what business he was really in, and it had nothing to do with ships or optic fiber.

Winnick was doing nature's work: separating fools from their money. And he was good at it.

Supposedly, Winnick knew the undersea cable business well. Likewise, the people from whom he raised money were the "best pros" on Wall Street and were supposed to be capable of managing big bucks. After all, if they did not know how to place money to get a decent return, what did they know? And those who provided these "best pros" with money were also supposed to know what they were doing. As it turned out, no one had a clue.

We tell the forgotten story of Global Crossing now as a cautionary tale; a look inside the minds and motives of the chief executive officers (CEOs), traders, and analysts of the first great boom and bust of the twenty-first century. There are, of course—and will always be!—others.

Let us set the stage of the turn of the "New Era," a couple of decades ago. There are so many parallels in our current market to the "dot com bubble," it feels almost foolish to be writing about the same subject. At the same time, we dove back into history then, in the original manuscripts. And we will do it again now, to provide perspective and depth to what has amounted to a whole lot of confusion in the markets.

## THE END OF HISTORY

It was in 1806 that Wilhelm Friedrich Hegel first proclaimed history to be at an end. He saw in Napoleon's defeat of Prussia at the battle of Jena the same victory Fukuyama thought he saw in the summer of 1989—the triumph of the ideals of the French Revolution. Mass participation in government, both Hegel and Fukuyama believed, brought permanent peace and prosperity. History must be over.

But history did not end in 1806 . . . (nor in 1989). Instead, in 1806, "history" in the sense that we know it today had barely begun. Never before were so many people caught up in the collective exercises that fascinate historians. As the nineteenth century developed, more and more people—by fits and starts—became involved in politics through the growth of democratic assemblies and parliaments. This democratization of the Western world threw no obstacle in history's path. To the contrary, it cleared the way and paved the road for the most historical century in mankind's experience. It was in the twentieth century that the world became saturated with politics, democracy, and, not coincidentally, war.

For the first time, armies of citizen soldiers were available to almost all European powers . . . along with the full resources of thoroughly collectivized societies. Thanks to modern communications—railroads, telegraphs, telephone, newspaper, television—the mobs, which had heretofore been limited by the range of voice and rumor, spanned time zones. As we have already seen, whole nations became engaged in mob sentiments and took up adventures that even the lowest village idiot might have previously regarded as hopeless.

Fukuyama was as wrong about economics and democracy as he was about history. The popular view—which he took up—was that the demise of communism signaled the total defeat of Marx's ideas.

"The century that began full of self-confidence in the ultimate triumph of Western liberal democracy seems at its close to be returning full circle to where it started," he wrote, "not to an 'end of ideology,' or a convergence between capitalism and socialism, as earlier predicted, but to an unabashed victory of economic and political liberalism." National socialism was destroyed in World War II, he pointed out. The Union of Soviet Socialist Republics fell apart in the late 1980s.


## RAGING BULL

One of the great marvels of life is not that fools and their money are soon parted, but that they ever get together in the first place. Life goes on, we note, for no particular reason other than the vanity of it all. One lie replaces another like cars along a Paris street (where a parking spot rarely remains vacant for long).

Over the course of the twentieth century, and trudging on and into the first two decades of the twenty-first, a simple idea stuck in investors' minds: everything worked like a machine, especially the economy.

If the economy was growing too fast, Chairman of the Federal Reserve Alan Greenspan would "put on the brakes" by raising interest rates. If the economy was growing too slowly, he would "open up the throttle" by lowering interest rates. The idea was so simple, almost anyone could understand it. The mechanical metaphor seemed to describe perfectly how the Fed—and the economy as a whole—worked. There were no experiences in the prior two decades to contradict it. The metaphor had worked so well for so long: it was almost as if it were true.

The trouble is, the market may look mechanistic, but it is not. The market is an unbounded, organic system. Mastering it is a human science, not a hard science. The financial markets reflect the activity of the human order of things; they are unbounded, chaotic systems.

The best metaphor for understanding such a system is the nature of which they are a part—infinitely complex and ultimately uncontrollable. Markets are neither kind nor forgiving. If they do the work of God, as has been suggested, it is the unforgiving Him of the Old Testament, not the New.

But by the turn of the twenty-first century, we lived in a wonderful world. It was rich and lush . . . the sun shone every day. Progress seemed inevitable and unstoppable, and compiling information in digital form was thought to hold the secret to an ever-increasing abundance of resources for mankind. A massive increase in productivity would lead to more prosperity and leisure time for everyone.

It seemed so simple: computers and telecommunications would provide people with increasing amounts of "information." Information in turn would allow goods to be produced faster and at lower costs. The whole system would benefit.

Humans, once Neanderthals in a low cave hunched over in darkness and ignorance, would now be able to stand upright and edge a little closer to perfection every day. There was no chance that they would slip up, as they had always done in the past, we were told, for this was a more fully evolved species, better adapted to the Information Age. This really is a "New Era," we were assured.

By the year 2000, fifty years of progress and a 3-decade-long bull market had created a race of geniuses. Americans were on top of the world. Their armies were unbeatable. Their currency was accepted everywhere as though it had real value. Dollars were and remain[1] the United States' most successful export, with a net outflow of nearly $3.5 trillion in 2022, up from $1 trillion in 2000. Dollars are the product on which the nation enjoys its biggest profit margin. It costs less than a cent to produce a dollar. Yet, each one is valued at par.

America's perceived greatest strength at the beginning of the New Era was its economy. It was not only the strongest in the world, but the strongest the modern world had ever seen.

The United States had increased its economic lead over the competition in the 10 years running up to the end of the century. In the minds of many, the US economy was unstoppable, and its continued success inevitable. They believed that the nation's leadership position was not merely cyclical, but eternal. It had achieved a state so nearly perfect that improvement was hardly imaginable. American music, art, films, democracy, and American-style market capitalism were everywhere triumphant.

"America is the world's only surviving model of human progress," President George W. Bush boasted to the graduating class of West Point in June 2002.

"America has its faults," wrote Thomas L. Friedman in the *New York Times* at about the same time. "But without it," he continued, "nothing good happens."

No one even bothered to ask any questions. You'll find that is one of the comforts of a great boom; question marks disappear.

When things go well, people are content not to ask questions and not to look too hard. They think they know how the world works and are happy with the jingoisms and dumbed down metaphors that explain it.

And at the end of September 2001, ominous drafts of cold weather came in like a front. Sifting through the debris of the dot .com bust, we find the Nasdaq down 73% from its high. The Dow had dropped 32%. A recession had begun in March. And America lost 2,996 innocent lives to an act of terrorism.

Although at first it was reported to have ended after a single quarter, later revisions showed that it lasted through the end of the year. Investors had no way of knowing, for they had no crystal balls, but they were in for a spell of ugliness.

Yet only a few people began rummaging through their cupboards for their coats and mittens. Such was the climate when we began following the booms and busts of the modern era.

We humans understand things by analogy. Indeed, since before Noah built his ark, humans have tried to understand the world by extrapolating from the known to the unknown. Comparison was the only tool they had to explain what they observed. Once upon a time, a bear might have been said to run "as fast as a lion," for example, or "like a holy hellcat" because it was not possible to time an animal's running speed precisely. After a period without rain, villagers might have remarked that it "was just like the Great Drought" of a few years earlier.

They had no way of knowing what might happen, of course, but the analogy warned them to conserve their food. By comparing one thing we don't really understand to another we understand only slightly better, we think we understand both.

Back then, we imagined Alan Greenspan, for example, pulling levers and turning knobs as if the economy really could be run like a machine. The metaphor is the easiest way for the financial scrivener to get his point across.

Yet, curiously, in the early years of the New Era, the metaphors from years ago or from across the wide Pacific did not seem to matter. Things were different. Not only did the old rules and old lessons no longer apply, analogies and metaphors themselves were now out of fashion.

This was the New Era indeed. But it was so much more than just "digital." It was deeply human. Deeply emotional. Deeply flawed and cumbersome and confusing. At the dawn of the new millennia, the people of the world were optimistic, truly believing that nearly all of life would soon be digitized and that mankind would grow better informed, richer, and morally superior every day. Its wildness lied in wait.[2]

## GURUS OF THE NEW MILLENIUM

The history of the New Era will read that Robert Metcalfe and Gordon Moore, like Moses and Aaron, led their followers out of the bondage of the Old Economy and into the land of stock options and mocha lattes. Who wouldn't want to follow?

We know Robert Metcalfe now for inventing "ethernet." Gordon Moore gave his name to "Moore's Law"—that immutable fact about the proliferation of computing technology in the 1970s and 1980s.[3] Metcalfe and Moore handed down the laws by which the people of Silicon Valley lived by so fruitfully in the 1990s.

For his part, Metcalfe envisioned an easy-to-understand phenomenon: each element of a system or collectivity becomes more valuable as it expands.

You can see this by thinking about the phone system. When the Bell Telephone Company was founded in May 1877, its products were almost useless because subscribers could not call anyone who did not also have a telephone. But 3 years later, there were 30,000 phones in use. And everyone wanted one.

This led to the further insight by Bell that his company could afford to spend a great deal of money selling and installing telephones because it would earn a profit later on. What's more, it was critical that people purchased Bell telephones rather than a competitor's. Ultimately, the most valuable, and presumably the most profitable, service would be the one that was most ubiquitous.

This New Era insight cleared the way for a new and popular business plan: do not worry about profits—fight for market share.

At the time, few noticed the flaw: the telephone system was a quasi-monopoly. It made sense to pay a lot of money to put it in place, because the company could expect monopoly-level profits for a very long time. Bell Telephone and many of its derivatives are still in business; we know them by their new name, AT&T.

In the early 2000s there were thousands and thousands of internet start-ups that had no hope of getting a monopoly—or anything close to it.

Globe.com, launched by the *Boston Globe* never reached anywhere near the market share promised by first mover status. Soon every publisher of any genre had a website. Webvan.com went the way of the dodo bird. One barely remembers their business model. Most readers probably don't even remember these companies. Amazon.com, however, proved to be the "unicorn"—a company that succeeds despite insurmountable odds.

During the more heady days of the tech boom, Moore handed down his own law: he stated that computational power would double every 18 months—which, thus far, it had. This growth rate astonished everyone and led to the other major delusion of internet investors—that just because computer power increases exponentially, so should internet businesses and stock prices.

Moore's law only applies to the speed at which computers process information. Government quants assumed, wrongly, that this was equivalent to an increase in the nation's wealth, as expressed by gross domestic product (GDP). As we see later on, this in turn led to distortions in other measures, such as productivity and inflation levels.

## JOHN THE BAPTIST OF THE DIGITAL AGE

If Moore and Metcalfe were the Old Testament prophets of the New Era, George Gilder was its messiah. Every revolution needs its intellectuals, its firebrands, its executioners, and its victims.

A speechwriter for Romney, Rockefeller, and Nixon, Gilder authored several well-read books, including *Wealth and Poverty* and *Life After Television*. He was quoted more often by Ronald Reagan, the record shows, than any other writer. His book, *Microcosm*, took him further than anyone had ever gone into the distant reaches of new technology and the enterprising spirit.

Gilder's articles in *Forbes ASAP* were hard to read, and often incomprehensible. But never mind. He was a genius, and he was right about a great many things. His reports were followed by many of the shrewdest investors of the time. . . to such an extent that this "pale, nervous Yankee" was seen as a demigod or "John the Baptist of the Digital Age," as one article put it. But he had worked himself into such a state of rapture over the possibilities of the internet that he seemed to have gone a little mad.

One important caveat: "I don't do price," Gilder commented. Too bad, the hubris of man. As investors would discover later, price is important. A novel technology may be spectacular, the company that owns it may be a great company, but the stock is only a good investment at the right price.

"Listen to the technology!" Gilder's Caltech physics professor, Carver Mead, had advised the New Era messiah. Listening carefully, Gilder believed that, if he strained his ears enough, he could almost hear the cosmos speaking.

"Buy Global Crossing!" he thought he had heard.

Gilder did not usually buy, and judging from the press reports, he had little interest in picking stocks. But this Ulysses of the Telecosm had forgotten to plug his ears or have himself lashed to the mast. Thus, the sirens at Global Crossing got him. . . and drove him mad with euphoria. Nowhere was this more manifest than in his book, *Telecosm,* in which he announced the emergence of a new economy "based on a new sphere of cornucopian radiance—reality unmassed and unmasked, leaving only the Promethean light."

To this day, we do not know what that sentence was supposed to mean. It was all very well to gush about how Global Crossing helped to bring about "a new epoch of spirit and faith" with its "majestic cumulative power, truth, and transcendence of contemporary science and wealth." But with a profit/earnings (P/E) ratio of negative 130, an investor would have been a fool to bet money on it.

Yet in June 2001, George Gilder continued to praise Global Crossing, qualifying the stock as "no surer bet in the Telecosm." Remember, Gilder didn't "do price."[4]

## "NO SURER BET" IN THE TELECOSM

Our friend Gary Winnick had been a former Drexel Burnham bond trader before he got into the fiber-optic business almost by accident.

He had seen the possibilities of bandwidth after financing an undersea cable for AT&T in 1997. His first cable took 14 months to lay; it was extremely profitable. Thus the business plan for Global Crossing emerged: raise money and lay fiber-optic cable! Simple enough.

Early estimates of construction costs were around $2.7 billion. The money was soon coming into Global Crossing's Bermuda headquarters at the speed of light (pun intended). The stock went public in August 1998 at $9.50. Eight months later, it hit $60 a share, giving the company a market capitalization of $54 billion. Winnick's personal stake in the company rose to $4.7 billion. He was soon dreaming of building an undersea broadband network that would link continents and serve global carriers like Deutsche Telekom and Bell's legendary AT&T.

Just 3 years later, in November 2001, Global Crossing "shocked and angered" investors by reporting a loss of $3.35 billion—more than six times greater than the loss from the same quarter a year earlier.

Included in the loss was a $2 billion write-down of its stake in another star-crossed company of the new economy, Exodus Communications, then operating under protection of the US Bankruptcy Code. Global Crossing common stock traded at only $1.24 in mid-November—up from the 38 cents rate of October 9, but down from the $13.30 level set in June when George Gilder believed it to be a sure thing. In a year and a half, investors had lost about $52.9 billion on the stock.

Still Gilder held on. "If you bought Global Crossing in 1998," he had written just a few months earlier (in June 2001), "you bought one 5,000-mile cable. Today you are buying a 102,000-mile network." He continued in reverence:

> If you bought Global Crossing in 1998, you bought $400 million in revenue. Today, you are buying over $5 billion in sales and more than a billion dollars in adjusted cash flow, growing at 40% a year. If you bought Global Crossing in 1998, you bought into static transatlantic STM1 sales. Today you are buying an IP backbone with traffic growing at 450% a year and 20% ownership of Exodus (the Web's key hub for exafloods of content, storage, and services) which almost doubled year-to-year revenues in the March quarter. If you bought Global Crossing in 1998, you bought the dream of a global web of glass and light. Today you are buying that Web."[5]

"If you bought Global Crossing in 1998," a cynic—like us—might have retorted, "you would have lost 98% of your money." (See Figure 1.1.)

The dream turned out to be a better investment than the web itself. As Global Crossing raised an increasing amount of money and laid ever more cable, it hastened its day of reckoning.

With Gilder's "exaflood" of profitable content, the cable companies were soon swamped with excess supply, and they were so deeply underwater financially that they had no hope of escape.

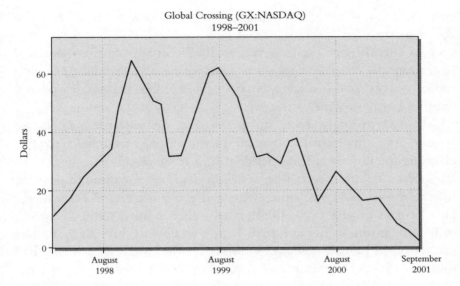

Global Crossing (GX:NASDAQ)
1998–2001

**FIGURE 1.1**  The New Era's Promethean Light

Global Crossing was George Gilder's favorite stock. Unfortunately for investors, Gilder did not "do price." Global Crossing declared bankruptcy in January 2002. Founder Gary Winnick banked some $700 million before resigning as CEO. On resignation, he stated: "I deeply regret that so many good people involved with Global Crossing also suffered significant financial loss."

While Gilder watched the stars of the Telecosm, smart industry insiders turned their own eyes earthward and saw the deluge coming.

Thus, in November 2001, investors were not the same warm-hearted, generous naïfs who lent money to Global Crossing and other wunderkinder at the height of the tech boom.

After all, lenders had marked Global Crossing's bonds down to a suspicious 18 cents on the dollar. Its secured bank debt traded at 67 cents on the dollar. Preferred shares were priced to yield 177%—if they yielded anything at all.

"Bandwidth"—that great promise of Metcalfe and Moore—had seemed like a good investment . . . when investors had a lot of money and little bandwidth. But soon, investors had less money and more bandwidth to choose from. Global Crossing was, as they say, "in a pickle."

Prices of bandwidth plummeted because of their availability. Meanwhile, according to experts, less than 10% of fiber-optic cable was used or "lit." And despite this fiber glut, Global Crossing continued to spend $500 million every quarter to finance more construction.

Not surprisingly, on January 28, 2002, Global Crossing declared bankruptcy, leaving lenders with losses of nearly $4 billion. Adding more capacity at this stage was akin to a drunken partygoer opening another bottle of wine.

More surprisingly, many still believed. A *Fortune* article published June 9, 2002, for example, lamented the collapse of Global Crossing, claiming the company had a "decent shot at survival."

So whose fault was it? Winnick, who had had the gumption to ask for the money? Or the patsies who had given it to him? They might have ponied up the $2.7 billion; maybe then Global Crossing would still be in business. Instead, they kept shoving big bills in Winnick's pockets until he had raised $20 billion. By the time his company had folded, its long-term debt had swelled to $7.6 billion (with total liabilities of $14 billion), and it simply did not have the cash to make its interest payments.

What happened to the $20 billion that Winnick had raised?

He had spread the money around—acquiring other overpriced telecoms, giving Wall Street a way to earn massive fees by keeping the money coming his way. From 1998 through 2001, the top Wall Street firms earned more than $13 billion in telecom underwriting and investment-banking fees.

And so both the juice and hokum whirled around. Salomon's technology analyst, Jack Grubman, talked up the stock. Gilder talked up the stock. Investors bought it for more than it was worth. Winnick continued to buy other telecoms for more than they were worth. Everybody made money. But it was a vanity. People do not get rich by spending money on things they do not need and cannot afford at prices that are too high. All they do is move money around . . . and waste a great deal of time.

At the time, and in the telecom sector alone, far more dark fibers were put down than the world really wanted. And when the bust finally came, Global Crossing alone had torn a $54 billion hole in investors' pockets.

By the time Global Crossing declared bankruptcy, Winnick had sold $735 million of stock and received another $15.8 million in other emoluments. He must have felt pretty smart. He had done what he had set out to do; Winnick and family had pocketed more than $600 million by cashing in stock during 2000 and 2002, even as Global Crossing struggled with a severe debt load, falling prices, and an industry in upheaval. He had also arranged to sell 10 million shares at $12 in May 2002, a decision wryly qualified by *Forbes* as "good timing" when it saw the company's shares drop below the 2 cent level at the end of 2002.

"As of 2015," our quick search of Wikipedia reports, "Winnick was chairman and chief executive officer of Winnick & Company, a Los Angeles–based private investment firm founded in 1985. In 1999, Winnick was listed by the *Los Angeles Business Journal* as the wealthiest Angeleno with a net worth of more than $6 billion; as of 2002 his net worth was listed at $550 million."[6]

There are some things, as Mae West observed, of which a man can have too much and suffer no harm. But too much money can be a clear and present danger to a man . . . or even to an entire economy. Telecom in the early 2000s was not the first, nor will it be the last industry to be ruined by an excess of good fortune.

"Most of us know, intuitively, that these young web companies minted by the hour will not survive and prosper," Michael Malone, then editor of *Forbes ASAP* and author of several books on business and the new economy, wrote. It seems obvious a couple decades and a few financial panics later, but what Malone was writing, especially for a leading tech publication, was blasphemous at the time. The "new economy" bubble did not seem real or right to him.

Malone had even received founders' shares from both Tom Siebel, founder and CEO of Siebel Systems Inc., with whom he coauthored *Virtual Selling,* and Pierre Omidyar, founder of eBay. He had no idea what the shares were worth and was astonished to find himself a wealthy man. But he lacked faith; he sold his shares as soon as he could.

Malone predicted, moreover, that in the "coming reckoning," investors' money would be lost, retirement funds would be erased, and that the valuations ruling the stock market would come back down to earth from their irrational heights. We remember getting hate (e)mail at the time for having expressed our own skepticism.

In hindsight we know by the late 1990s, Metcalfe and Moore shared this sentiment.

It was as if they had returned to the Valley and found that their tribesmen had turned the Internet Age into an absurd parody. Instead of using the power of the silicon chip and the internet to launch real businesses and create real wealth, they found investors dancing recklessly around the graven image of enterprise—the initial public offering (IPO): gain money before the company actually does anything.

Metcalfe described himself as hung up on the stock market bubble. "There's stuff going on out there that I just don't get yet," he explained. He considered the bubble "distorted" and expressed concerns that this distortion would eventually "blow up."

His writings show a concern for entrepreneurial obsession with IPOs:

> I'm frequently asking [entrepreneurs] the question, "So, what's your company going to be?" The answer these days usually contains the letters I-P-O. That's the wrong phrase to have in the first five sentences explaining what your new business is going to be about. If you're thinking IPO, you've got your eye on the wrong ball. . . . These people think that an IPO is a significant event. I view it as a minor financial event. They view it as what life is all about.[7]
>
> Would there be a day of reckoning coming?

"The [venture capitalists] get in on the ground floor," Metcalfe continued, "and they get out early. [But] these poor schmucks in the public markets. . . They are going to start looking for profits and they're not going to find them. It's all going to come crashing down."[8]

According to the popular thinking of the time, Malone, Metcalfe, and Moore had become out of touch.

Reading our words about these events today—the New Era! Unicorns! The world connected!—we are left with a strange feeling, like craving a baguette with brie and some *jambon* while motivating through the dusty dirt roads of Phoenix, Arizona. That is, nostalgia for a life that was and could be but is not. As they say, *C'est la vie.*

# CHAPTER 2

# *HOMO DIGITALIS,* OR "IF YOU KNOW, YOU KNOW"

You may be wondering, "Seriously, what were we all thinking"?

In the summer of 2000, the financial analyst Ed Yardeni categorized us humans of the New Era into two different types: the "forward-looking camp" and the "backward-looking crowd."[1]

According to Yardeni, the first camp believed that the digital technology revolution was transforming our economy into the New Economy, and the second viewed the New Economy as mostly hype and considered the technology revolution to be a stock market bubble.

These views were further explored by the chief economist at Deutsche Bank, Alex Brown, who concluded: "The first group gets it, the second group doesn't." It became fashionable for the delusional to refer to their fellow lunatics as those who "get it" and to dismiss everyone else.

We saw this market-driven delusion appear again leading up to the Panic of '08 and then again in 2018–2019 prior to the COVID-19 pandemic. The emergent banking crisis of 2023 looks like yet another chapter in the "Anatomy of a Bust." But it's hard to tell, as of yet. At some point, books about finance meet deadlines. Life, the economy, and history roll on.

## THE "AUGHTS" (AND OUGHT-NOTS)

The 2000s, or "the aughts," as they were called, were a funny time to be alive. Fortunes were made. Hearts were broken. The financial press did not help, at all, trying to figure out what was actually going on. Too much money was foisted into the system. Value had taken a vacation. Looking back, value may have just retired to Miami.

To us *aught* meant zero. There's some irony there. Certainly, at the time, we didn't get the aughts.

Typically, the expression "getting it" described a position considered so hip and correct that there was no need (and little hope) of ever justifying it by appeals to reason or experience.

Men who wondered at the extreme claims of radical feminism, for example, were told that they just didn't get it. The term "woke" with all its accusatory *-isms* hadn't been offered up as a legitimate term yet. But the precedent was well ensconced. You either got it or you didn't. And it wasn't even clear who was "the decider" on these issues back then.[2]

Whether by checking the bumps on human heads, the activity in their email accounts, or their voting habits, Ed Yardeni identified a whole new subspecies of human—*homo digitalis*—the "digital man." The first group—those who get it—"is composed of digital humans," Yardeni wrote, "who believe the New Economy's secular trends are overwhelming the Old Economy's business cycles." The second group, in contrast, "is mostly analog-type (*homo analogous*) personalities who believe that fluctuations are wired into our brains and collective behavior."[3]

His comments were just as annoying back then as they are now. Did human behavior somehow mutate because we now have the internet?

## THE YEAR 2000

Before Yardeni's taxonomy of man and other such leveling denominations, he was best known as the man who had made Y2K hysteria mainstream.

Remember Y2K? That was one for the dustbin of history, as well. Of course, that's easy to say now.

Yardeni predicted that the computer problems associated with the year 2000 would cause a great recession. Of all the Y2K personalities, perhaps none was proven more wrong than Yardeni. Not only were there no Y2K problems of any economic significance—the effect of the whole scare actually created a boom, not a recession—an extremely perverse boom and one that got the heart pumping.

Huge spending on Y2K prophylactics masked itself as a big balloon in productivity, thanks to the miracle workers at the Bureau of Labor Statistics. Yardeni must have been astounded: two little digits on the Gregorian calendar—and BOOM! The world's biggest economy took off. Government and corporate spending on new code and hardware boosted GDP in the third quarter of 1999 by 8%. All that fear and spending ended up amounting to one big huge "nothing burger," as the millennials like to describe events that don't really seem to matter after all.

"The New Economy," echoed David Denby in the *New Yorker,* "seems to be producing a New Man who, in imitation of the economy itself, is going through wrenching changes in the way he lives, works, buys and interacts with other people."[4]

Fast-forward to the post-pandemic economy, and we see another dramatic shift in the way people live, work, interact with one another, and spend leisure time.

The technology being rapidly developed during the early decades of the twenty-first century were implemented in rapid, ubiquitous fashion during the lockdowns. By early 2023, 65% of the workforce refused to return to the office full-time. Businesses looking to hire new talent had to resort to additional incentives just to get them to agree to pre-pandemic workplace norms.

This trend is a dream come true to *homo digitalis*. There they were—a new race of humans walking among us. All we knew about them was that they "got it" and that they were digital. We also knew something of their whereabouts—there were evidently many digital humans on Wall Street and very few in Japan! "Information wants to be free," they chided. "Speed changes the meaning of information. Our goal is to achieve ubiquity." What they said did not seem to matter; they were the young, the hip, the plugged-in. And they got it. Good.

## "GETTING IT"

Someone once said that you only make big money from people who are stupider than you.

*Homo digitalis* figured this out early . . . and were fortunate in having such a large market. Like the hustlers and *chutzpahs* who sold modern art to Fortune 500 corporations, they went right for the high ground.

Everyone—from top corporate CEOs to cab drivers—wanted to throw money their way. Michael Wolff in *Forbes ASAP* described what it was like when the absurd pretensions of the New Era techies met feeble, empty-headed corporate America:

> I wish I could communicate, however guilty I feel about it now, the sheer joy of sitting in meetings with well-established businessmen representing billions of dollars of assets and multimillion-dollar profit streams and being able not only to high hand them because I got it and they didn't, but also to be able to actually humble them, to flagrantly condescend to them, to treat them like children. On the basis of this knowingness, hundreds of billions of dollars have traded hands.

Why didn't the big finance guys get it? Could it be, quite simply, because there was nothing to get? Then, as now, the techies had no real knowledge—just a pretense of knowledge—big, hollow ideas that in the end, meant nothing. Granted, they had technology, but they had no more idea of what it might do or what it might mean than anyone else. Probably less—since they tended to have so little real experience. And even the technology they mastered was often shown to be ineffective, or quickly superseded by more, yet newer technology of an impact and significance that was even less certain. Those trends have continued to this day as every new wizardry

Each revolution seems to demand a New Man to go with it . . . or go along with it. The French Revolution produced the citizens *sans culotte* eager to crucify the priests—from whose hands he formerly took the sacraments—and chop off the head of the aristocrat whose land he had tilled. The Russian Revolution produced a New Man too—the Soviet Man, who not only could do the tasks of 14 normal men, but was above the reach of normal emotions and bodily functions. As Trotsky put it, he would be able to "master even the semi-conscious and unconscious systems of his own body: respiration, the circulatory system, digestion and reproduction."

Those who got it were supposed to know, deep down, an inchoate and indescribable truth that the rest of us could not quite fathom.

As a result, Digital Man—a race of mutant *Homo Sapien*—was supposed to not merely inherit the world, but to take it by adverse possession. But none of the New Men in history (from Russia, France, or elsewhere) ever succeeded in eliminating the weaknesses and sins to which we humans are the heirs.

And even if there were a New Man for the New Economy, he was apparently very similar to the old one: "Greedy, obsessed, and ignorant"[5] were the words that David Denby, writing in the *New Yorker,* used to describe the *homo digitalis* he saw around him.

Like Marx, Engels, or Lenin, the New Era revolutionaries helped convince the average investor that they could get rich without working by buying into technology they did not understand, and stock in companies they did not know the names of, with money they did not have.

What was talk of gigabits of photons flying over glass fiber and multiplexing, pulsating transits other than the information revolution's answer to Marxist claptrap about dialectical materialism? Bear with us.

To the average investor, it was all weird and unfathomable. But if it made him rich, why ask questions?

The revelation was. It happened. Many who invest in tech and Silicon Valley and cryptocurrencies still believe it.

To those who did ask questions—whether they were the reactionary bourgeois elements of Russia in 1917 or the reactionary conservative investors, such as Warren Buffett in 1999—the answer was the same: *they didn't get it.*

The fault was not so much intellectual, for no one accused Buffett of being stupid. It was deeper than that. The New Era demanded investors who understood it in their heart, bones, and guts—with no need for question marks or explanations. Investors who just got it.

## THE WORLD WIDE WEB (OF LIES?)

Don't get us wrong, the information revolution had its people working feverishly to make the world a better place.

"This is real," we recall a lunch companion telling us in early 2000. She had been a commodities trader. But commodities had gone down in price for so many years that it scarcely seemed worth the effort to trade them anymore.

What the world craved was intangibles, not tangibles. "But no one is interested in commodities trading," she explained. So, our friend gave up commodities trading and followed the money. She was now working as an advisor to dot-com entrepreneurs, providing them with information on how to go public. "These guys work 24/7," she explained. "They think they're building a whole new world."

Again, we reprise these comments to reveal what, strangely, predated our current time of anxiety and skepticism in the markets.

Of all the messianic madmen of the era, Michael Saylor of MicroStrategy certainly stood out—perhaps as the most insane, and certainly as one of the richest. Saylor brought entertainment to millions. . . and helped separate countless fools from their money.

"We're purging ignorance from the planet," Saylor exclaimed, setting a lofty goal for himself. He was on a "crusade for intelligence," he claimed;[6] he wanted to make information free and have it run like water. He planned to write a major book on the subject, to be entitled *Intelligence*.

In a contest between ignorance and stupidity on the one hand, and information and intelligence on the other, we know how to bet.

A certain level of madness is often an advantage in the business and entertainment world, but this was too extreme for that. Purging the planet of ignorance? Only a buffoon or a Pollyanna would say such a foolish thing. Saylor was clearly one or the other—maybe both.[7]

Saylor made a public spectacle of himself every time he opened his mouth: "I think my software is going to become so ubiquitous, so essential, that if it stops working there will be riots," he had told a writer for the *New Yorker*.[8]

MicroStrategy had merely developed software that helped businesses figure out who was buying their products. The software allowed McDonald's, for example, to evaluate how many more (or less) Big Macs a Chicago franchise would sell on a winter Friday than would a franchise in Miami.

Saylor also had a less visible corruption; he had hidden massive indiscretions in his company's financial statements.

The stock market had gone mad over companies such as MicroStrategy. Shares were offered to the public on June 11, 1998. Nearly 2 years later, the stock hit $333. Saylor made $1.3 billion that day and $4.5 billion in the preceding week—bringing his personal net worth to $13.6 billion. At the time, MicroStrategy, with sales of only $200 million and a reported profit for 1999 of $12.6 million, was worth more than DuPont. This made Saylor the richest man in the Washington, D.C., area—wealthier even than Oracle founder, Larry Ellison. At $333, the stock price was as insane as the company's CEO.

While we were mocking MicroStrategy, its share price, and its dizzy CEO in our daily email missives (shameless plug: jointhesessions.com), the rest of the financial press was praising him. Hardly a single report failed to find something flattering to say. The English language has thousands of negative words, but before March 20, 2000, the ink-stained hacks, analysts, and TV presenters could not seem to find a single one that applied to Michael Saylor.

Then came March 20, 2000. That day, the financial reporters reopened their dictionaries as Michael Saylor made history.

Under pressure from the Securities and Exchange Commission (SEC), he was forced to admit that MicroStrategy had cooked its books for the previous two years. Instead of a profit of $12.6 million in 1999, the company would now show a loss of $34 million to

$40 million. Revenue, too, was downsized. Never before had a man lost so much money in such a short time.

In 6 hours, his net worth dropped by $6.1 billion.

From that day on, Saylor's life changed. Instead of being praised by investors and the financial media, he was whacked hard. Investors were out $11 billion. Some of them were angry. Others were suicidal. "I never thought I could lose like this," said one investor on the Yahoo!/MicroStrategy message board . . . before declaring that he was going to kill himself. (Remember "message boards"? They were the primitive ancestor to the likes of Reddit.)

Before Y2K, Saylor could do no wrong; for years after, he could do no right. Most prominently, *Fortune* listed him as number one in the "Billionaire Losers Club," with total losses of $13 billion.

But a difficult failure does a man more good than an easy success. On the evidence, Saylor was a better man in the fall of 2001 than he had been a few years earlier. According to *Washington Post* reports, he turned to drinking to drown his losses.[9] When not drinking, he was nursing his business. The stock was still overpriced, but at $3.36, a lot less overpriced than it had been.

So was he still a visionary? An "older, wiser" one, he replied. Saylor would continue his New Era crusade well into the crypto era— becoming one of the most outspoken Bitcoin evangelists in a sea of converts.

Saylor raised eyebrows across the business world in 2020 when he made a $4 billion bet on Bitcoin with MicroStrategy's money. During a correction in the Bitcoin price in early 2022, the firm's balance sheet lost $1 billion on losses in the crypto coin alone. His faith holds strong, however.

The excesses of the dot–com bust, and those that have become the financial norm since, have been well documented elsewhere. By 2001, economists and analysts had already conceded that the "whole internet thing" had gotten out of hand.

Of course, they had no way of knowing that Saylor had fudged the numbers. Nor could they be blamed for not realizing how quickly many of the tech companies would collapse or how far the whole sector would fall. Who could have predicted such things? But, most of those who had seen no reason to resist buying MicroStrategy at more than $110 per share in December 1999 now claimed that they had known all along that there was a bubble in the tech sector. With the wind blowing from a different direction, they found it all too easy to change tack.

We recite the excesses of this era not merely to gawk, scold, or even shrink. It was not just the worst minds in America that were caught up in the bubble delusion, but many of the best. Nor was the bubble a perversion of human nature or an aberration in human history.

Episodically, such things happen. People begin to believe that the old lessons no longer apply and the old rules no longer work. And the misappropriated lessons of that time live with us today, don't they?

Nobody learned from the period of "helicopter money" that followed the implosion of tech stocks after the tech boom. Who, we ask, learned from the bailouts that followed the Financial Panic of 2008? That might seem like a pedantic question, as we gag through another bust today.

By 2000, the bubble economy comprised virtual companies with virtual revenues and virtual profits. A truly digital economy, as *homo digitalis* promised. Companies that had never made a dime of profits, and never would, were valued as if they were worth billions.

We could already see that by the fall of 2001, and yet we were pariahs for saying so. The worst of these companies had already crashed, and the best were on their way back down to where they had started.

Many dot-com entrepreneurs had turned to driving cabs or waiting tables. A few of the era's wheelers and dealers were already being hunted down by ambitious prosecutors to be locked up for their fraud. Some had moved into real estate. Meanwhile, many of the intellectuals who directed, rationalized, hyped, and often profited from the Information Revolution receded, still at large, but poorer and humbler. Not many gave up the quest.

Who are these people who are "changing the world?" It wasn't always for the better.

# CHAPTER 3

# DREAMERS AND SCHEMERS

Jeffrey Preston Bezos was 35 when *Time* magazine awarded him "Person of the Year" in January 2001. *Time* gushed, "Jeff peered into the maze of connected computers called the World Wide Web and realized that the future of retailing was glowing back at him. . . . Every time a seismic shift takes place in our economy, there are people who feel the vibrations long before the rest of us do," prattled the magazine, "vibrations so strong they demand action—actions that can seem rash, even stupid."

In the summer of 2000, *Harry Potter and the Goblet of Fire* arrived (in hardback) on the nation's bookshelves. It was such a hit that many stores quickly ran short of copies. Parents turned to the internet and to the internet's most famous company, Amazon.com, to secure a copy. Amazon was able to take advantage of this success story to bring on 63,550 new customers.

But even the most popular book of the season proved a loss for the company.

Harry Potter sales resulted in losses for Amazon of about $5 million, or about $78.68 per sale (more than three times the purchase price). Company spokesmen promptly claimed that there was no cause for concern as they would make up for the losses through all the new customers the book had brought.

But how, we recall wondering at the time, by selling the next Harry Potter book at four times what it would cost in Barnes & Noble? And how, we pondered, could you put any reasonable value on these money-losing internet companies?

But the summer of 2000 was not yet the time for questions. It was an interesting—wild, even—time for faith.

## THE VALUE OF A SMILE (OR AN EYEBALL)

The value of a stock is determined, ultimately, by the stream of earnings it is expected to produce. The same is true even for internet stocks.

But Amazon, the great big river of internet reverie, produced no stream of profits. Not even a trickle.

Moreover, a report by McKinsey & Company found that the best way to value dot-coms was to return to economic fundamentals with the discounted cash flow approach. But it is hard to discount a flow of cash that does not exist.

It was the nonexistence of cash flow that made Amazon.com (AMZN) and many other internet companies so peculiar and attractive, the object of our imagination.

Lacking facts, investors were left to use their guts. Cash flow could be anything they wanted it to be. Analysts could imagine any price target that suited them. No company stimulated this feeling more than Amazon.com.

The company flowed through the landscape of Internet-Land—Gilder's "Telecosm"? Zuckerberg's "Metaverse"? From the glacial melt high in the high Andes of technological innovation and speculative imagination to the darkened dens of *homo digitalis* . . . to the bug-infested jungle of monopoly, competition, and creative destruction . . . to the mansions of the first-mover advantage and hedonic price measures . . . to the Mount Olympus of the New Man, New Economy, New Metrics, and New Era . . . right down to the delta of washed-out dreams, where all those hyped-up humbugs eventually settle in the mud.

Amazon.com flowed through it all. And never, during this entire spell of absurdity, inanity, and chicanery, could anyone say with any assurance what the company was worth.

In place of a bottom line that could have been multiplied to produce a meaningful price comparison, AMZN had only a sinkhole.

Looking at its financial details more closely, Amazon might have had sales of $574 million in the first 3 months of 2000, but it also had a net loss of $308 million and an operating loss of $198 million. Moreover, compared with the same period of the previous year, although sales had doubled, operating losses had come close to quadrupling. Granted, the company boasted $1 billion in cash and securities, but against that, it had $2 billion in debt, an accumulated deficit of more than $1 billion, and only $25.6 million in stockholders' equity.

Lacking the fulcrum of profits on which to lever a reasonable price, a number of approaches were used over the years to come up with an unreasonable one.

Enter "eyeballs." In the real world, these visual portals were once considered a means of establishing the value of an internet stock. So was "stickiness"—the amount of time the eyeballs stayed glued to the site. Another common approach was multiplying the rate of sales growth.

But, finally, the confederacy of dunces that passed itself off as a group of stock analysts went back to fundamentals. They began to value internet companies in the same way publishers value a subscriber—in terms of lifetime value. Smiles you might say.

Indeed, both publishing companies and internet companies operate on the same basic premise: they spend money to bring in customers. Then, they expect a stream of income (sales, renewals, advertising) from each customer. The value of a company can be determined by calculating the net value of each customer over the lifetime of the relationship and multiplying by the number of customers. Amazon had about 15 million customers at the time. But how much was each one worth?

In February 2000, Jamie Kiggen, an analyst with Donaldson, Lufkin, & Jenrette, dreamed his way to a figure of $1,905. We wondered how, in an industry noted for aggressive competition and razor-thin margins (so thin, in fact, that Amazon's margin was negative—minus 39%—meaning it lost money on each sale), could the company possibly make nearly $2,000 per customer? It couldn't. The idea was preposterous. Still, it gave investors a price target of $140 a share for AMZN.

Another analyst, Eric Von der Porten of Leeward Investments (a California hedge fund, with less of an attachment to the big river), used Kiggen's model and priced the lifetime value of each customer at just $26. Multiply that by the number of customers, and you get a capital value for the company of about $440 million—or a stock price of about $1.25.13.

Bezos, Amazon's founder, would have argued that Kiggen's model was wrong and that it was too early to try to put a value on Amazon because he was not even trying to make a profit. As he explained to *Playboy,* "We are a customer store."[1] He meant that the company focused on the customer instead of on making a profit or even a product. This was another commandment of the internet.

Sales might have continued rising at Amazon. But profits?

In the fourth quarter of 2000, Amazon lost $545 million, a figure $222 million higher than that of the same period the year before. Cumulative losses for the company almost exceeded $3 billion. For *Time,* Amazon's losses were "a sign of the New Economics of internet commerce" and "the idea that in the new global marketplace whoever has the most information wins."

"It's a revolution," *Time* exclaimed. "It kills old economics, it kills old companies, it kills old rules."[2] At the time, all it did, initially, was kill investors' money.

The company claimed to be "the planet's" largest virtual store. It had 23 million registered customers, and Bezos said it would continue getting bigger and bigger—growing at a compound rate of 50% for the next 10 years. That would give it more than 1.3 billion customers by the year 2010. And sales would hit more than $100 billion. It would be the biggest virtual store in the whole blooming galaxy.

Imagine that you had never heard of Amazon or of the New Economy. Imagine that Bezos came up to you and offered you his company for $14 billion. It has $2.1 billion in revenue. Assets of uncertain value. Billions in debt. And it loses more than $1 billion a year. What would be your reaction? Would you pay $14 billion for the privilege of losing $1 billion per year? Would you want a piece of that deal? In the heyday of the New Era, many people did.

Some people get rich in a revolution. Some people get killed. By October 2001, it was becoming clear who would be the victims—those who believed in Amazon.com and the Information Revolution.

Bezos was, of course, one of those victims. In 2001, he was awarded the "Fame Is Fleeting Award," by Gretchen Morgenson in the *New York Times,* "for one of the fastest falls from grace in recent history."[3] She considered it sadly ironic that he was facing irate shareholders only a year after being honored as *Time*'s Person of the Year. There is a greater irony in Bezos' rocket ship flying to space in 2021.

At the end of 2000, Amazon's stock price showed a decline of 89% to the $7 to $10 range (from its December 1999 high of $113). Thus, a pin had pierced the bubble in high technology, and those who "got it" were getting it good and hard. Their day of reckoning had come.

Of course, like Saylor, Bezos would live to fight another day. Perhaps that is another lesson of the boom-and-bust cycle: hold on for dear life; we've got a hell of a bumpy ride.

Following the new economy playbook, Amazon was losing money on every book sold. In order to do what most companies are meant to do—post profits—they had to change their business plan.

In 2006, Amazon launched Amazon Web Services (AWS). The new business strategy leveraged its web technology and logistics business by consulting with other corporations who were trying to get online.

Amazon didn't capture investors' imagination until 2016—15 years after we first started writing about it. By 2021, when the stock hit its historic high of $178, AWS accounted for 83% of the company's profits.[4]

On July 27, 2017, Bezos' unicorn briefly made him the world's richest man, surpassing Microsoft cofounder Bill Gates' $90 billion. On the strength of the stock price, Bezos' bank account blew past $100 billion for the first time on November 24, 2017, and he was formally named by *Forbes* magazine the world's richest man on March 6,

2018, with a net worth of $112 billion. A very public divorce and drop in the stock price soon knocked him down a few notches on the billionaires' billionaire list.

The COVID-19 pandemic was Bezos' friend as well. His company's prowess in logistics was able to deliver any number of goods to house-bound, claustrophobic families on lockdown. One of the darlings of the New Era, it turns out, was really good at delivering material things. Of course, he still had enough money to blast Star Trek's Captain Kirk (actor William Shatner), into space for real on his oddly phallic Blue Origin spaceship on October 13, 2021.[5]

## COUPLES WHO ENGINEER TOGETHER

Of all the companies that might have been able to harness the new advantage given them by the Information Age, perhaps none was better placed than Cisco. The company was so admired by investors that they gave it a market cap higher than any other company had ever received. Even after the Nasdaq had crashed, Cisco's CEO John Chambers explained to investors that the company would nevertheless continue to enjoy 30% to 50% annual sales growth for as far as the eye could see.

But the all-seeing eye could not see very far. It saw only what it wanted to see. Neither Greenspan, the world's most celebrated macroeconomist, nor Cisco Systems, one of the most envied corporations on Wall Street, really understood what was going on.

As was becoming obvious, the New Era was a capital spending boom that made Wall Street's numbers look seductive.

In the late 1990s, businesses all over the planet felt the need to get into the swing of the New Era by spending on information technology (IT). In the perverse logic of the late tech bubble, if they could spend enough, fast enough—their share prices would rise.

But sooner or later, companies had all the routers and multiplexers they needed—even more than enough. Business capital investment fell between 2000 and 2001. And unsold equipment piled up on the shelves.

Meanwhile, Cisco sales, which analysts had expected to grow 30% per year for the next 10 years, began falling instead. In fact, in 2001, it was down 25% on the preceding year. Like an auto dealer in a downturn, Cisco found itself with its lot full of various makes and models that it wanted to unload—new and used.

"Cisco Systems Capital," reported the company's website, "now offers refurbished Cisco equipment with the same warranty protection and support as new . . . but at a lower price." Discounts listed at www.usedrouter.com ranged from almost 70% to as little as 20%.

"I can buy the equipment for 10 cents on the dollar," said one regular customer. "The stuff we are seeing right now is very often less than a year old and still under warranty."

At its peak in early 2000, Cisco (CSCO) was worth nearly half a trillion dollars. This is the equivalent of about $4,000 for every household in America, or about $75 for every *Homo sapien* on the planet. Meanwhile, Cisco shares traded hands at about 190 times earnings. This implied a growth rate for the company of about 190% according to the conventional analysis. In reality, this figure was about 3.5 times the company's actual growth rate. It was also mathematically unsustainable: the higher the rate of growth, the faster the market opportunity would be exhausted.

Cisco's story is well known. In 1984, Sandy Lerner and Len Bosack got together to solve a problem. They needed to make the computers in Stanford University's business school capable of talking to those in the engineering school. They built routers, cobbled together some software, and solved the problem. Henceforth, Stanford's business students could send dirty jokes to the guys in the engineering department via computer. It was not long before other computer users were showing up at Lerner and Bosack's door to get the communications equipment. The couple got married and set up shop in their home—manufacturing the devices themselves and using credit cards as a source of capital.

By 1990, CSCO was a player in Silicon Valley. The Lerner and Bosack team brought in a venture capital group that took the company to the public markets and then forced the founding couple out. Lerner and Bosack divorced in the early 1990s. So they had neither the company they founded nor each other's company.

But if the marriage did not prosper, the company certainly did, and Cisco figured that it needed to offer more than just routers. So in the mid-1990s, it began purchasing other companies involved in the computer communications trade.

Cisco acquired one company in 1993, three companies in 1994, four companies in 1995, and seven in 1996, including the $4 billion acquisition of StrataCom, then the largest purchase in the history of Silicon Valley. It picked up six more companies in 1997, nine in 1998, eighteen in 1999, and bought ten in 2000, for a total of 58 acquisitions.

The Cisco kids were certainly on a buying binge. The idea was pretty simple. Customers did not want routers. They wanted solutions to their communications problems. And since the problems had varied solutions, Cisco needed to offer a variety of products.

Cisco, in other words, was not a router company. It was a marketing channel for computer communications. When it bought some small company with a useful, but largely unknown, device, the product was marked with the Cisco brand and launched to the customer base. Negligible sales could go to monster sales almost overnight. One company, for example, that had $10 million in revenues at the time of acquisition, gave Cisco technology that soon generated more than $1 billion in revenues.

This was all very well, but when two new companies a month were being purchased, they were not all likely to produce such spectacular results. In fact, most were likely to be duds. A lot, it turned out, depended on how the accounting was done.

Moreover, Cisco's appetite for acquisitions drove up prices to preposterous levels. It bought ArrowPoint for shares worth $5.7 billion—a lot of money to pay for a company that had a negative book value, had never earned a penny, and had sales of only about $40 million. But what did the Cisco kids care? The company's funds did not represent real money; it was "Cisco scrip"—a new currency provided by delusional investors.

Each share of CSCO stock was thought to be worth about $63. But an investor would earn no dividends, and the company itself earned only 38 cents per share. Even if profits continued to increase at the 1999 rate, Cisco would earn only $3.74 per share in 5 years. If the stock price had continued apace, the company would have been worth nearly $5 trillion, an amount equal to half of the entire US GDP.

What's more, the process of creative destruction, of which Cisco was such an extraordinary beneficiary, was not likely to stop dead in its tracks the moment the company finally reached a level of profitability that justified its price (if ever). That is the trouble with new technology, after all.

There is always newer technology, as well as newer and better Cisco kids just waiting for their moments of fame and fortune.

## THAT'S SOOO "OLD ECONOMY"

Then there was General Motors (GM). They make cars. But Carl Icahn, corporate raider of 1980s fame, was in the news again at the end of the century for a more financial reason. He was attempting to force GM to sell its stake in Hughes Electronics in order to "unlock shareholder value."

GM had more sales, in dollar terms, than any other company in the world—$177 billion worth. But it only earned a profit of $6 billion (3% of sales). Not only were earnings low, but the other news was not good. GM was losing market share, and its unionized workers seemed ready to revolt.

GM did have a few things going for it. Even in September 2000, $6 billion was a lot of money. Plus, the company had $10 billion in cash. Its pension plan was overfunded by $9 billion. And it owned a stake in Hughes that was worth $15 billion.

Icahn's idea was obvious. He would buy a big enough block of GM stock to be able to force the company to sell the Hughes shares. The entire company—at its then current stock price—had a value of about $36 billion, less than one-tenth of Cisco's.

Imagine that you, personally, could have bought the company. For $36 billion, you would have bought a company with $10 billion in the cash register. So, you would only really be $26 billion out of pocket. And then, you could have sold the Hughes holding for $15 billion, so the rest of the company would really have cost you only $11 billion.

You would have had the world's biggest company (producing cars, trucks, and other things you could actually put your hands on) as well as a spare 1966 Corvette in a garage somewhere for you to drive around. Factories, real estate, giant machinery . . . you've got it all. Plus, you would have earned about $6 billion each year.

Expressed in conventional terms, the operating part of the world's largest company had a P/E of just 1.83. From your point of view, as owner, you would have gotten back your investment money in about 20 months and have earned about $6 billion every year after that. Or you could have bought 10% of Cisco.

If you relied on the slogans and feebleminded dicta of the financial media, you would have avoided GM. GM was so "old economy." It was a has-been company that seemed unable to get its act together. Owning GM was definitely not cool.

Icahn did not worry about being cool. He had a PhD in philosophy from Princeton. In his thesis, he developed the idea that collective thinking is invalid: "Knowledge is based only on what you observe. You talk to me about something, you must relate it to something that's observable." There was nothing to get unless it was right in front of you.

Of course, George Gilder had no interest in GM. He was interested in Global Crossing, and he couldn't get enough of it when it was trading at 33 times sales and $60 per share. The man must have been beside himself with joy when, in October 2001, he could buy as many shares as he wanted for only 50 cents apiece. Investors had lost 99.9% of their money already, but the losses did not stop there. An investor who held on at 50 cents would have lost another 96% of his money by the end of the following year, when the stock traded for only 2 cents.

Maybe the promise of the Information Age would come true at last. Suddenly, late at night, when sensible men had taken to their beds and only techies, terrorists, and teenagers were still awake, the world's dark fibers would light up with data. And maybe then, Global Crossing's stock would rise. . . to 3 cents!

GM proved to be one of the most prominent victims once the tech bubble morphed, aided and abetted by the Feds, into a much larger bubble, a bubble who's detritus—once popped—dripped all over Icahn's "real" economy as well as the financial markets. In 2009, GM received $12.5 billion in bailout funds as the company was forced to declare bankruptcy. All told, by 2014 the US Treasury Department spent $50 billion to save the moribund carmaker and its 1.2 million employees.[6]

By 2014, the government admitted it had written off $11.2 billion in losses because it could not save the "old" GM.

Icahn is an investor at heart. He was the primary investor in GM prior to the 2008 crisis. GM had gone bust. The government ended up taking over. When we wrote this chapter, he was the majority shareholder.

He was a financier making a big bet on the old economy. Which failed. The only way that they could fix it was through government intervention.

GM was put into receivership and relaunched. In the end, when it all fell apart, GM had to reengineer its cars and entertain the new prospect of green electric vehicles.

It was one of the largest nonbanking corporate bailouts in US history.

The fall of GM represented a true falling away from the New Economy, encouraging investors to further delude themselves in the fervor of all that is the finance of the internet and its myriad technologies.

## THE PRICE WE PAY

Today, we might laugh, but Gilder, a messiah of the New Era, was still in the wilderness, and who can fault him for that? After all, he did no harm.

Behind his *pensées* was an even nuttier idea—that information in the form of digitized data could make people rich. His thinking was very much in the spirit of the times, when a powerful sense of optimism pervaded American civil society.

But in every revolution, the real mischief was done by the small cadre of cynical gun runners who followed in their messiah's visionary footsteps. Who can blame Gilder for his disciples' excesses?

A former Global Crossing employee described Winnick and his Global Crossing cronies as "the biggest group of greedheads in an era of fabled excess."

Winnick made money on Global Crossing—again, by selling rather than buying its stock.

When the telecoms blew up, he managed to walk away with $730 million before the bomb detonated. But other investors were not so lucky: they lost $2.5 trillion in market value. Somehow, Grubman forgot to tell them when to sell. Instead, as late as spring 2001, he wrote about the "historic opportunities to buy world-class assets such as Global Crossing that are evolving into world-class operating businesses at compelling value." On that same day, Global Crossing shares sold for $7.68. If they were "compelling" then, you would think the shares would be absolutely irresistible later on! Alas, after the company went bankrupt, Grubman, who owned a $6 million townhouse in Manhattan, with neither mortgage nor lien, simply "discontinued coverage" of the stock.

All of this did not mean much to Gilder. No, no—he really was not to blame. For he was still staring at the skies, thinking about gigabits, and scribbling away. . . even when creditors pulled up in front of his house and wondered how much they could get for it.

But how had it come to this? he asked himself.

After all, he had listened to the technology and had begun hearing voices just as the Information Revolution was getting underway.

In a better world, things might have gone differently, he convinced himself. After all, he had been earnestly blathering before large crowds and making good money at it. Almost 400 people had paid $4,000 each to attend his Telecosm conference in 1997; his speeches, heard by thousands, earned him $50,000 per talk. Moreover, in 1999, his list of recommended tech stocks had averaged more than a 247% return, and by the end of 2000, his newsletter boasted 70,000 subscribers paying $295 a year. At the bubble's peak, just one "gildered" word could boost a stock price 50% in a single day.

But then the New Era messiah had stumbled over a bit of bad luck. Tech stocks crashed, and suddenly people were not interested in attending his conferences or reading his newsletters, for they no longer seemed to care how many bits you could crowd onto the head of a silicon chip.

Worse, in January 2002, came the news that his favorite corporation—the company he thought would "change the world economy"—had filed for bankruptcy protection. Gilder reflected on his fortunes over those past few years:

> You can be just fabulously flush one moment, and then the next, you can't make that last million-dollar payment to your partners, and there's suddenly a lien on your house. . . . For a few years in a row there, I was the best stock picker in the world. But last year you could say . . . I was the worst.[7]

Poor George, very rich when things were going his way, had gone broke when they changed direction.

But to his credit (not his benefit), at least the guru had put his money where his mouth was. He had not merely misled investors; he had misled himself too. He had bought into everything—Global Crossing, the New Era, his own publishing business.

Still suffering from New Era hallucinations, he continued to have faith in the wonders of technology, even after the Nasdaq's crash. He later expressed his belief in the power of his "Telecosm," claiming that it was "transforming the world economy and every existing political and cultural arrangement," and could significantly improve productivity. He wasn't wrong, per se: "Its ability to transmit any amount of information, to anyone anywhere, anytime, at a negligible cost" unleash surges of productivity as yet unimagined.[8] It's just that Gilder didn't do price.

It's not only the mentality that made us think our humanity had reached it pinnacle in the new millennium. Our monetary policy too seemed to think we had achieved greatness.

# PART TWO

# THE FABULOUS DESTINY OF ALAN GREENSPAN

*We know that the gold the devil gives his paramours turns into excrement after his departure.*

—Sigmund Freud

# CHAPTER 4

# IN THE BATH BLOWING BUBBLES

"How do we know when irrational exuberance has unduly escalated asset values, which then become subject to unexpected and prolonged contractions?" asked Fed Chairman Alan Greenspan, speaking that foreign language of datasets and economic politics. The occasion was a black-tie dinner at the American Enterprise Institute in December 1996. In translation, he asked: "At what point will the Fed come in and spoil the stock-go-up party at the end of the world?"

"We as central bankers," Greenspan continued, "need not be concerned if a collapsing financial asset bubble does not threaten to impair the real economy, its production, jobs, and price stability. But we should not underestimate or become complacent about the complexity of the interactions of the asset markets and the economy."

The answer: Never.

In 1996, the bear market of 1973 to 1974—and the market crash of 1987—were still blaring caution signs to Greenspan. Consequences spindled their grasping fingers, to which he turned the other cheek.

The Chairman spoke on the evening of December 5. On the morning of December 6, markets reacted. Investors in Tokyo panicked, giving the Nikkei Dow a 3% loss for the day, its biggest drop of the year. Hong Kong fell almost 3%. Frankfurt 4%. London 2%.

But by the time the sun rose over New York City, investors had decided not to care. After a steep drop in the first half-hour, as overnight sell orders were executed, the market began a rebound and never looked back.

By the spring of the year 2000, the Dow had almost doubled from the level that had so concerned the Fed chairman.

The last thing "the Maestro," as he was heralded, wanted to do was to upset the way things were going. He was alarmed at Dow 6,437, serene at Dow 11,722.

In 1996, he had been pressured by politicians of both parties to go along with the gag. Stocks were rising, and everyone was happy. The last thing they wanted was a sourpuss at the Fed ruining the party. Conveniently, Greenspan came to believe—as many other around him—in the New Era and all that came with it, including a newfound power to guide the economy.

## TALKING YOUR BOOK

Wall Street has an expression for fund managers whose conversations seem intended to support their current market holdings. "They are talking their book," say the old-timers.

A fund manager with a huge short position says he is sure the market is going to fall; another whose beat is precious metals says he expects a raging bull market in his sector come tomorrow; and one who specializes in technology is almost certain to tell you that tech stocks are the only way to make money on Wall Street.

All of a sudden, after his comment on "irrational exuberance," Greenspan seemed to wake up and realize what business he was in. Whatever else he might be doing, he was the lead PR man for American consumer capitalism, the US economy, the dollar, and capital markets.

Stocks were already expensive in 1996. But they were getting even more expensive and no one—not the politicians, the brokers, or the investors—wanted to see the process come to an end. The

Fed chief had momentarily forgotten that what benefited Alan Greenspan was not objective commentary on the level of stock prices, but helping stock prices go up even further.

The higher stocks rose, the more convinced people became that the top man at the central bank knew what he was doing. Greenspan's "book" was long stocks, not short.

Appearing before Congress a few weeks later, the Fed chief saw his mistake clearly.

Jim Bunning, a Republican senator from Kentucky, must have thought he had a direct link to the market gods. Somehow, he knew that the stock market was not overpriced. Greenspan's position was "misguided," he said, adding that it might "become more of a threat to our economy than inflation ever will be."

Phil Gramm, a Republican from Texas, was more modest. Still, he did have an opinion, and it was at odds with the Fed chairman's. "I would guess," he ventured, "that equity values are not only not overvalued, but may still be undervalued." Confusing, yes, but telling about a feeling of deep uncertainty over the grandiose nature of Greenspan's monetary policy. Bunning put it to the Maestro straight: "If we get prime interest rates at double digits, we are going to stop this economy in its tracks. I don't want to see that happen on your watch, and I surely don't want to see it happen on mine."[1]

Greenspan got the message. "I have the same view," he replied.

The chairman had learned his lesson quickly. Once skeptical of the New Economy, he began talking his book: "This is the best economy I've ever seen in 50 years of studying it every day," he told Bill Clinton in May 1998.[2]

"What we may be observing in the current environment," he said in December of that year, "is a number of key technologies, some even mature, finally interacting to create significant new opportunities for value creations. New technology has radically reduced the costs of borrowing and lending across traditional national borders," he added.[3]

Even in mid-2001, after trillions had been lost in the capital markets and a recession had begun in the United States, the chairman still sounded like the Wall Street analyst Abby Joseph Cohen: "There is still, in my judgment, ample evidence that we are experiencing only a pause in the investment in a broad set of innovations that has elevated the underlying growth in productivity . . . The mildness and brevity of the downturn are a testament to the notable improvement in the resilience and the flexibility of the economy."

## SPIKING THE PUNCHBOWL

Greenspan's predecessor, William McChesney Martin, once remarked that the real job of the Fed was to "take away the punchbowl"[4] before the party got out of control.

While the country was beginning to really feel the pangs of a hangover from the tech boom and bust, instead of taking away the punch bowl, Sir Alan[5] did the exact opposite: he spiked it with the high-proof gin of cheap and easy credit.

Every time the head of the Federal Reserve faced a problem, he slunk over to the punchbowl and poured more in, until Americans were wobbling under the influence of the lowest interest rates in 45 years: a 1% key Fed lending rate for only the second time in history.

The tech bust of Wall Street in the late 1990s into the new millennium was a lot of things. Silly, embarrassing, most of all enlightening.

The people who should have lost money did. And they probably would have lost a lot more had not the Feds, led by Greenspan, stepped in and did what they do best—they began moving money around, "papering over" the ramifications of the bust to keep the party going.

In this sort of environment, skeptics had a hard time. No one has perfect information, and people—quite rationally, in fact—infer a great deal from the actions of others.

As a bubble expands, some skeptics begin to disregard their own judgment because they feel that everyone else simply couldn't be wrong. Contrarian voices become softer, which only makes it harder for the remaining skeptics to justify their views. Over time, the quality of information that can be gleaned from the behavior of others becomes worse and worse.[6]

The tech boom made cab drivers and shoe shiners feel like stock market geniuses, if only for a short while. Throw a dart at the screen, and you would make money.

The housing boom that followed made the tech boom and consequent bust seem quaint. It involved more than just speculators in the stock market; it sucked in everyone who was either trying to buy a home, manage their home equity, or rent. In other words, most of the US adult population.

All of a sudden, even buying a home—once seen as the ultimate responsibility—was available to everyone and the pool boy. The housing markets took over the public's imagination, turning their eyes away from what should have been a long and painful correction following the irrational exuberance of the dot-com bubble at the turn of the century.

"Alan, you're it," Bob Woodward, author of *Maestro: Greenspan's Fed and the American Boom,* quotes E. Gerald Corrigan on October 20, 1987.[7] "Goddamit, it's up to you. This whole thing is on your shoulders," Corrigan continued.

In his book, Woodward observes the scene like a ground squirrel watching a bank robbery. He notices every movement but seems to have no idea what was going on.

Greenspan, however, knew exactly what he was doing: Greenspan never put the interests of others ahead of his own. He was just going along.

"The Federal Reserve, consistent with its responsibilities as the nation's central bank, affirmed today its readiness to serve as a source of liquidity to support the economic and financial system," said Greenspan's press release.

Forget the gold standard, the Fed chief seemed to say; we'll make sure there is plenty of paper money and electronic credit for everyone. And so there was.

In every subsequent crisis that came along—the Gulf War and recession of 1993, the Asian Currency Crisis, the Russian Crisis, the collapse of LTCM, the threat of the Y2K computer bug, and finally, the Great Bear Market of 2000 onward, the Greenspan Fed reacted in the same way: by providing the market with more money and more credit.

The figures are breathtaking. Since assuming control of the nation's currency, Chairman Greenspan added $4.5 trillion to the money supply (as measured by M3)—doubling the total amount printed by all the Fed chairmen before him (see Figure 4.1).

"He helps breathe life into the vision of America as strong, the best, invincible," gushed Woodward. But it was the hot breath of nearly unlimited credit that caused the United States to get a little light-headed.

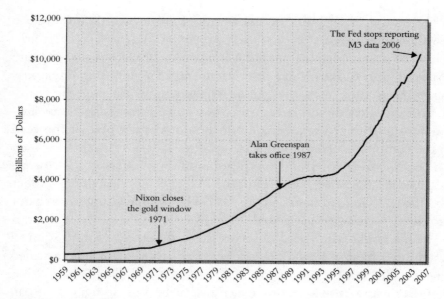

**FIGURE 4.1** Fast Cash from the Greenspan Fed

Sixteen years after Nixon closed the gold window, Randian acolyte and onetime gold bug, Alan Greenspan began authorizing more paper money than all previous Federal Reserve chairmen combined.

*Source:* Federal Reserve.

The effect of all this money and credit was to spur the biggest boom in financial assets in world history.

Paul Volcker had broken inflation's back; now the Fed could ease almost at will. When stocks and real estate prices rose, as they had in the United States in the Roaring 1920s, no one complained.

It was only inflation in consumer prices that brought howls of discontent and rumors of a personnel change at the nation's central bank. Asset prices could rise to the point of absurdity; no effigies of the Fed chairman would be burned. No search would be begun for his replacement.

## WHERE THE PAPER AT

Most economists will tell you that the economic system is controlled by mood changes at the Fed. But sometimes things happen even when US central bankers are not particularly in the mood for them.

When the Fed governors feel the need for a little more bustling about in the nation's shops and factories, they administer a little "coup de whiskey," as Fed Chief Norman Strong once put it.

When they are in the mood for calm, by contrast, they take away the whiskey bottle, and the party soon dies down.

Since World War II, the Fed's mood swings have seemed to correspond well with the ups and downs in the economy. An associate of Greenspan, John Taylor, had codified the observation in what was called the Taylor Rule. As the economy, and inflation, heated up, the Fed's overnight lending rates also rose.

As the economy, and inflation, cooled, the Fed's shortest rates came down too. But sometimes things happen even if US central bankers are not particularly in the mood for them.

Despite a flood of money and credit creation, as well as widespread predictions of recovery, in the first years of the twenty-first century the markets refused to cooperate.

Whatever was ailing the US economy, it did not seem to yield to a shot or two of whiskey. For the first time in the postwar period, monetary easing—even the most aggressive easing in the Fed's history—proved a flop.

Throughout 2001, the Greenspan Fed did what it had to do and the only thing it could have done: it cut rates. Month after month, sometimes 25 basis points were cut, sometimes 50 basis points. At first, nearly every economist and every investor expected a "second half recovery." But a genuine recovery never came. Unemployment went up; profits went down.

Consumers took the bait offered to them by the Fed: lower interest rates. Debt continued to rise. By mid-2001, private-sector debt equaled 280% of GDP—the largest debt pile in economic history. Then, in the first quarter of 2002, consumers borrowed at an annual rate of $695 billion—breaking all previous records.

Their incomes, on the other hand, rose at an annual rate of only $110 billion. And for the 12 months ending in April 2002, $5.9 of debt was added for every $1 of growth in GDP. By the end of 2002, private sector debt had hit 300% of GDP.

Dallas Fed Governor Robert McTeer told the Richardson, Texas, Chamber of Commerce in February 2001, "If we all go join hands and go buy an SUV, everything will be all right . . . preferably a Navigator."

After the terrorist attacks, the calls for consumer spending began to sound as much like patriotic jingos as economic analysis. Thrift came to be seen as an enemy of the state, almost as diabolical as Osama bin Laden.

"On Long Island," the *Los Angeles Times* tattled on a man 3,961 kilometers away, "bakery worker Carlos Gaviria said the market collapse has caused him to rein in his personal spending. 'If enough people do the same,' he said, 'it could add up to something big.'"[8]

"What's going on on Wall Street . . . tells me that whatever money I have, I have to hold on to, because it isn't predictable what's going to happen tomorrow," Gaviria told the *Times*. "By holding my money, maybe I am affecting the economy itself."

Even McTeer recognized it. Later in the year, he explained: "With industry already in a slump, the only thing that has kept the nation out of recession has been the willingness of consumers to dig into their pockets and buy. That spending has been fueled by an ever increasing use of credit."[9]

"They [Americans] have been doing something that's probably irrational from the point of view of the individual consumer," said McTeer, speaking of the trend he and other Fed governors had helped put in motion, "because they all need to be saving more: saving for retirement, saving for college and all that. But we'd be in bad trouble if they started doing that rational thing all of a sudden. We're happy they're spending. We wish that they didn't run up a lot of debt to do it."[10]

But in the fall of 2001, instead of falling, US consumer confidence took its biggest jump in more than 10 years. Nearly every price and every statistic revealed a startling lack of worry.

The absence of qualms or question marks was unsettling. Consumers increased personal consumption at a 6% rate in the fourth quarter of 2001—the same quarter in which the economy was supposed to be reeling from the recession and the terrorist attacks of September 11. "Never before have consumers spent with such abandon during a recession," commented Stephen Roach, chief economist at Morgan Stanley.

Consumers go more deeply into debt only when they are pretty sure the extra debt will be no problem for them. In 2000 alone, they borrowed another $198 billion against their own homes. The total in

2002 was $1.2 trillion. Even following a recession, they were sure jobs would be plentiful. Nor did they fear that interest rates would rise. Not that rates couldn't rise—they just didn't seem to think about it.

Nor were investors greatly worried that stocks were too expensive. They were more concerned about how they would feel if stocks rose and they missed out on the bull market. They bid up stocks to price levels the world had never seen and was unlikely to see again in their lifetimes. At the end of 2001, the S&P traded at 44 times earnings. And the P/E ratio of the median Value Line stock reached 20.3 (as figured by Ned Davis Research)—a new record high.

The confidence of US consumers and investors was taken as good news throughout the world. People thought it meant good things to come. A contrary view was that it was merely a sign of good things that had already come and gone. Confidence is a trailing indicator. The more there is of it, the greater the boom left behind and the greater the trouble that lies ahead.

Why were consumers and investors so confident? Looking backward, they had plenty of good reasons for optimism. The Dow had seemed to go nowhere but up for the previous two decades (with a little leveling off in the most recent 2 years). Inflation and interest rates had been going down for about the same length of time. The Soviet Union had capitulated. The United States was in a class of its own militarily—not merely the world's only superpower—but the world's only real power of any sort. Never before had there been such an imbalance between US military spending and that of the rest of the world. Challenges to the US military and economic might had been feeble; both the battle against recession and the War Against Terror had been waged with a few casualties. Was it any wonder that Americans looked back with pride and the warm glow of confidence?

But looking forward was another matter. In a bull market, "stocks climb a wall of worry," say the old-timers, but on this polished stone of self-satisfaction, stocks found few footholds. Not that there wasn't plenty to worry about. There was the current account deficit, for example, and the dollar. Sooner or later, the rest of the world would begin to ask questions, even if Americans did not. Then, the dollar would fall . . . and so would US financial assets.

And, of course, there were stocks themselves, esteemed so highly by ordinary investors that there was almost no chance that they would be able to live up to the expectations that had been set for them. Sooner or later, it was reasonable to think, disappointment would lead to disinvestment. Jeremy Grantham told Barron's that every bubble episode was eventually fully corrected. He challenged readers to think of a single counterexample. None came forward. But these things did not seem to worry Americans. They drove ahead confidently. Hands on the wheel . . . foot on the throttle pedal . . . and their eyes fixed on the road behind them!

In the fall of 2001, encouraging consumer confidence was easy work. Consumers were ready for it. For 20 years, they could not help but notice that interest rates had been coming down—lowering the burden of debt. Inflation, little by little, reduced the weight of it. Except for a slight recession in the early 1990s, consumers had known nothing but economic expansion and nearly full employment since 1982.

Who could doubt that there would always be work available for anyone who wanted to do it? Who imagined that Greenspan's aggressive cutting of interest rates would not quickly put the economy on the road to recovery? Who would have thought that lower interest rates would not be a godsend for consumers—enabling them to continue spending?

The problem with consumers was not that they lacked confidence, but that they had too much. Their apparent financial success combined with the success of the Fed, had made them confident to the point of recklessness. Thus, they were ready meat for the innovators in the financial industry. Never lacking ingenuity, innovators came up with new and better ways to turn consumers' confidence into consumer debt—just as Minsky had predicted. Soon auto manufacturers were offering 0% financing. And mortgage mongers were allowing customers to borrow up to 100% (2002 figures) of the appraised value, pay interest only for up to 15 years, and even skip payments from time to time.

Almost unnoticed, homebuilders had even found a way to bypass the typical mortgage requirement that a prospective borrower must at least be able to pony up the down payment.

A borrower with none of his own money at stake seemed a poor credit risk. But a loophole in the Fannie Mae rules allowed a nonprofit group to put up the down payment in order to encourage home ownership among disadvantaged groups. Homebuilders soon realized that they could fund down payment assistance (DPA) groups themselves and sell more houses to more marginal home buyers. By the end of 2002, DPA plans were involved in 20% of new mortgages.

And where stocks were concerned, even after 9 months of recession, instead of sinking to recession levels, during which you can buy a dollar's worth of earnings for 8 to 12 bucks, a dollar's worth of earnings would have cost you about $40. Stocks were so high that earnings could double in 2001—as most analysts were predicting—and P/E ratios would still be at the top of the bull market range even if stock prices went nowhere.

What kind of recession was this? Perhaps it was the perfect one—as phony as the boom that preceded it. We remind readers that the boom was built on a lie: that thanks to a cluster of New Era stars, the earth would never again sleep in darkness. Things would get better and better, forever and ever, amen. So brightly did these stars sparkle that investors went mad looking at them—sure that they were going to get rich without working! And so, they bid up stock prices and thought they saw their wealth go up. And thus the promises of the stars seemed to be coming true.

Greenspan did not agree with the idea that a bust is necessary to correct the mistakes of a boom. Rather, to him, the Fed's job is to mitigate the amplitudes—the highs and the lows—of the business cycle. By pumping credit into the system through loosening monetary policy, Greenspan found that he could stimulate a business cycle uptrend *ad infinitum*, absolving risk, papering over losses, and keeping the party going.

Like all night's out, however, a hangover is waiting in the morning.

# CHAPTER 5

# "FREE MONEY" AND OTHER NEW ERA HALLUCINATIONS

Easy money is in its own way a mass psychology event. As more and more money was spent on information technology, and computational power continued to follow Moore's law—doubling every 18 months—GDP and productivity numbers began to look like someone with too many facelifts—grotesque and unrecognizable.

But it was not until the last quarter of 1999 that this hedonic measure really put the productivity numbers in their most flattering light. Info tech spending went wild in the last half of 1999—urged to excess by the Y2K threat. This activity was amplified by the Bureau of Labor Statistics to such an extent that its message could be heard all over the world: 6% productivity was a triumph—the New Era was paying off!

The third and final quarters of 1999 produced some very healthy numbers for labor productivity. The Bureau of Labor Statistics recorded the rate of increase at 5% in the third quarter and 6.4% in the fourth. It was partly on the basis of these numbers that the historic shift of money from the Old Economy to the New Economy was justified and explained. The Old Economy was said to be growing sluggishly, while the new one seemed to be propelled forward at ever-faster speeds by the incredible productivity gains made possible by IT.

"Incredible" was the operative word. When the productivity numbers were deconstructed, they looked less than credible, if not outright fraudulent.

As Kurt Richebächer put it, "After three years of near-stagnation between 1992 and 1995, productivity growth all of a sudden began to spurt in [the last quarter of 1995]. What caused that?"[1]

What caused it was that the Bureau of Labor Statistics changed the way it calculated productivity. It began to look at what it called a "hedonic" price index that took into account not just the price of computer equipment, but its computational power. On the surface, this makes some sense. If a dollar buys twice as much computational power one year as the next, it is as if the price of computing power had fallen in half.

The third quarter of 1995 was the first time this change took effect. It miraculously transformed $2.4 billion in computer spending into $14 billion of output, instantly boosting GDP by 20%, lowering inflation, and increasing productivity (output per hour).

The number for the fourth quarter, to repeat, was spectacular. Incredible. It was revised later to an even more incredible 6.9%.

The only trouble was that it was not real. It was, like the New Era that supposedly made it possible, a fraud. More computational power is not the same as economic growth. And being able to turn out more computational power for each hour of labor input is not the same as an increase in labor productivity.

Like the millions of lines of code and the millions of miles of fiber-optic cable, computational power is only as valuable as the money that people are willing to spend to get it. And that is measured not by hedonic numbers, but by real dollars and cents.

What was true for the nation's financial performance was also true for that of individual companies. Companies engineered their financial reports to give investors the information they wanted to hear. What they were often doing was exactly what Alan Greenspan worried about—impairing balance sheets in order to produce growth and earnings numbers that delighted Wall Street. Curiously, during what was supposed to be the greatest economic boom in history, the financial condition of many major companies actually deteriorated.

## THE MYTH OF PRODUCTIVITY

But by 2000, Greenspan no longer noticed; he had become irrationally exuberant himself.

"Markets make opinions," as they say on Wall Street. The Fed chairman's opinion had caught up with the bull market in equities. As Benjamin Graham wrote of the 1949 to 1966 bull market: "It created a natural satisfaction on Wall Street with such fine achievements and a quite illogical and dangerous conviction that equally marvelous results could be expected for common stocks in the future."

Stocks rise, as Buffett put it, first for the right reasons and then for the wrong ones. Stocks were cheap in 1982; the Dow rose 550% over the next 14 years. Then, by the time Greenspan warned of irrational exuberance, stocks were no longer cheap. But by then no one cared. Benjamin Graham's giant "voting machine" of Wall Street cast its ballots for stocks with go-go technology and can-do management. Stocks rose further; and people became increasingly sure that they would continue to rise.

"Greenspan will never allow the economy to fall into recession," said analysts. "The Fed will always step in to avoid a really bad bear market," said investors. Over the long term, there was no longer any risk from owning shares, they said. Even Greenspan seemed to believe it. If the Fed chairman believed it, who could doubt it was true? The more true it seemed, the more exuberant people became.

"What happened in the 1990s," according to Robert Shiller, author of the book *Irrational Exuberance,* "is that people really believed that we were going into a new era and were willing to take risks rational people would not take . . . people did not feel they had to save. They spent heavily because they thought the future was riskless."[2]

But like value, risk has a way of showing up where it is unexpected. The more infallible Greenspan appeared, the more "unduly escalated" asset values became. Having warned of a modest irrational exuberance, the maestro created a greater one.

"Greenspan Arrests Wall Street Collapse," said a headline in the French financial journal, *La Tribune,* in early December 2000. Greenspan had apparently done it. He had saved the day.

But Greenspan had done nothing yet. And what could he do? Lower short-term rates? Would it work? Why would people, and businesses, who were already deeply in debt, want to borrow even more?

Perhaps lowering the price of credit would do no more to alleviate credit problems than lowering the price of Jim Beam whiskey would help cure dipsomania. In both cases, the problem was not the price of the elixir, but the use to which it has been put.

## JUNK BONDS AND BAD BETS

In the late 1990s, every silly idea that came along could belly up to the credit bar and imbibe almost as much as it wanted. Trillions of dollars worth of capital were raised, spent, and then disappeared. What was left were IOUs, stocks, bank loans, and bonds. The quality of these debt instruments was falling rapidly.

By 2000, the junk bond market was suffering through its worst funk since at least 1990. The average junk bond mutual fund lost 11% that year, its worst performance since 1990. So-called TMT companies (telecommunications, media, and technology) were the worst creditors in the junk bond market. They borrowed huge sums to build out promising new communications networks. ICG Communications Inc., for example, had borrowed $2 billion by the time it filed for Chapter 11 bankruptcy protection in November 2000.

Falling prices for junk bonds meant rising costs of credit for the borrowers—and not just TMT borrowers. J.C. Penney's bonds yielded 18%, Tenneco Automotive's bonds yielded 21.3%, and the gold producer Ashanti's bonds could be bought to yield 27%. These were all troubled companies. But that is what you get after a credit binge: companies with problems because they have taken up too much capital and spent it too freely. You also get consumers with problems, for the same reasons.

When credit is too cheap, people treat it cheaply. The result is trouble. But was it not the sort of trouble that can be cured by even cheaper credit? In 2000, the US economy was near the end of one of the biggest credit binges in history. The headaches and regrets could not be dodged or ignored. The zeitgeist of the market was changing. Instead of dreams, there would be nightmares. Venture funds were being replaced by vulture funds. And hard-nosed, bitter-end investors and workout specialists were taking the place of naïve amateurs. The focus of these serious investors was no longer on cleaning up in the market, but on merely cleaning up. Moreover, investors, who used to believe everything was possible and who accepted every fairy-tale business plan, chapter and verse, were beginning to believe nothing and accepted only Chapters 11 and 7.

Among the sad stories making their way around the World Wide Web at the time was one from Philadelphia concerning Warren "Pete" Musser—one of Wall Street's most aggressive promoters during the Internet mania.

Musser was no fool. The 73-year-old investor built one of the most successful new-tech incubation companies in the nation—with huge stakes in the well-known stars of the internet world—such as ICG, VerticalNet, and US Interactive. He did not get to this position overnight. Instead, he began the firm decades ago and knew his business well. "Of all the guys who should have known better," commented Howard Butcher IV, an investor, who had been a longtime Internet skeptic, "he's a consummate stock promoter. You'd think he would have unloaded it and had his big nest egg of cash instead of being in debt."[3]

But Musser apparently succumbed to the risk that all stock promoters take (and maybe even Greenspan): he came to believe his own hype. And to his own disadvantage. He was forced to sell 80% of his shares to cover an old-fashioned margin call. The shares, worth $738 million a few months before, brought in less than $100 million. It was too late for Musser, but the financial press worldwide continued to report that Greenspan was on his way with help.

Shareholders also believed that Greenspan still held the big put option that would save them from losses. But did he? Could a change in policy by the Fed save the Mussers of this world? Or were their investments so suicidal, so hopeless that they could not avoid self-destruction? In finance, there is smart money, dumb money, and money so imbecilic that it practically cries out for euthanasia.

Pets.com spent $179 to acquire each dog food customer. After the company had gone belly-up, what was left? How could a change in interest rate policy bring back the millions that had been spent? Likewise, TheStreet.com lost $37 million in the first 9 months of 2000—or nearly $400 for every one of its paying customers. TheStreet.com announced the closing of its UK office and a 20% cut in employees. Maybe someday it would find a business model that worked. But how would a lower Fed funds rate help investors recover the $37 million? And, how would lower rates bring back the $100 billion that AOL/Time Warner lost in 2002?

A cut in the Fed funds rate does not suddenly make borrowers more creditworthy. No one was going to jump at the chance to lend money to TheStreet.com or Amazon or other CWI (companies with issues) borrowers just because the Fed cut rates. For if a man borrows more than he can afford and spends the money on high living instead of on productive investments, lower interest rates do not make you want to lend him more. He needs to put his financial affairs in order first—and he cannot do that by borrowing more money.

The way to make money, according to George Soros, is to find the trend whose premise is false and bet against it. The premise of 2001 prices on Wall Street was that Greenspan, public servant, would be able to do what no one has ever been able to do before—prevent stock prices from regressing to the mean.

Many reasons were offered for his likely success: the "productivity miracle" was popular, until most figures showed productivity growth regressing to the mean. "Higher GDP growth rates" was also a winner, until GDP growth also slowed. "Information technology" had a ring to it, but it needed the objective correlative of higher productivity and economic growth to give it substance. How about "higher corporate profits?" Alas, that fell into the gutters of Wall Street as corporate profits slipped up along with everything else, including the myths of the "endless expansion" and the "perfect inventory control systems." Only one thin reed remained standing—the idea that Greenspan was in control of the US dollar and its economy.

Yet, little in the history of the Fed justified the confidence people seemed to have in it.

As January 2001 began, economists must have been on the edge of their chairs. Would the Fed, which had debased the currency it was supposed to protect, now turn out to be the savior of the whole economy? Nowhere in the Federal Reserve–enabling legislation is there any mention of a "chicken in every pot." There is no discussion of "protecting Wall Street's commissions," of "bailing out underwater businesses," of "stimulating consumers to buy," of "helping Americans go further into debt," nor of "reinflating leaky bubbles." Yet, those were the things the Fed now aimed to do.

## CHICKEN IN EVERY POT

Drunk on Greenspan's easy credit, Y2K blood scrubbed clean off the streets. Where were American investors to turn?

To real estate, of course. And with serious conviction.

Housing mania took over the United States—and everyone was getting in on the action. Yale professor Robert Shiller explained the phenomenon as "infectious exuberance."

Speculative bubbles are fueled by the contagious delusions of boom thinking and are only encouraged by rising prices. Sooner or later, some factor boosts the transmission rate high enough above the removal rate for an optimistic view of the market to become widespread.

Arguments that "this boom" is unlike past bubbles—said "New Era hallucinations"—become more prominent and seemingly credible. In the housing boom, such optimism was much in evidence.

Our parents and grandparents viewed owning a home as the goal of financial life. The hallmark of the American Dream.

By 2004, the S&P/Case-Shiller Home Price Index revealed the prospect of home ownership was rapidly becoming a pipe dream for most in the market.[4] Consistent with the market, a "home" was no longer just a place to live and raise a family—it had become an investment. That pile of bricks and granite countertops, once the symbol of nuclear families and American ideals, was now going to make you big money.

For many, it seemed like a sure thing. Home prices, which had already begun to rise as far back as 1997, picked up pace. Nationwide, the average year-over-year was at around 8% per year, but in some areas—most notably, Los Angeles County, Las Vegas, and Miami—homes were going up 20% to 30% in a single year.

Speculators swooped in, buying up houses just to "flip" them for a profit. In Florida, for instance, buyers were taking up condos that hadn't even been built yet. In Miami, flipping condos came to be a profitable speculation.

Speculators would buy a group of 5 or 10 condos even before a single shovelful of dirt had been displaced. The idea was to sell the contracts to other speculators while the place was being built. The second buyer would then sell to yet another buyer when it was completed. Neither the first, nor the second, nor the third buyer had any intention of living in the condo.

The trouble was that the object of their speculation looked rather lonely and forlorn when the jig was finally up. Driving by at night, it was noticeable that few of the condos had lights on. Most were empty, waiting for their ultimate buyer, the poor sap who would actually live in the place and, presumably, pay for it.

This eventually became such a problem for developers that they tried to squeeze out the speculators, insisting that buyers take up only one of the condos and move in within a specified period. In some projects, developers announced special offers, which had prospective buyers camping out all weekend in order to get a good place in line to buy when the doors opened on Monday morning.

The special offers and incentives, not to mention the creative financing that was being thrown at them, made it impossible for the average homeowner to resist the siren song of the real estate market. They weren't going to sit idly by and watch their home rise in value and not take advantage of it somehow. After all, from 1997 to 2007, total housing values rose from $8.8 trillion to $21.5 trillion—nearly threefold in 10 years.[5]

Your home became your own personal ATM, and the allure of this "free money" was so great that homeowners hopped over to their local banks to get at them and then whined their way deeper into debt. The financial industry, ever ready to separate a fool from his or her money, rushed to the scene with the offer of home equity lines of credit that could be used "for everyday expenses, like groceries and gas."

Thus did the world's mouth (as the United States has been called) gobble down its own houses one brick at a time. Homeowners, thinking they were getting something for nothing, believed they were merely taking some of their gains off the table—like selling a few shares of appreciated stock. Little did they realize they were selling the table itself . . . along with the kid's bathroom and the family room.

If, for example, the house went from a $100,000 price to a price of $200,000, the homeowner may feel he can "take out" $100,000 of equity and still be living in a $100,000 house. But what he is actually doing is selling half the house to the mortgage lender. Even if the higher prices stick, he still has to live somewhere, and now he has to "rent" half his house from the mortgagor.

When a real estate bubble bursts, there are at least two losers—the borrower as well as the lender—and neither walks away easily. The borrower still has to pay his mortgage or he loses his house, and often must pay a mortgage that is higher than the value of the house. Many cannot or will not pay, which bounces the loss back onto the lender.

But such is the cold, cold world we live in that the appeal of rising asset values—whether real or paper—is almost irresistible.

## AS CALIFORNIA GOES . . .

At the height of the boom, the average house in San Jose, California, sold for half a million dollars.

How many people in the San Jose area can afford a $500,000 house? We don't know, but we suspect that the number is less than the number of owners.

Americans have become convinced that buying as much house as you can—even more than you can comfortably afford—is a shrewd financial move.

At the peak of the real estate boom, in 2005, NAHB/Wells Fargo Housing deemed LA County the least affordable metropolis in the nation, where only 14% of the population could afford to buy a home.[6]

To plug this gap between affordability and purchase prices, the California boom relied heavily on exotic financing, such as an adjustable-rate mortgage, and because of this reliance, the gap between affordability and purchase prices widened to insurmountable proportions.

By 2005, almost 40% of the state's homeowners—compared to 29% nationally—paid at least one-third of their income for housing, according to the Public Policy Institute of California.

Even worse than that, one-fifth of all homebuyers paid more than half of their incomes for housing.[7]

"Without easy credit, and lots of it, California real estate could never have achieved its epic valuations," recalled Eric Fry, a colleague, living at the time in Laguna Beach:

> Credit not only enabled first-time buyers to "stretch" a bit, it also enabled and emboldened speculative builders, second-home buyers, second-home builders and every other variant of housing market participant/speculator.
>
> But because financing became so exotic, and speculative participation in the market became so great, the simultaneous unwinding of both has been as pleasant as hanging out with your in-laws during a root canal.[8]
>
> The number and variety of nontraditional mortgages flourished from 2001 to 2007. Adjustable rate mortgages became common, as did zero-down payment mortgages, mortgages with alluringly low starter rates, including interest-only mortgages, flexible payments, and "stated income" applications, in which the borrower is left to use his own imagination in describing his financial circumstances. You know the deal. At this point, it is rote learning, engrained in our memories. We can't possibly fall victim again!

The actions and innovations of the lenders, along with the federal government's housing policies, were to help Americans buy their own homes. Easy credit was meant to increase homeownership.

Renting a house was seen as a kind of social failure, like dropping out of high school or driving an outdated Sonata. They had "democratized" the credit market, lenders and government officials alike claimed.

Now, not only rich speculators could lose their shirts. The common man could lose his too! The obvious effect of all these innovations was to turn America into a nation of unwitting housing speculators, not of homeowners. Instead of actually buying and paying for a house, marginal buyers were enticed into these innovative mortgage products, which were more like options to buy a house rather than an actual purchase of one.

As time went on, more and more homeowners became gamblers, betting that property values would rise fast enough so they could refinance again, all of them forgetting one important fact: a house is a house. It provides a service, but it doesn't provide any more service if it is quoted at $500,000 than if it is quoted at $300,000. Same roof. Same air-conditioning. Same everything. Except, when it is said to be worth more, two noxious things result. First, the homeowner can "take out" some of the equity and feel like he is still ahead of the game. He doesn't worry about it when prices are rising; when the loan comes due, he can always take out a little more. Gradually, he gets deeper and deeper into debt. And then, inevitably, his house goes down in price, and he gets into trouble.

The other awful consequence is the cost of owning the home goes up.

As the house becomes more "valuable," typically the cost of property taxes, insurance, and upkeep mount. Thus, the net value, or net service, an owner gets from his house actually goes down. He has the same roof over his head, but it costs him more.

What the housing mania pointed out, like the tech boom before it, is that a man can make a fool of himself whenever he wants. Generally, he pays the price himself and the rest of the world goes on with its business. But in order to get a real public spectacle going, you need to separate cause from effect. It is only when a fellow thinks he can get away with something that he really lets loose.

Is it just a coincidence that mass and public thinking emerged with mass and social media . . . or that collective groupthink has consequences all of its own?

In the waning glory days of the housing boom, we wondered if there was anyone in the United Kingdom or the United States who still lived within his means. Did anyone even know what their means were?

Only occasionally did they even bother to find out. Like a middle-age man hunting around in closets for a beat old suit, when he put on the pants, he realized he has outgrown them. In fact, he spills over the top and nearly rips the back trying to fit.

Of course, you couldn't blame people for not living within their means—the whole idea is as quaint as thrift, as antique as spats. New credit card offers came every day. And when the offer to buy a house for no-money-down on a teaser-rate ARM was right in front of you, allowing you to afford much more house than you thought you could—at least for a while—who could pass that up?

Most of the time, most people get by, just as most of the time, most people don't get themselves into serious trouble with the law. They know what they can get away with and what they can't. But occasionally, the old standards and guideposts get knocked down. Then, they run into trouble.

Junk bonds, margin buying, program trading, portfolio insurance—each one eventually leads to trouble. People get excited about it . . . they think it is the answer to their prayers. . . they think it is going to make them rich. They do it. And then they overdo it.

In 2007, the same was true for the innovation of easy mortgage credit. Now you can get a mortgage, apparently, over the internet. Lender and borrower never meet. And then, of course, Wall Street created a whole industry—another new innovation—to take these mortgages and turn them into new and titillating products.

First the mortgages—then the securities derived from them—landed themselves in trouble. What began as a problem for borrowers has turned into a problem for lenders too.

The slump in the housing market began to make it tough for borrowers to sell or refinance. Or from another perspective, it made it hard for people to buy houses; homebuilders were so depressed that their wives were hiding their hunting rifles. They have not been in such a funk for 16 years. And the people who financed the homebuilders were not feeling so good either. Countrywide Financial Corporation, one of the nation's biggest mortgage lenders, said conditions "became increasingly challenging" in the second quarter of 2007.[9]

Meanwhile, the homeowners are often stuck—with a nice house, but no way to pay for it. Finally, the long arm of the law stretches out and takes their house away from them. But that is hardly the end of the story. It is only the beginning. Because then the mortgage goes unpaid, and the whole bunch of dodgy sausages that were packaged up as "Collateralized Debt Obligations" begins to stink.

"Up until now, hedge funds have been creating a great deal of the miraculous 'liquidity' sloshing around the globe," offers Dan Amoss, a short-side analyst with Agora Financial (www.agorafinancial.com). "By buying the highly leveraged equity and mezzanine tranches

CDOs, they've greatly strengthened the buying power that's been bidding up the prices—and lowering the yields—of risky debt instruments. George Soros' theory of reflexivity was at work during the financing stage of the housing bubble; now it's working in reverse to 'de'-finance the housing bubble."[10]

"Indigestion tends to lower an appetite, and institutional investors' appetite for junk bonds is spoiling just as Wall Street tries to serve them heaps of acidic securities," continues Dan.

"While CDOs have shifted risk away from the banking system by linking borrowers with lenders from around the world, they have not lessened default risk; they've merely transferred it to unsuspecting lenders that are just beginning to push back."


## A RICH MAN'S MARXISM?

On the heels of the nationalization of Fannie and Freddie were the murmurs coming from the investment bank Lehman Brothers. In September 2008, they reported a quarterly loss of $4 billion—their worst since going public and second consecutive loss.

Immediately, there was a din on Wall Street. Would Lehman follow in the footsteps of Bear? We didn't have to wonder long.

The Federal Reserve invited financial CEOs from far and wide to Wall Street, hoping to entice a buyout or merger to keep Lehman afloat. Bank of America made a bid, but ultimately walked away. Barclays did the same.

On September 15, 2008, after 158 years in business, Lehman Brothers filed the biggest bankruptcy in Wall Street history with $613 billion in debt.[11]

Yes, yet another falls prey to their own devices. Like all hustlers, they weren't smart enough to ignore their own lies. They were the ones who packaged up all that subprime debt—mortgage loans on overpriced property to people who couldn't pay the money back; they knew what was in that "mystery meat." Then, they got the useful stooges at the rating companies to call it Grade A. And then, they bought it themselves! What were they thinking? Not only that, they bought it on leverage—so that if it went bad, the whole company would go belly-up!

And now, mothers no longer want their babies to grow up to be stockbrokers and investment bankers. Now they want them to grow up to be bankruptcy lawyers! That's where the money is!

Governments used to talk of providing "safety nets" for citizens in trouble. That meant offering assistance to people on the margins of society. A man who lost his job would get unemployment compensation. One who was injured would get workman's comp. Poor people were offered food stamps and surplus food from government farm support programs.

Now, the feds offer a safety net for people with money—a kind of rich man's Marxism—in the form of protection against financial losses.

The logic of the safety net—whether used to catch a poor man or a rich one—is that whatever mess you've gotten yourself into, someone else pays for it. You forget to save money; you lose your job; bingo, someone else provides emergency assistance. During the 1970s and 1980s, Americans began to realize that providing unlimited assistance to the poor had its drawbacks; many people actually seemed to prefer a life of easy poverty to a life of hard work. Many people were "hooked" on public assistance, with several generations of welfare recipients in a single family. We recall, in the early 1980s, asking a young woman in the ghetto of Baltimore what she did for a living.

"I get a check," was her reply.

Poor thing. She never knew the pleasure and pride of a job well done. She never enjoyed the boost to her confidence and self-esteem that minimum wage employment can give.

Later, the Reagan administration reformed the welfare system. We don't know if it did any good or not, but people stopped getting so many checks . . . and stopped talking about it. Now what they are talking about is the safety nets for the rich—and everyone is in favor of them. So far, we've seen the central bank act with remarkable speed to help bankers, speculators, and hedge fund managers. Stockholders have been given a boost too. And if the housing slump worsens, the government will probably rush out some safety nets for homeowners.

Now, capitalists, proles, and the bourgeoisie all get checks.

"Stimmy" checks paid directly to US citizens during the COVID-19 pandemic era were accepted as if that were not just an acceptable role of the US Treasury but expected.

Is that progress or what?

We've already seen the onset of the housing bubble and subsequent subprime mortgage crisis it incited on Wall Street. But to fully understand how it came about we have to go back a decade, before the 2000 Tech Wreck was an event.

In August 1998, Bill Krasker, John Meriwether, and two men who had just won the Nobel Prize in Economics, Myron Scholes and Robert Merton, were deeply concerned about swap spreads. Their computer models had told them that the spreads might move about a point or so on an active day. But on that Friday, the spreads were bouncing all over the place.

This was bad news for the Long Term Capital Management (LTCM) hedge fund managers. They had as much as $1 trillion in exposure to various positions. Most of their positions were bets that prices in the future would regress to historic means. Prices that seemed out of kilter with past patterns, reasoned the geniuses at LTCM, would sooner or later come back to more familiar levels (see Figure 5.1).

The LTCM team was making history. They had an edge. They were the smartest people on the planet, and everyone knew it. The money

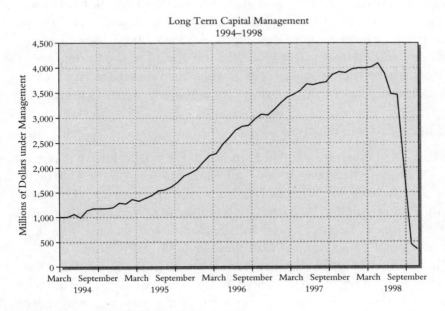

Long Term Capital Management
1994–1998

**FIGURE 5.1**  Nothing Fails Like Success

At its peak, LTCM's balance sheet was in excess of $100 billion. But the firm was leveraged to the very limit with more than 1.25 trillion in derivative contracts.

they were making—as much as 40% per year since the fund began—just proved it. It was hailed as a new "computer age" by *BusinessWeek*, and the professors were its masters.[12] Scholes and Merton were driving fancy new cars. "Merton had dyed his hair red, left his wife and moved into a snazzy pad in Boston," Lowenstein reported in his book, *When Genius Failed*. The whole world—and the world's money—seemed to lay at their feet.

The professors' insight was as useful as it was obvious: An investment that is unusually cheap—or unusually expensive—represents a form of potential financial energy. Sooner or later, it will be less unusual.

Their mistake was obvious too: they thought that the world was more reasonable than it actually is and assumed that "regression to the mean" applied only to markets. Bond prices might regress to the mean, but so would the professors' reputations and their investors' fortunes. Regression to the mean modestly predicts that things usually return to where they usually are. Few things are excluded.

The professors presumed that spreads between, say, long bonds and short ones, or between Italian bonds and German ones, were like throws of the dice. Will the spreads widen or narrow? You could look at the historical record, they believed, and compute the odds. If current prices seemed out of line with the odds, they took it as an absurdity and bet that prices would be less absurd in the future.

And maybe they would. But as Keynes once noted, the market can stay irrational longer than an investor or a business can stay solvent.

## In Greenspan We Trust(ed)

By late 2000, investors still had high hopes for stocks. That was not to deny that there had been losses—substantial losses. Almost $1 trillion had already been lost on the Nasdaq. Companies such as Theglobe .com, Career Builder, Webvan, and Audible, Inc. were already nearly out of business. Investors were still exuberant but thought they had become much more rational than they were the year before.

It was one thing for the loopy dot-coms to go belly-up. The Dow was quite another matter. "There is no way," investors would say, "Alan Greenspan will allow a serious bear market or a serious recession." Wasn't that the real bargain that had been struck with the central bank, after all? Americans would allow the bankers their profits, their limousines, and boardrooms; they would permit a gradual ruin of the nation's currency too. But in exchange, the Fed would manage the economy so that people did not have to worry about a serious decline. That was why savings rates were low in the United States. People did not have to save for a rainy day—because it never rained.

"In effect," wrote Paul Krugman in *Upside,* "capitalism and its economists made a deal with the public; it will be okay to have free markets from now on, because we know enough to prevent any more Great Depressions."[13]

And so it was that the entire world turned its weary eyes to Greenspan. The *capo di tutti capi* (boss of bosses) of central bankers was meant to save not merely US investors, but the entire world. Everyone knew that, worldwide, the United States was the "engine of growth" and that Americans were the best consumers—always ready to buy what they did not need with money they did not have. And despite the damage done to the Nasdaq, it was widely known that Greenspan had what it took to keep the US wealth machine delivering the goods.

Investors bought the Dow in the year 2000, confident that Greenspan would not allow prices to fall. He would not want prices to fall because falling stock prices would make people feel poorer; and poorer people would buy less—threatening the entire world economy.

## The Greenspan Put

That he had the will to prevent stocks from falling was beyond question. Almost everyone agreed that he had the means, too—the so-called "Greenspan put."

A put option allows its holder to sell at a predetermined price, that is to "put it to" the person on the other side of the trade. In a falling market, a put option is a way to make profits by forcing the other fellow to buy at an above-market price.

Greenspan's put option was his control of short-term interest rates. Lowering rates, so nearly everyone thought (including central bankers), was the way to stimulate demand for money, which, in turn, would increase consumer spending and business investment, and practically force investors to buy stocks. "In Greenspan We Trust," proclaimed a *Fortune* cover in late 2000.[14] Before the rate cuts began, the knowledge that the Fed would begin to cut seemed to be enough.

Like a cross-dresser, Greenspan had everything he needed to do the job, except the essentials. The nine telecom giants had borrowed approximately $25.6 billion by the end of 2000, and the Fed chief had no way to make telecom debt worth what people paid for the stock. He could not replenish consumers' savings accounts. He could not make Enron a healthy business, erase excess capacity, or make investment losses disappear.

In addition to the bad theory at the top of the bubble, Greenspan had bad information. The Information Age brought more information to more people—including to central bankers—but the more information people had, the more opportunity they had to choose the misinformation that suited their purposes.

Before Keynes and Friedman, economists believed in a Newtonian economic world. A boom could be expected to produce a nearly equal and opposite reaction. The more people got carried away in the up part of the cycle—that is, the more they borrowed and spent unwisely—the more they would suffer in the ensuing downswing. Economics and moral philosophy were in harmony, both of them elements of the most human science—the study of what people actually did. The Great Depression was seen as an inevitable repercussion of the 1920s boom, made worse by governmental interference with the market's corrective mechanisms.

But with the publication of their book, *A Monetary History of the United States* (1963), Milton Friedman and Anna Jacobson Schwartz reinterpreted the Great Depression. They offered policy makers and investors the hope of resurrection without crucifixion, Easter without Lent, gluttony without fat, boom without bust.

"The US economy's collapse from 1929 to 1933 was by no means an inevitable consequence of what had gone before during the boom," wrote Friedman and Schwartz. "It was a result of the policies following those years. Alternative policies that could have halted the monetary debacle were available throughout those years. Though the Reserve System proclaimed that it was following an easy-money policy, in fact, it followed an exceedingly tight policy."

"The monetary authorities could have prevented the decline in the stock of money," they continued, "indeed, could have produced almost any desired increase in the money stock."

Greenspan was determined not to repeat this mistake. He would follow Friedman's advice and gun the monetary stimulus until the muffler melted. But what if Friedman were wrong? What if policy could not produce any outcome the policy makers wished? What if the crash and depression were not merely monetary phenomena, but market and economic (and human!) events? What if it was not the banking crisis that caused the losses in the markets, but the other way around?

A lower Fed funds rate—the rate that the Fed charges member banks to borrow money—allows the banks to lend at lower rates too. But in a deflationary bust, people lose jobs; the values of stocks and other investments fall; sales and profits decline, while there are still big debts to pay. Lowering the price of money might have some effect, but not necessarily the desired one.

If only Greenspan were really at the controls of some vast machine! He might twist a knob . . . or push a lever . . . and the machine would do as he wanted. Instead, Greenspan's lever sent the machine going in an unexpected direction.

Great markets work like best-selling novels—with a plot that involves an ironic twist or two. We cannot imagine a blockbuster novel in which the dramatis personae get exactly what they expect. (Suppose Scarlett had married Ashley Wilkes and lived happily ever after? Margaret Mitchell would have sold a few copies to her friends and relatives and that would have been the end of it.) Nor would we want to live in such a world; it would be as dull and earnest as a poem by Maya Angelou.

"The mildness and brevity of the downturn are a testament to the notable improvement in the resilience and the flexibility of the economy," said Alan Greenspan to a congressional committee during hearings in July 2002.

"The fundamentals are in place," he continued (as the stock market rose) "for a return to sustained healthy growth: imbalances in inventories and capital goods appear largely to have been worked off; inflation is quite low and is expected to remain so; and productivity growth has been remarkably strong, implying considerable underlying support to household and business spending as well as potential relief from cost and price pressures."

Again, Greenspan spoke with no smile on his face. Nor, as far as we know, were his fingers crossed. He said what he said as though he meant it, as though he believed it himself. Certainly, his listeners seemed to believe it. The politicians looked grave when the cameras turned in their direction. They posed silly questions prepared for them by eager staffers. And laughed at their own dull jokes. No one seemed to have the slightest idea of how ridiculous and pathetic the whole show really was.

The spectacle seemed designed for prime time, to reassure the Shareholder Nation that it faced nothing more troubling than a temporary "failure of confidence" on the part of skittish investors and that as soon as a few miscreants were behind bars, the whole nasty episode would soon be forgotten. No one was rude enough to point out that it was the star witness, Greenspan himself, who bore much of the blame for the bubble and its aftermath. Nor did anyone seem to wonder how the nation's central banker could correct his mistake.

After the crash of 1929, similar hearings were held by similar groups of Washington hacks. That was before the days of air-conditioning. Few matters were important enough to sweat through a summer in the nation's capitol. But when the weather softened, the politicians turned up the heat for the benefit of the rubes and patsies in the home districts. Albert Wiggins, head of Chase National Bank, was discovered to have shorted his own shares and made millions. Sam Insull presided over the WorldCom of the 1920s—Commonwealth Edison—a $3 billion utility company whose books were audited by Arthur Andersen. He fled the country when the cops came looking for him. And poor Richard Whitney, who had once headed the New York Stock Exchange, went to prison for embezzling as much as $30 million from the exchange's pension fund.

Seventy years on, Greenspan, by contrast, was still greeted as a hero in congressional hearing rooms. The politicians—and the *lumpeninvestoriat*—were still counting on him to save the world as we know it.

People expected so much—perhaps too much—of Greenspan. They expected his aim to be perfect. But in his first 11 tries, he failed to set interest rates at the precise level needed to revive the stock market.

In every respect, Greenspan's rate cuts were doomed. They caused qualified borrowers to hesitate, while inviting unqualified ones to go more deeply into debt. And they produced a new round of inflation in an unintended sector: real property.

A recession is supposed to lower consumer spending and increase savings levels. But the recession of 2001 had not. Instead, consumers borrowed and spent more than ever before, confident of clear skies tomorrow. Instead of being alarmed, Greenspan told Congress that this reckless behavior was "an important stabilizing force for the overall economy."[15] No one was heard to guffaw. But by mid-2002, consumers were nearly as helpless and desperate as the central bank. Paul Kasriel, an economist at Northern Trust, pointed out that for the first time since World War II, the average net worth of Americans was going down. It rose by about $3,700 per year in the last few years of the 1990s. But in the first two years of the new century, it had fallen by about $1,000. The stock market had wiped out between $5 trillion and $7 trillion. Only real estate prices seemed to defy the general deflationary trend.[16]

The consumer was the last man standing in the US economy. Greenspan was compelled to do all he could to hold him upright— even if he was already dead. No longer was the Fed chairman merely luring rich investors into blowing themselves up. By knocking 475 basis points off short-term rates, he enticed millions of innocent consumers deeper into debt—urging them to buy new SUVs and refinance their homes as if the fate of the nation depended on it. Consumers did themselves no favor by taking on bigger mortgages and auto loans, and a few were beginning to realize it. Greenspan, meanwhile, was beginning to look less like the world's savior and more like the ambitious rascal he actually was.

The lenders were flush, but the borrowers were up to their necks and having a hard time keeping their footing in the swirling water. By the close of 2002, foreclosure rates were at 30-year highs, bankruptcies were at a new record, and business profits were still falling.

And Greenspan? From comedy to tragedy . . . from poetry to pure doggerel . . . Greenspan's oeuvre seemed to find its most farcical moment on August 30, 2002, when the Fed chairman addressed a Fed symposium in Jackson Hole, Wyoming.

Six years earlier, he had described stock market investors as "irrationally exuberant." Now he claimed he could see nothing untoward, even with the Dow 100% higher. He would not know a bubble if it blew up in his face, he seemed to say; he would have to wait and check in the mirror for bruise marks.

And even if he had been able to spot the bubble expanding, the Fed chairman continued, he would not have been able to find a pin. The hundreds of economists at the Fed were powerless, "confronted with forces that none of us had personally experienced . . . aside from the recent experience of Japan, only history books and musty archives gave us clues to the appropriate stance for policy."

Greenspan—the only member of *Time*'s "Committee to Save the World" triumvirate still in office, the Caesar of central banking—could not last much longer.

The pundits were edging his way, golden daggers in their hands. From Paul Krugman in the *New York Times* to Abelson in *Barron's*, they were escalating their attacks—from criticism to open contempt.

The Maestro had given the nation exactly what it had asked for; he had struck up the band and puffed up the biggest bubble in world history.

On November 14, 2000, Bob Woodward's hagiography of Greenspan, *Maestro*, went on sale. Greenspan's reputation was never greater than on that day. On that same day, an ounce of gold—the reciprocal of Greenspan's reputation—could be bought for just $264. Who knew that gold was about to begin a major bull market? After an initial drop, to below $260 in February and again in April of 2001, it rose sharply.

While gold had entered a bullish phase, Greenspan's reputation was in decline. Not only did he help inflate the bubble and fail to prick it, he rushed to supply additional air pressure whenever it began deflating on its own.

Only days after his Wyoming speech in 2002, the price of gold rose to $320. By the end of the year, it hit the $330 mark.

A photo in the summer press showed the titan of central banking looking a little tired. Even an hour soaking in his bubbles did not seem to be enough. Absurdity takes energy. In his pictures, the Fed chairman rested his chin against his arm, as if he were running low.

The minutes of past meetings of the Fed's Open Market committee reveal a surprisingly more confident and energetic chairman. In September 1996, for example, Greenspan told his fellow central bankers: "I recognize there is a stock market bubble at this point." Then, referring to a suggestion that margin requirements be raised to dampen speculation: "I guarantee that if you want to get rid of the bubble, whatever it is, that will do it."

What became of these insights? What became of the Alan Greenspan of that era? He was no Volcker; the former Fed chief was made of sturdier stuff and was willing to go against the mob. Greenspan bent.

The Fed chief already had reinvented himself to suit his ambitions. Had not the gold-buggish Ayn Rand devotee remade himself into the greatest paper-money monger the world had ever seen? Had not the man who once wrote that gold was the only honest money already betrayed his own beliefs as well as the nation's currency?

Who knows what Greenspan really thought. Maybe it was among the fluffy suds of his bathwater that he came to believe the nation's capital markets had been transformed by a "productivity miracle."

And maybe, while searching for the soap in the warm, slippery embrace of his own tub, he allowed himself to believe that there was no need to raise margin requirements, or to warn investors about the dangers of a bubble market, or to try to prick it himself.

## THE MESS THE MAESTRO MADE

Murray Rothbard had Greenspan's number a long time ago.

"I knew Alan thirty years ago," Rothbard wrote in 1987, when Greenspan was first appointed to head the Fed. "and have followed his career with great interest since . . . Greenspan's real qualification is that he can be trusted never to rock the establishment's boat . . . at no time in his twenty-year career in politics has he ever advocated anything that even remotely smacks of laissez-faire, or even any approach toward it . . . Alan is a long-time member of the famed Trilateral Commission, the Rockefeller-dominated pinnacle of the financial-political power elite in this country. And as he assumes his post as head of the Fed, he leaves his honored place on the board of directors of J.P. Morgan & Co. and Morgan Guaranty Trust."[17]

We are annoyed at Alan Greenspan, not because he set the US middle class on the path to destruction but because his book, *The Age of Turbulence*, got so much more attention than the book we wrote with Lila Rajiva, *Mobs, Messiahs, and Markets*. Greenspan's empty tome came out right after ours and promptly knocked ours out of its brief moment in the limelight.

But now others are getting annoyed at Greenspan too—for more serious reasons. Says Nobel Prize winning economist Joseph Stiglitz:

Alan Greenspan really made a mess of all this. He pushed out too much liquidity at the wrong time. He supported the tax cut in 2001, which is the beginning of these problems [deficits didn't matter to him, either] . . . He encouraged people to take out variable rate mortgages.[18]

The critique we leveled against the Greenspan Fed 3 years ago is now widely accepted; the feds saw the little recession of 2001 and panicked. They put out too much money and too much credit for much too long, causing bubbles all over the world. So free and easy were US banks and credit institutions during this period that bank robbers stopped wearing ski masks and carrying guns; all they had to do was to ask for the money like everyone else.

The free-floating loot produced a holiday atmosphere that looked to most people like real prosperity. "See," they said to each other, "the free market works."

"Greed is good," said Gordon Gekko. Financial incentives were thought to be the key to everything—higher productivity, higher profits, growth . . . everything. You want an executive to perform? Give him stock options! You want an investment manager to make you money? Give him a piece of the action. You want to win over the poor and minorities? Let them get in on this great money-making machine. Columnist Thomas L. Friedman keeps telling us that the terrorists would come over to our side if they just had more financial incentives . . . if they had jobs . . . if they had university degrees . . . if they had credit cards and mortgages. But it emerged in England that of the terrorist suspects nabbed so far, the average one was a doctor working for the National Health Service!

Money isn't everything. Especially the kind of money that the Fed creates.

## Bernanke: Helicopter Money

In November 2002, when new Fed member, Benjamin Bernanke took up the subject of the threat of Japan-style deflation, he not so much proposed inflation as promised it.[19] The financial press had finally picked up on the Japan example. Fed officials were now routinely asked: "Well, how come the Japanese have been unable to avoid deflation? And how will the Fed do better than the Japanese Central Bank?"

Bernanke didn't wait for the question. The Japanese could have avoided its bouts with deflation if it had targeted higher inflation rates, he maintained.

"Don't worry about that here. Even if we get down to zero rates [real rates were already below zero]," said the Fed governor, there are plenty of other things the central bank can do. Print money, for example. "Sufficient injections of money will always reverse deflation," said Bernanke.

"In the 1930s," he continued, "Roosevelt ended deflation by devaluing the dollar 40% against gold." He might have added that deflation ended after the worst depression in America's history had forced 10,000 banks to go bust and left one out of every four workers jobless.

Was it comforting to know that the Fed could beat deflation by destroying the dollar and the economy? Ben Bernanke followed up by saying, "There is virtually no meaningful limit to what we could inject [from the money supply] into the system, were it necessary."

Technically correct, for the Fed could always charter a fleet of helicopters and drop $100 bills over lower Manhattan, but as a monetary policy, printing money is not without its drawbacks.

The essential requirement of money is that it be valuable, which requires that it be of limited supply. But that is also the essential problem with all managed currencies. Its managers may create more of it when it suits them, but they should never create so much that they destroy the illusion of scarcity.

"What the US owes to foreign countries it pays—at least in part," observed Charles de Gaulle in 1965, a full 37 years ahead of Greenspan and Bernanke, "with dollars it can simply issue if it wants to."

De Gaulle was first in line at the "gold window" at the Fed, where he exchanged his dollars for gold and brought the world's monetary system crashing down. Nixon then slammed shut the gold window, and the price of gold began to move upward (30% per year from 1968 to the peak in January 1980—exceeding the return on stocks in any 12-year period in history).

Goldbugs were so excited by this that they bought—even as gold reached $800—and regretted it for the next 22 years. But in 2002, the price of gold moved up cautiously; the goldbugs had less money and more sense. Still, on the open market—if no longer at the gold window—the neo-de Gaulles of this world had a way to exchange their dollars for gold. Greenspan and Bernanke must have made them think about it.

So imagine the world's surprise when Fed governor, Ben Bernanke, announced that the Fed would create an almost unlimited supply of new dollars—if it thought necessary—to head off deflation. Dennis Gartman said the speech by Bernanke was "the most important speech on Federal Reserve and monetary policy since the explanation emanating from the Plaza Accord a decade and a half ago."[20]

Bernanke told the world—including foreigners, who held as much as $9 trillion of US assets—that the Fed would not permit a more valuable currency. How would it avoid it? By inflating as much as the situation required. There was effectively "no limit" on how much inflation the Fed could create, or would be willing to create, to avoid deflation, he said.

It was almost like the moment when German central banker, Dr. Rudolf Havenstein, had announced in the early 1920s that Germany intended to destroy the deutschmark in order to skip out of its war reparations. From August 1922 to November 1923, consumer price inflation rose by 10 to the 10th power so that by the end of November, a single dollar was worth 4.2 trillion marks. Now Bernanke proposed a similar feat to finance the United States' imperial and lifestyle ambitions: the United States would take its tribute in the form of an inflated currency.

In the 60 days following Bernanke's speech (on November 21, 2002), the dollar fell 6.4% against the euro and 10.1% against gold. It continued to slide for another 6 years . . . that is until the real crisis hit and for a brief period in the fall of 2008 the greenback reasserted itself as the reserve currency of the world.

## THE PROGRESSIVE ERA OF MONETARY POLICY

In order to understand the "Yellen Fed"—those years when Janet Yellen served as the chairman of the Federal Reserve—we have to step back in time more than a hundred years to the Progressive Era.

The Progressive Era refers to a period in American history that spanned roughly from the 1890s to the 1920s. As in our own time, the history of that time is pockmarked with widespread social and political movements. Today, the movements on the fringe are equally as pronounced—Black Lives Matter on the one hand, Proud Boys on the other, to name just two—and concerned with media bias, social injustice, and cultural identity.

During the Progressive Era of the turn of the twentieth century, significant changes in monetary policy occurred as well. Foremost was a shift in the United States from the classical gold standard, known also as the Victorian gold standard, to a "more flexible" and interventionist approach. The classical gold standard, which had been in place for much of the nineteenth century, tied the value of a country's currency to a fixed amount of gold.

The limitations of the gold standard became increasingly apparent as the economy grew. . . and Europe prepared for war. You can't fight a war on the gold standard. It's expensive, first. But secondly, the production of armaments and other tools of war are destined to be destroyed. Who knows the cost of a war at the outset? A more flexible credit-based system is necessary to achieve victory.

The legendary financier and banker JP Morgan had bailed out the US government in the financial panics of 1893 and more recently 1907. Tired of using his own checkbook to keep the free market open for his businesses, Morgan sided with a group of more progressive bankers and supported the establishment of the Federal Reserve in 1913. The Federal Reserve was created to serve as the central bank of the United States and to provide a more flexible and stable monetary system. It was given the authority to regulate the money supply, set interest rates, and act as a lender of last resort to banks in times of financial crisis.

From the outset, the Federal Reserve had a dual mandate: defend the dollar, thereby keeping prices in check, and ensure full employment among citizens. The "flexible" part of the equation required the introduction of fiat money. "Fiat money," to be clear, is currency that is not backed by a physical commodity like gold but derives its value from the "full faith and credit"—the trust—earned by the federal government. A fiat currency must have the confidence of the people using it. The nation's new fiat money allowed for greater "flexibility" in managing the money supply and responding to economic conditions, whether they be favorable to business or not.

In her tenure as chairman of the Federal Reserve between 2014 and 2018, Yellen introduced a new mandate to the Fed's agenda. She wanted banking to conform to the new progressive era chimera of "diversity, equity, and inclusion" (DEI) in addition to the original mandates. She cemented the idea too that Fed decisions should be "data-driven," which sounds logical, but as we'll see time and again, data are imperfect and often late. Yellen kept the Greenspan Put in her back pocket too.

On February 27, 2018, Bernanke and Yellen appeared together before an audience at the Brookings Institute in Washington, DC. The subject was monetary policy as practiced by the Federal Open Market Committee (FOMC) during the 12 years they collectively served as chairmen. Bernanke served from 2006 through the panic years 2008–2009 and on until 2014. Yellen picked up where Bernanke left off and served from 2014–2018. Historically, these years will go down as the years Bernanke and Yellen presided over an aggressively experimental monetary policy scheme.

The conversation was easy-going, lighthearted even. And why not? The duo had served their time. They were comfortable letting bygones be bygones. Still, the conversation revealed a few key insights to Yellen's belief in an "activist" Federal Reserve—pushing for equity in the banking system and using Fed policy to prop up the stock market.

"Tobin was my teacher," Yellen replied when asked about her mentor, professor James Tobin, whom she'd studied under at Yale. "But I will have to say he was more than my teacher. He was actually an inspiration to me. I think what impressed me was not only his analytic skills and his knowledge of macroeconomics and the work that he did, but also his very strong commitment to social justice and to the view that economics is magical and it's about making the world a better place."[21]

James Tobin, a self-described "neo-Keynsian" economist won the Nobel Memorial Prize in Economic Sciences in 1981 for "creative and extensive work on the analysis of financial markets and their relations to expenditure decisions, employment, production and prices."[22] Translation: Tobin believed adopting an accurate monetary policy was inherently a science not unlike chemistry or ornithology. He also believed policy could, and should, be used to support the stock market during bear markets and goose them during bulls.

Reducing economics to a mathematical equation also helped both Bernanke and Yellen claim their policies were data-driven. "I was on record [in 1996] as saying that I thought we should adopt a numerical inflation target," Yellen told Bernanke, "and that I thought it should be 2%." Yellen went on to explain:

> I articulated the reasons about the zero lower bound and nominal wage rigidity that later became central to our decisions. Alan [Greenspan's] view was that we should not adopt an inflation target at all. And, of course, he was successful in stopping that from happening until you [Ben Bernanke] and I worked together. I think it had long been your desire to see this happen as it had been mine, and I think you especially should feel proud that you were able to put in place what I think has been a successful framework."[23]

The concept of an "inflation target" was first posited by the Stanford economist John Taylor in 1993. While Taylor did not go as far as to pinpoint 2% as the desirable rate of inflation, he did concede it was a "concept." He tried to reduce it to an algebraic formula that strategy policymakers could use to aim for maximum sustainable growth and achieve the economy's productive potential. We include the formula here for entertainment purposes only:

**The Taylor Rule**

$$r = p + 0.5y + 0.5(p - 2) + 2$$

Where:

- $r$ = nominal fed funds rate
- $p$ = the rate of inflation
- $y$ = the percent deviation between current real GDP and the long-term linear trend in GDP

Following Taylor's rule, Bernanke and Yellen arrived at the 2% inflation target even current Fed Chair Jerome Powell alludes to during his post FOMC announcement press conferences.

Alas, economics is not an exact science. It's made up of millions of instantaneous decisions deliberated over by millions of people every second. To paraphrase the economist Fredrick Hayek, our knowledge is a priori imperfect. We cannot have enough knowledge at any given time to make accurate to-the-minute decisions. Hayek asserted it's better to let the market, which is itself a measure of all these decisions, decide by establishing natural "equilibrium" through prices.

Yellen, in her own way, acknowledges the conundrum any Fed chair faces. Her solution. . . wait for the data to pour in after the Fed begins lowering or raising interest rates, then adjust accordingly. The Fed is always behind the curve on inflation or deflation because it collects data for 6 weeks at a time before each FOMC meeting. Yellen:

> Further, in the conversation with Bernanke, Yellen likened arriving at a policy decision to trying to select a color of paint a designer might paint a room.
>
> You have 19 people around the table, and you want to come up with a decision we can all live with on what color to paint the room. And we'd go around the table. Ben, what would you like? You think baby blue is just absolutely ideal. David, what do you think? Chartreuse you think is a lovely color. And we go around the room like that. And the question is, are we ever going to converge? I would feel my job is get everybody to see that off-white is not a bad alternative.

Once the color of paint has been agreed upon then the policy needs to be put into action.

Having inherited the post financial crisis economy from Bernanke, Yellen continued to manhandle the tools bestowed upon her by her predecessors: interest rates and quantitative easing (QE).

The results in our view lead directly to the historic inflation the global economy experienced during and after the pandemic lockdowns. During the better part of her tenure, Yellen presided over lower bound interest rates at near zero, so-called "zero interest rate policy" (ZIRP). (See Figure 5.2.)

The Fed raised interest rates once in December 2015 and then again a year later in 2016. It wasn't until 2017 that Yellen get serious about raising interest rates to slow the economy. The trajectory she'd embarked on was rudely interrupted by the COVID-19 pandemic and dramatic lockdown of the global economy.

Interest rate policy is one lever the Fed chair can pull or push. Directly buying assets in the stock or bond markets thereby creating price stability for financial assets.

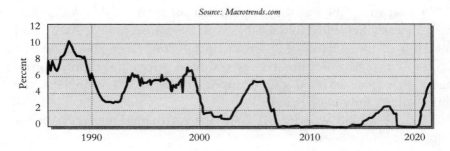

**FIGURE 5.2** Fed Fund Rates Before and During Janet Yellen's Tenure at the Fed, Including Under Powell During the Pandemic and Beyond

In 2008–2009, the Fed bought mortgage-backed securities (MBS) to bail out Wall Street banks who'd gambled on these synthetic assets. As the Fed propped up the financial system with direct purchases, its own balance sheet ballooned to historic levels.

Markets make opinions. Under Janet Yellen's tenure at the Fed, a whole generation of home buyers, college students, stock traders, and speculators got used to low and all but zero interest rates. Banks have come to believe that no matter how risky their own strategies, they will be supported and bailed out by an activist Fed. Risk has been socialized—spread out across the economy impacting even those who did not participate in risky behavior.

When it came time for Jerome Powell to negotiate the pandemic lockdowns, subsequent supply chain issues, and then fight a 40-year high inflation rate, things got messy real fast. (See Figure 5.3.)

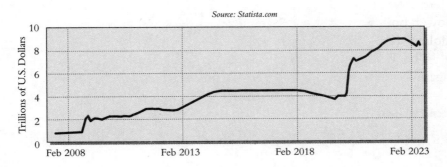

**FIGURE 5.3** Fed Balance Sheet Under Bernanke, Yellen, and Powell

"I was wrong then about the path that inflation would take," Yellen, now Treasury Secretary, told CNN's Wolf Blitzer on June 1, 2022. "As I mentioned, there have been unanticipated and large shocks to the economy that have boosted energy and food prices, and supply bottlenecks that have affected our economy badly, that I didn't—at the time—didn't fully understand."[24]

How, we're left wondering, does one mathematically account for imperfect information?

# CHAPTER 6

## A THEORY OF MORAL HAZARDS

A reasonable man expects things to happen that ought to happen. A fool ought to be separated from his money. A thief ought to go to jail. A man who abuses a child or double-crosses a friend ought to roast in hell. Whether they do or not is not up to us, of course . . . but we can hope. And what better way has a man of running his own life than figuring out what ought to happen and then making his decisions as if it really will? Of all the systems, secrets, formulas, charts, graphs, and models that help a man invest, we have found none more rewarding than this: assume what ought to happen will happen: buy low, sell high . . . and don't worry about it too much.

But what ought to happen? Alas, it is not always easy to know . . .

"The great judge of the world," wrote Adam Smith in his *Theory of Moral Sentiments*, "has, for the wisest reasons, thought proper to interpose, between the weak eye of human reason, and the throne of his eternal justice, a degree of obscurity and darkness . . . [which] . . .

renders the impression of it faint and feeble in comparison of what might be expected from the grandeur and importance of so mighty an object."

If "Ought" were a person, Ought would not be a bartender or a good-hearted prostitute. Ought is not the kind of word you would want to hang out with on a Saturday night or relax with at home for it would always be reminding you to take out the trash or fix the garage door.

If it were a Latin noun, Ought would be feminine, but more like a shrewish wife than a willing mistress. For Ought is judgmental—a nag, a scold. Even the sound of it is sharp; it comes up from the throat like a dagger and heads right for soft tissue, remembering the location of weak spots and raw nerves for many years.

Ought is neither a good-time girl nor a boom-time companion, but more like the I-told-you-so who hands you aspirin on Sunday morning, tells you what a fool you were, and warns you what will happen if you keep it up. "You get what you deserve," she reminds you.

A man who lets himself be bossed around by Ought is no man at all, in our opinion. He is a dullard, a wimp, and a wuss—a logical, rational, reasonable lump. Thankfully, most men, most of the time, will not readily submit. Instead, they do not do what they ought to do, but what they want to do. Stirred up by mob sentiments or private desires, they make fools of themselves regularly. They cannot help themselves.

Of course, Ms. Ought is right; they get what they deserve. But sometimes it is worth it.

Modern economists no longer believe in Ought. They do not appreciate her moral tone and try to ignore her. To them, the economy is a giant machine with no soul, no heart . . . no right and no wrong. It is just a matter of finding the accelerator.

The nature of the economist's trade has changed completely in the past 200 years. Had he handed out business cards, Adam Smith's would have borne the professional inscription "Moral Philosopher," not "Economist." Smith saw God's "invisible hand" in the workings of the marketplace. Trying to understand how it worked, he looked for the Oughts everywhere. Everywhere and always people get what they deserve, Smith might have said. And if not . . . they ought to!

Today, the "Ought to" school of economics has few students and fewer teachers. Most economists consider it only one step removed from sorcery. But here at our offices on the rue de la Verrerie in Paris, the flame is still alive, flickering.

"Call it the overinvestment theory of recessions of 'liquidationism,' or just call it the 'hangover theory,'" Paul Krugman began his critique of the "Ought to" school. "It is the idea that slumps are the price we pay for booms, that the suffering the economy experiences during a recession is a necessary punishment for the excesses of the previous expansion . . .[1]

"Deep economic problems are supposed to be a punishment for deep economic sins," Krugman continued in June 1998.[2]

Krugman elaborated the concept in December of the same year. The "hangover theory," he called it—referring to the way a man feels after he has been on a drinking binge. The hangover theory is "disastrously wrongheaded," Krugman explains. "Recessions are not necessary consequences of booms. They can and should be fought, not with austerity but with liberality—with policies that encourage people to spend more, not less."[3]

What kind of world is it? Is it one in which a man can cure a hangover by getting drunk or get out of debt by borrowing more? Or is there a price to be paid for foolishness, collectively as well as individually?

Is the world just a fine-tuned machine where a capable public servant can simply turn a screw or tighten a knob to make history turn out the way he wants? Or is it an infinitely complicated, natural thing as prone to error as a mob of teenage delinquents.

"The hangover theory is perversely seductive—not because it offers an easy way out, but because it doesn't," Krugman continued in his December 1998 attack. "Powerful as these seductions may be, they must be resisted, for the hangover theory is disastrously wrong-headed," he concluded.

In Krugman's mechanistic world, there is no room for Ought. If the monetary grease monkeys after the Great Depression of the 1930s or in Japan of the 1990s had failed to get their machines working, it was not because there were invisible hands at work or that there were nagging moral principles to be reckoned with . . . but because they had not managed to turn the right screws!

It is completely incomprehensible to Krugman that there may be no screws left to turn or that the mechanics might inevitably turn the wrong screws as they play out their roles in the morality spectacle.

Krugman is hardly alone. As the twentieth century developed, mass democracy and mass markets gradually took the Ought out of both politics and markets. In the nineteenth century, a man would go bust, and his friends and relatives would view it as a personal, moral failing. They would presume he did something he oughtn't have. He gambled. He drank. He spent. He must have done something.

But as economies collectivized, the risk of failure was removed from the individual and spread among the group. If a man went broke in the 1930s, it wasn't his fault; he could blame the Crash and Great Depression. If people were poor, it wasn't their fault; it was society's fault, for it had failed to provide jobs. And if investors lost money, that too was no longer their own damned faults . . . but the fault of the Fed . . . or the government. If consumers spent too much money, whose fault was it? Perhaps the Fed had set rates too low. In any case, the masses recognized no personal failing. Instead, the failure was collective and technical—the mechanics had failed to turn the right screws. Ought had disappeared.

In politics, the masses recognized no higher authority than the will of the sacred majority. No matter what lame or abominable thing they decided to do, how could it be wrong?

Likewise, in markets, economists won a Nobel Prize for pointing out that mass markets could never be wrong. The perfect market hypothesis demonstrated that the judgment of millions of investors and spenders must always be correct. The whole method of modern economics shifted from exploring what a man ought to do to statistical analysis.

"There is more than a germ of truth in the suggestion that, in a society where statisticians thrive, liberty and individuality are likely to be emasculated," wrote M.J. Moroney in *Fact from Figures*. "Historically, statistics is no more than 'State Arithmetic,' a system by which differences between individuals are eliminated by the taking of an average. It has been used—indeed, still is used—to enable rulers to know just how far they may safely go in picking the pockets of their subjects."

Economists attached sensors to various parts of the great machine, as if they were running diagnostics on an auto engine. Depending on the information, they twisted up interest rates or suggested opening up the throttle to let in more new money. Of course, it was absurd. Had not the perfect market already set rates exactly where they needed to be?

We note, ominously, that even though modern economists took the moral ought out of their calculations, they could not take the moral hazard out of the market. The masses, the *lumpeninvestoriat*, scarcely noticed; but the more economists and investors ignored the ought, the more the hazard grew.

In a small town in the Midwest, a man would have to sneak around under the eyes of his neighbors in order to get up to something. Then, word would get around, and soon the whole thing would be over.

But here in Paris, moral hazards are on every street corner, which is what we like about the place. Here, a man can get into trouble and stay there for a long time before it catches up with him. And if he had no vice when he arrived in town, he can pick one up quickly and develop it into a lifelong companion.

After work, your authors could sit across the street at the Paradis Bar, have a few drinks, a cigarette or two, and then wander over to the infamous rue St. Denis and enjoy ourselves with Brigitte or Françoise for a modest outlay. If we were more ambitious about picking up vices, we could take up gambling, stock market speculating, or even theft. We might begin picking pockets on the metro and work our way up: first, we could rob our partners or defraud investors—and then, moving on to the big time, we could go into politics.

But there is a certain rhythm to moral hazards. Whether petty or great, all are exhilarating at the beginning and heartbreaking at the end. For there is always a price to pay.

## ALL THE UNIVERSE IS MORAL

"All the universe is moral," wrote Emerson early in the nineteenth century. Now, no one seems to believe it . . . except us. And yet, the cycle is the same for market booms, empires, and even an individual life. What tickles the fancy so much at the debut saddens it at the finale.

"Whatever is your weakness," says Richard Russell, "the market will find it."

Greedy investors wait too long to sell—and lose their money. Fear keeps others from ever buying in the first place. Laziness gets others who fail to do their homework and get carried along by mob sentiments into buying the most popular stocks at their most absurd prices.

"I ought to have sold at the top," says the one. "I ought to have bought at the bottom," says the other. "I ought to have looked at the balance sheet," says the third. "I ought not to have drunk that last bottle," says the fourth.

But modern economists act as if the story had no moral . . . as if there were no "oughts." Everything happens according to cause and effect, they believe. There is no such thing as a stock that is too expensive or too cheap: the stock market is perfect. It finds the exactly ideal price every minute of every day. There is no such thing as moral failing either. A man cannot be faulted for buying a stock at its perfect price.

And prices would indeed be perfect if, as economists seem to think, men carefully weighed the available information and calculated the odds as coldly as a sniper. But real men rarely weigh anything carefully—except perhaps sirloin steaks when they buy them by the pound. Many have never met a moral hazard they did not like. And when they participate in collective undertakings—such as politics, war, football games, or stock market booms—they immediately become even bigger boobs.

Economists imagine that the economy functions as a sort of machine too, with rational men popping up and down like valve lifters. No moral hazards present themselves, for a machine is as indifferent to larceny as it is to a short skirt.

You can put a pack of cards or a fifth of whiskey in front of a machine, come back an hour later, and the machine still will not have touched them. Not so a human being. All he needs is an opportunity, and he is on his way to hell!

The term *moral hazard* has a special meaning as well as a general one. "The idea is simple," explains Jeffrey Tucker, in an article published by the Mises Institute in December 1998. "If you are continually willing to protect people from the consequences of their own errors, your benevolence will be factored into the future decisions of the persons rescued. In the long run, they will make even more errors. The principle exists at all levels. The teacher who changes grades when students plead hardship isn't helping in the long run. The teacher is rewarding and thereby encouraging poor study habits. He is creating moral hazard."[4]

The new, collectivized world of the late twentieth century was full of accommodating teachers and forgiving wives. Investors paid too much for stocks. Businesses and consumers borrowed too much. And the whole world seemed to believe what could not be true—that the dollar was more valuable than gold. For nearly 20 years, gold went down while the dollar went up.

Gold ought to have gone up. Since the beginning of Alan Greenspan's term to the end of 2002, the monetary base almost tripled. In the most recent few years of Greenspan's term, short-term interest rates were driven down to barely a fifth of what they had been 2 years before.

"[L]owering rates or providing ample liquidity when problems materialize, but not raising them as imbalances build up, can be rather insidious in the longer run," conceded a working paper from the Bank of International Settlements. "They promote a form of moral hazard that can sow the seeds of instability and of costly fluctuations in the real economy."

By the beginning of 2003, as much as $9 trillion of US dollar assets were in foreign hands and three times as many were in circulation as there had been in 1987. The hazards had never been greater . . . nor ever harder to discern.

In the late 1990s, even after Alan Greenspan noted that investors had become irrationally exuberant, they seemed to become even more irrationally exuberant. And then, when recession and bear market threatened, these irrational investors were sure that the very same central banker, who could not prevent a bubble from forming, could nevertheless stop it from springing a leak.

Alas, this proved a vain hope; a bear market beginning in March 2000 had reduced the nation's stock market wealth by $7 trillion as of January 2003. But another remarkable thing happened at the same time—nothing much.

"The 2000 to 2002 stock market slump failed to produce a financial crisis," wrote David Hale, chairman of Prince Street Capital hedge fund, in an early 2003 issue of *Barron's*. "Wealth losses in the US equity market since March 2002 have been unprecedented. They have been equal to 90% of GDP, compared with 60% during the 2 years after the 1929 stock-market crash. But during the past 2 years, only 11 banks failed in the United States, compared with nearly 500 [from] 1989 to 1991 and thousands during the 1930s."

And in the economy, there was the same remarkable lack of anything special. Unemployment lines grew longer, but not so long as you might reasonably expect. And consumer borrowing and spending did not fall, as could have been expected, but rose. "In 2002, mortgage refinancing shot up to $1.5 trillion compared with a previous peak of $750 billion in '98," Hale tells us.

Following a mild economic downturn in 2001—and after the opening shots in the War Against Terror—"it is difficult to imagine a more benign scenario than the 3% growth in output that the economy actually enjoyed during the past year," Hale concluded.

What bothered us about this situation was precisely what delighted Hale—we could not reasonably expect it. What ought to follow a spectacularly absurd boom is a spectacularly absurd bust.

But the Japanese bubble wasn't completely destroyed in a year or two, either. Economists were still reluctant to cast their eyes toward Japan—because they could not explain it. Neither monetary nor fiscal stimuli seemed to have done the trick. But if you could grab their heads and turn them toward the Land of the Rising Sun, they would see that after a mild recession, GDP growth continued in Japan following the stock market peak in 1989—at about 2% to 3% per year. This went on for several years. But then the economy went into a more prolonged slump. By 2000, GDP per person was back to 1993 levels.

In both cases—Japan and the United States—there ought to have been a correction worthy of the preceding boom. In Japan, eventually, there was. In the United States, we presume, there will be.

Japan's example, we are told, does not apply anywhere outside Japan because the Japanese created a form of capitalism that was almost unrecognizable to Westerners. It was a system of cross-holdings, state intervention, cronyism, and a stock market that had become a popular sensation. In the financial frenzy of the late 1980s, Japanese companies ceased to act like capitalist enterprises altogether, for they ignored the capitalists. Profits no longer mattered. Assets per share had become an illusion. All that seemed to count was growth, market share, and big announcements to the press.

What kind of capitalism could it be when the capitalists did not require a return on their investment? Was it so different from the US model? US businesses in the late 1990s seemed to care even less about their capitalists than Japanese ones had. As stock prices peaked out on Wall Street in early 2000, profits had already been falling for 3 years. They continued to fall, sharply, for the first 2 years of the slump. Executive salaries soared, first as profits fell, and later as many of the biggest companies in the country edged into insolvency. Plus, the managers gave away the store in options to key employees— further disguising the real costs of business.

Despite all the hullabaloo about investing in New Economy technology, actual investment in plants, equipment, and things-that-might-give-investors-higher-profits-in-the-future declined. In the late 1990s, net capital investment dropped to new postwar lows.

As described earlier, instead of paying attention to the business, US corporate executives focused on deal making, acquisitions, and short-term profits—anything that would get their names in the paper.

You'd think an owner would get upset. But none of this mattered to the capitalists—because they had ceased to exist. Old-time capitalists who put money into businesses they knew and understood— with the reasonable hope of earning a profit—had been replaced by a new, collectivized *lumpeninvestoriat*, whose expectations were decidedly unreasonable. The patsies and chumps expected impossible rates of return from stocks about which they had no clue. Management could run down the balance sheet all it wanted. It could make extravagant compensation deals with itself. It could acquire assets for preposterous prices; it could borrow huge sums and then wonder how it would repay the money. It could cut dividends . . . or not pay them at all; the little guys would never figure it out.

The *lumpeninvestoriat* in Japan, as in the United States, ought to have jumped away from stocks, debt, and spending immediately following the crash in the stock market. The market should have plunged and then recovered. But government policy makers and central bankers were soon out in force—spreading so many safety nets, there was scarcely a square foot of pavement on which to fall.

Of course, the little guys never knew what they were doing in the first place. Was it such a surprise that they did the wrong thing again, resisting change by holding on, dragging out the pain of the correction, and postponing a real recovery? In Japan, analysts got weary waiting. Then, the slump continued, slowly and softly, like a man drowning in a beer tank.

Having looked at what ought to have happened to the stock market and the economy and what really did happen, we now peek under the hood of the imperial currency, the US dollar. What ought it do, we ask ourselves? To make it easy for readers, we give our verdict before presenting any evidence: it ought to go down.

The *lumpeninvestoriat*, that is, the hoi polloi of common investors, tend to believe things that are not true. In the heydays of the great boom, they believed they could get 18% return on their money invested in stocks—even though they had no idea what the companies really did or how they operated. They believed they could trust corporate executives to make investors rich, rather than just making themselves rich. They believed that stocks always went up and that Greenspan would not permit a major bear market. They believed that the US system of participatory capitalism, open markets, and safety nets was the finest ever devised and that it represented some sort of perfection that would remain on top of the world . . . if not forever, at least for a very long time.

They believed also that the US dollar was as real as money gets and that it would be destroyed in an orderly, measured way. A little inflation, they had been told, was actually good for an economy.

Of all the lies that the new *investoriat* took up, none was more provocative than the dollar. In order for anything to retain any value—particularly a currency—it must be in limited supply. If there were millions of paintings by Monet or Rembrandt, for example, they would be worth a lot less than they are today. Back in the nineteenth century, currencies were backed by gold. This had the effect of limiting the quantity of money, for there was only so much gold available.

After getting into the habit of accepting paper backed by gold, people barely noticed when the paper no longer had any backing at all. Governments still printed and distributed the new, managed currencies. Governments would make sure that they did not print too much, or so people assumed.

But while central bank reserves increased only 55% between 1948 and 1971 (the Bretton Woods period), they rose more than 2,000% during the next 30 years. This explosive growth in money and credit can also be measured by the increase in the bond market. Worth $776 billion in 1970, the global bond market had grown to $40 trillion by the end of the century. But who complained? The money found its way first into stock prices . . . and later into real estate. People looked at the house that just sold down the street and felt richer, not poorer—just as the Japanese had 10 years before.

And yet, since John Law first test-drove the idea in 1719, it has not been possible for a central bank to create trillions in new money—out of thin air—without driving the currency itself into the ground. "The dollar ought to fall," economists began saying as the 1990s passed. Finally, in 2002, the dollar did fall—against other currencies, particularly the euro and gold, against which it went down about 20% in 2002 alone.

What ought it do next, we ask again?

Here we add two complicating details. First, as described in previous chapters, for as much as the American *lumpeninvestoriat* was deceived by the dollar's apparent strength, foreigners were even bigger dupes. They could not get enough of them.

How could a country balance its books when it was buying more from foreigners than it was selling? It had to make up the difference by bringing the money back home as investment funds. Foreigners did not dump their dollars for their home currencies; instead, they used the money to buy dollar assets—US stocks, real estate, businesses. By the end of 2002, the total of foreign holdings of dollar assets had risen to a Himalayan high. With the dollar now falling and US stocks also falling, foreigners ought to want to lighten up on their dollar holdings.

Even tossing off a small percentage of these holdings could have a devastating effect on the dollar's price. On average, the dollar fell only 10% against foreign currencies in 2002. In the 1980s, with far less provocation, it dropped nearly 50%.

The other complication is that in addition to the $9 trillion worth of existing foreign holdings, the current account deficit grew by

$1.5 billion every day. However successful the United States has been as a military superpower, this power pales against its success as a monetary super superpower. Every day, Americans struck a bargain with foreigners in which the latter traded valuable goods and services for little pieces of paper with green ink on them. They had no intrinsic value, and their own custodians had pledged to create an almost infinite supply of them, if need be, to make sure they did not gain value against consumer goods!

"There is a crack in everything God made," Emerson keeps reminding us. The crack in this bargain is that it undermined the profitability of US companies. Spurred by the Fed, consumers spent their money at full gallop. They even spent money they did not have. But profits at US companies continued to fall. In fact, as a percentage of GDP, profits had been falling ever since the early 1960s, not coincidentally as the percentage of the economy devoted to consumer spending and the current account deficit increased.

What was happening was obvious. Americans were spending money, but the funds ended up in the coffers of foreign businesses. US companies had the expense of employing US workers, but the money did not come back to them; it went to their overseas competitors. At the beginning of 2003, US profits were already at a post–World War II low. This was not a trend that could go on forever. And as Herbert Stein pointed out, if it can't, it won't.

## NOTHING FAILS LIKE SUCCESS

In December 2002, Greenspan spoke to the New York Economic Club and sounded, for a while, like the Randian acolyte he was circa 1963:

> Although the gold standard could hardly be portrayed as having produced a period of price tranquility, it was the case that the price level in 1929 was not much different, on net, from what it had been in 1800. But, in the two decades following the abandonment of the gold standard in 1933, the consumer price index in the United States nearly doubled. And, in the four decades after that, prices quintupled. Monetary policy, unleashed from the constraint of domestic gold convertibility, had allowed a persistent overissuance of money.

As recently as a decade ago, central bankers, having witnessed more than a half-century of chronic inflation, appeared to confirm that a fiat currency was inherently subject to excess.

Of course, Greenspan was setting the stage. He might have added that no central banker in all history had ever succeeded in proving the contrary. Every fiat currency the world had ever seen had shown itself "subject to excess" and then subject to destruction. Circa 2002, against this epic background, central banker Greenspan strutted out, front and center.

Each métier comes with its own hazards. The baker burns his fingers; the psychiatrist soon needs to have his own head examined. The moral hazard of central banking is well documented. Given the power to create money out of thin air, the central banker almost always goes too far. And if one resists, his successor will almost certainly succumb.

There are some things at which succeeding is more dangerous than failing. Running a central bank—like robbing one—is an example. The more successful the central banker becomes and the more people come to believe in the stability of his paper money, the more hazardous the situation becomes.

Warren Buffett's father, a congressman from Nebraska, warned in a 1948 speech: "The paper money disease has been a pleasant habit thus far and will not be dropped voluntarily any more than a dope user will without a struggle give up narcotics . . . I find no evidence to support a hope that our fiat paper money venture will fare better ultimately than such experiments in other lands. . . ."[5]

In all other lands, at all other times, the story was the same. Paper money had not worked; the moral hazard was too great. Central bankers could not resist; when it suited them, they overdid it, increasing the money supply far faster than the growth in goods and services that the money could buy.

When we went looking for a list of the world's defunct or failing paper money, we were soon overwhelmed. We found a good long list, in alphabetical order . . . but gave up when at number 318 we were still in the Bs.

Against this sorry record of managed currencies is the exemplary one of gold. No matter whose face adorns the coin, or what inscription it bears, or when it was minted, an unmanaged gold coin today is still worth at least the value of its gold content, and it will generally buy as much in goods and services today as it did the day it was struck.

Gold is found on earth in limited amounts—only 3.5 parts per billion. Had God been less niggardly with the stuff, gold might be more ubiquitous and less expensive. But it is precisely because the earth yields up its gold so grudgingly that it is so valuable. Paper money, on the other hand, can be produced in almost infinite quantities. When central bankers reach the limits of modern printing technology, the designers have only to add a zero, and they will have increased the speed at which they inflate by a factor of 10. In today's electronic world, a man no longer measures his wealth in stacks of paper money. It is now just "information." A central banker does not even have to turn the crank on the printing press; electronically registered zeros can be added at the speed of light. Given the ease with which new paper money is created, is it any wonder the old paper money loses its value?

For a while, Greenspan seemed to have God's light shining on him. His paper dollars rose in value against gold for two decades, when they ought to have gone down.

Greenspan explains how this came about:

The adverse consequences of excessive money growth for financial stability and economic performance provoked a backlash. Central banks were finally pressed to rein in overissuance of money even at the cost of considerable temporary economic disruption. By 1979, the need for drastic measures had become painfully evident in the United States. The Federal Reserve, under the leadership of Paul Volcker and with the support of both the Carter and the Reagan Administrations, dramatically slowed the growth of money. Initially, the economy fell into recession and inflation receded. However, most important, when activity staged a vigorous recovery, the progress made in reducing inflation was largely preserved. By the end of the 1980s, the inflation climate was being altered dramatically.

The record of the past 20 years appears to underscore the observation that, although pressures for excess issuance of fiat money are chronic, a prudent monetary policy maintained over a protracted period can contain the forces of inflation.[6]

Until 2001, Greenspan's genius was universally acclaimed. Central banking looked, at long last, like a great success. But then the bubble burst. People began to wonder what kind of central bank would do such a dumb thing.

"Evidence of history suggests that allowing an asset bubble to develop is the greatest mistake that a central bank can make," wrote Andrew Smithers and Stephen Wright in *Valuing Wall Street*, in 2000. "Over the past 5 years or so the Federal Reserve has knowingly permitted the development of the greatest asset bubble of the twentieth century."

When the stock market collapsed, Greenspan's policies began to look less prudent. During his tour of duty at the Fed, the monetary base tripled, at a time when the gross domestic product rose only 50%. More new money came into being than under all previous Fed chairmen—roughly $6,250 for every new ounce of gold brought up from the earth.

All this new money created by the Greenspan Fed had the defect of excess paper money; it had no resources behind it. Though taken up by shopkeepers and dog groomers as if it were the real thing, it represented no increase in actual wealth. The retailer and the groomer thought they had more money, but there was really nothing to back it up.

The new money was issued, light on value, but heavy on consequences. It helped lure the *lumpeninvestoriat* into their own moral hazard; they no longer needed to save—because the Greenspan Fed always seemed to make new money available, at increasingly attractive rates. And it misled suppliers into believing there was more demand than there really was. Consumers were buying; there was no doubt about that. But how long could they continue to spend more than they actually earned?

The effects of this moral hazard are just now being felt. The consumer is more heavily in debt than ever before and seems to need increased credit just to stay afloat. The trend couldn't be more pronounced than following both the Panic of '08 and again following the pandemic lockdowns.

In 2010, after the economy began opening again, consumer loans spiked vertically and continued to climb throughout the period of low to negative interest rates. Banks themselves began to loosen credit standards, consumer borrowing went straight up.

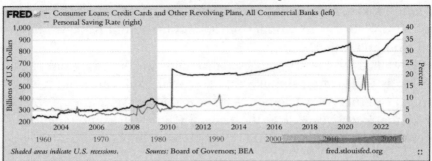

**FIGURE 6.1** Consumer Debt vs. Savings
Source: St. Louis Fed

Personal savings rates increased during the pandemic lockdowns in 2020, but consumer spending kept rising. This time, as the economy started opening up again, consumer debt shot up at a faster pace, while personal savings plummeted below 2008 levels (see Figure 6.1).

The post-pandemic result has been the most precipitous drop in disposable income since 1931, the onset of the Great Depression (see Figure 6.2).

There are signs that the trend is reversing, savings are coming back into fashion. But it's hard to ignore the disparity between consumer credit and the savings rate when the Fed is raising interest rates at the fastest pace in the past 40 plus years.

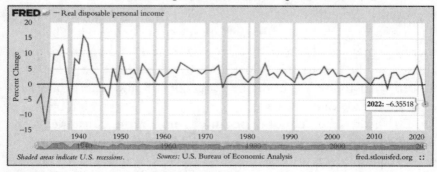

**FIGURE 6.2** Drop in Disposable Income
Source: St. Louis Fed

In reviewing our original observation of this phenomenon, we found it amusing that once the cracks in the subprime market, and the housing market as a whole, began to show, the press finally began to give credit where it was due. Two articles—one in *Forbes* and the other in the *Wall Street Journal*—single out our own dearly beloved former Fed chairman, Greenspan.

"Our present misery dates back to Alan Greenspan's easy money policy of a few years ago," wrote Martin T. Sosnoff in *Forbes* in 2007. "When the risk-free rate was pegged at 1%, financial market players, starved for higher yields, moved out on the quality spectrum for long maturity goods. Insurance underwriters, brokers, banks and some hedge funds that play the carry trade game have taken hits to their net asset value, but not enough to cripple them permanently."

"The housing debacle already has cut 1% out of GDP," he continued. "Fortunately, we are heading to the first anniversary of the decline in new construction, but there's more coming and no likely recovery before 2009. Existing home prices have peaked until the country absorbs new home inventory and coming defaults on mortgages outstanding."[7]

*The Wall Street Journal* added this:

> When the Fed cut interest rates to the lowest level in a generation to avoid a severe downturn, then-Chairman Alan Greenspan anticipated that making short-term credit so cheap would have unintended consequences. "I don't know what it is, but we're doing some damage because this is not the way credit markets should operate," he and a colleague recall him saying at the time.

Now the consequences of moves the Fed and others made are becoming clearer.

Low interest rates engineered by central banks and reinforced by a tidal wave of overseas savings fueled home prices and leveraged buyouts. Pension funds and endowments, unhappy with skimpy returns, shoved cash at hedge funds and private-equity firms, which borrowed heavily to make big bets. The investments of choice were opaque financial instruments that shifted default risk from lenders to global investors. The question now: When the dust settles, will the world be better off?[8]

And the question marks began to appear everywhere. But even so, without a hint of irony, the citizens of the United States turned to the instigators of the credit and housing meltdown—the central banks—to bail them out.

# CHAPTER 7

# FIRST IT GIVETH . . .

The Fed cut rates . . . central banks all over the world "injected liquidity" into the system. But no matter what action was taken, stocks and houses continued falling . . . and so did employment. In the beginning of 2008, the bull was bleeding to death.

So, in an effort to stop, or at least slow, the bleeding, on February 13, 2008, President Bush signed a $168 billion economic rescue program, calling it a "booster shot for our economy."[1]

This stimulus package meant $300 to $1,200 in tax rebates for many Americans . . . and most happily took that check.

But what actually happens to the money? It ends up overseas. The feds can stimulate . . . but what they are really stimulating is Asian factories . . . the gold market . . . and global speculators, not the US economy. Problems in the United States are too deep to be cured by a little more spending money. Besides, as we keep saying, the real problem in the United States is that people have borrowed and spent too much. Offering them more credit is not a solution; it's a temptation . . . like wearing a short skirt while counseling a sex addict . . . or turning your back on a kleptomaniac and then wondering what is missing.

Now, back to the rebate package. At $146 billion, it was almost exactly the same amount as Frederic Mishkin figures the US economy lost in 2007 in consumer spending due to the bear market in housing. Fed Governor Mishkin says that families cut back spending by seven cents for every dollar their houses go down in price (with a lag, we presume). That comes out to about $150 billion of reduced spending. Assuming consumers spend their rebate checks, the economy should have come out even.

But the drop in consumer spending caused by housing is just a small part of the deflation that was hitting the US economy. In the first few months of 2008, stocks were down 15% from their peak, and finance and housing industry leaders were reporting huge losses . . . with more to come.

What's more, the collapse in consumer purchasing power comes not just from a fall in their house prices, but also from the fact that they aren't rising. At the peak of the bubble, homeowners were taking out as much as $250 billion per quarter in refinancing, home-equity lines, and other housing-related credit. Now, that source is drying up.

The feds can try to replace that money, but they are not likely to succeed.

The feds can try to play out more lines of credit to strapped families, but what they are really doing is giving them more rope with which to hang themselves. The real problem is that US wages have not kept pace with inflation, which means, the average American is not as rich as he used to be. He can only pretend to be rich . . . by exchanging more of his leisure time for dollars . . . and by borrowing. Both of those "coping mechanisms," as Robert Reich called them, are now exhausted. Now, he's going to swing.

When the injection of money into the markets didn't seem to work—in fact, the markets seemed to just shrug it off, the Feds responded by cutting the discount rate on August 17, 2007.

The discount rate is what the Fed charges for banks that need to borrow funds from the Fed. They call this "having to go to the discount window." Now, normally, if you need to borrow from the discount window, the Fed doesn't take kindly to this. But if you need to go two times, then the Fed is looking into your books!

Well, this time, the Fed said, "Come on, borrow. And do it at a cheaper rate. We understand." Some financial commentators, including our old friend Marc Faber, were beginning to see the Fed's emergency rate cut as "Bernanke's first big mistake." He panicked, they said, and took the Fed in a direction it shouldn't go. Instead of holding the line against inflation, the Fed is now bailing out Wall Street financiers and speculators.

Where the Fed was headed is the direction Wall Street wanted it to go. Cutting rates suddenly, the Fed had come to the aid of speculators and the financial industry. Doing so, the Fed signaled that it offers what used to be called the "Greenspan Put" to investors—the assurance that it will always provide money on easy terms, when it is needed.

When do speculators need a helping hand from the Fed? When they are losing money, of course. And when do they lose money? When their bets turn out to be not as good as they thought they were. Why would the Fed want to protect speculators from their own mistakes?

Ah, dear reader, you must be either naïve . . . or a true capitalist. Otherwise, you wouldn't ask such a question.

There was a time when the business of the United States was business. Americans made things and sold them at home and on the world market. General Motors was our most important industry. So, what was good for GM was good for America.

Now the business of the United States is debt. Americans buy things they don't need with money they don't have. Financing debt—corporate, hedge fund, subprime, prime, mortgage, LBO, government—is our most important industry. So what is good for Wall Street, the reasoning goes, is good for America.

And things were just as bad on the other side of the pond. Poor Mervyn King. The man is the head of the Bank of England. He was just trying to do the right thing. When the credit crisis began that summer he, alone among central bankers, stood firm. No bailouts, said he. If we rescue reckless lenders and imprudent speculators, he opined, it could "sow the seeds of a future financial crisis."[2]

But integrity in a central banker is like honesty in a politician or chastity in a prostitute—the quality is completely at odds with his profession. Economists talk about the "moral hazard" of allowing investors to do the wrong thing and get away with it. But the hazard is greatest for central bankers themselves. Not since Paul Volcker has any central banker been able to stand up straight. Instead, they bow to pressure—from politicians, the public, the media, and the squirrelly economics profession itself. This has led to what some economists refer to as an "asymetrical response" from the financial authorities. When the going is good . . . they are reluctant to tighten up on credit. But when the going is not so good . . . they ease up quickly.

King resisted pressure for a few weeks. Then, in September, when the tabloids began running photos of depositors lining up to get their money back from troubled mortgage lender Northern Rock, he buckled. He turned to the cameras and offered to help out. "You need money . . . " he almost said. "Just come see me."

Little did he know, this would become the war cry in the battle of the coming months: Inflation versus Deflation; Markets versus Market Manipulators.

"We're in the helicopter phase now," said Howard Simons, a strategist at Bianco Research in Chicago. He's referring to Ben Bernanke's famous remark . . . that he would drop money from helicopters, if necessary, in order to avoid a deflationary meltdown. On March 11, 2008, Bernanke's helicopters dropped $200 billion. In the 2 days following, the hedge funds were still failing. What's worse, there were rumors that a big bank may be in big trouble.

We take a moment to explain how it works. The banks lent a lot of money to hedge funds. The funds didn't hedge; they gambled. As a result, many got themselves into trouble; they can't repay the money.

The banks sent out margin calls—asking for more cash from the hedge funds, but the funds don't have it. For example, in beginning of March, the Carlyle Fund got the "Margin Call from Hell" from its bankers. The banks wanted $97.5 million. That didn't seem like much a few months ago, but now money was hard to come by. Carlyle bet $31 for every single dollar it had in capital. With that kind of leverage, the managers stood to score a fortune if the markets went their way. But if prices went in the wrong direction, and the bets went bad, it didn't take much bad news before the fund went broke.

So, Carlyle went belly-up. It couldn't make its margin call. And all over town, other fund managers were biting their nails . . . and refusing to pick up the phone. The bankers paced the room, too. You know the old saying: when you owe the bank $100,000, you can't sleep at night. But when you owe the bank $1,000,000, it's the banker who can't sleep. Well, a lot of bankers lost sleep in Manhattan and London . . . wondering which of their clients would be able to repay . . . and which wouldn't. And the last thing the Fed wants is for some large bank to make the headlines with news that it is broke. That's what the Fed is for, after all. It's a banking cartel, designed to protect the banks from their own stupid mistakes.

Of course, the big mistake the banks made was lending money to people who lent money to people who lent money to people who couldn't pay it back. The subprime mortgage lenders didn't worry because they sold their loans on to packagers who sold them on again—often ending up in the portfolios of highly leveraged hedge funds, to which the banks had lent money. S&P now projected that the losses from subprime would rise to $285 billion, up about $20 billion from their last estimate. Our estimate at the time was that the losses would top $1 trillion . . . and if you wanted to throw in the collateral damage, lower house prices, the bill would rise to more than $6 trillion.

Ha! Were we wrong. It's funny when your projections are seen at the time as "gloom and doom." When the dust settled, the bill for the subprime crisis totaled $9.8 trillion as home prices plummeted and retirement accounts went *poof*.

Houses in Southern California lost 17.9% from March 2007 to March 2008. The median price sank to $408,000. In the summer, the median price was more than $500,000. As expected, by us, retail sales were slumping: unemployment reached a two and a half-year high. And America's CFOs believed the country to already be in recession.

But the question on everyone's mind was: will the Fed succeed?

First, there is the practical issue of how lending to impaired banks in the middle of a credit crunch actually stimulates the real economy. The presumption is that there are worthy projects—new factories, business expansions, new technological developments, new employees to be hired—just waiting for credit from the banks. Now, with their balance sheets restored (they laid their subprime-infected credits off on the Fed in return for Treasury bonds), they'll be able to lend again; that's the theory.

But what new factories? Who's hiring? What businesses are expanding? The country is in a recession, for Pete's sake. Besides, in the late stages of a credit bubble, few people borrow to actually expand the economy. The borrowers, instead, are hedge funds and speculators—just the people the banks are now afraid of. That's just the way a credit cycle works. At first, the borrowers are solid . . . with sensible plans for the money. Each dollar they borrow results in, say, another 75 cents to the nation's GDP. But as the cycle goes on, the borrowers become more and more reckless. Asset prices tend to move up quickly, so the borrowers figure they can't lose . . . and the lenders figure they have nothing to worry about because the collateral is becoming more and more valuable. As credit quality declines, each additional dollar borrowed adds less and less to the real economy. By the end, it may take an extra $10 worth of credit to produce a single extra dollar of GDP.

We take it as a given, at this stage, that more lending from the Fed cannot actually improve the real economy. In fact, it makes it worse—propping up failing companies, increasing speculation, misallocating resources, and adding to debts that will have to be paid, one way or another, by somebody or another, eventually. A better question is: how much damage will the Fed do to the real economy?

## CHECKING AND SAVINGS

Greenspan's real legacy was that he finally made central banking work. Bernanke has pledged not to mess it up. By targeting inflation, he says, he will be able to make the financial world even more stable and predictable. And if the party ever starts to wind down, he has told fellow economists that he will drop money out of helicopters, if necessary, to keep it going.

But of all the twisted concepts that came out during the end of the housing era, the explanation of the world's international financial system offered by Bernanke is perhaps the most elegantly preposterous. Americans are not spending too much, said Bernanke. The problem is that Asians are spending too little. As a result, they have a "savings glut" that Americans helpfully recycle into granite counter-tops and home entertainment systems.

Bernanke managed to condense a whole universe of lies, misap-prehensions, and conceits into two short words. Yet as compact as they were, they covered up a grotesque system of global finance so out of whack that even congresspeople are appalled: one nation buys things it doesn't need with money it doesn't have. Another sells on credit to people who already cannot pay—and builds more factories to increase output.

This idea of the savings glut encouraged the fantasy that Americans were doing the savers a big favor by taking their money. He made it seem like such a benign and salutary exchange. They do the saving . . . we'll do the spending. They do the producing . . . we'll do the con-suming. "They sweat," said one financial pundit. "We think."

The conceit of it had about the same effect upon US investors and consumers as finding an overturned liquor truck in the street. Soon, they were helping themselves to armloads of bottles—and the party was on!

"We are so clever, we no longer have to do the hard work," they told themselves. "We are such geniuses; we no longer have to save. We are so 'inventive' . . . we are so 'creative' . . . we have the most 'dynamic economy' and the most 'flexible' markets. Hey, let's face it—we're just smarter than everyone else."

But now, the cops are on the scene, and people are throwing up in the bushes. "The party is over," declares the financial media. US sub-prime borrowers (and lenders) no longer look like geniuses. Instead, they look like the yahoos they always were. Suddenly, many of the biggest players on Wall Street and in Greenwich don't look so smart. And the Europeans pat themselves on the back—"See . . . Americans are morons," they tell each other. "Just like we thought."

It would be much simpler for us if the world were set up in a more orderly and predictable way. But then, it wouldn't be nearly as much fun. Even the feds could control a simpleton's world. What a dreary place that would be!

Still, ships' compasses don't intentionally lead us onto the rocks. More money = more inflation, that's the rule. Besides, it's not just a matter of money. The feds are clearly sowing the wind with their quantitative easing. They deserve to reap the whirlwind.

But wait . . . it's inflation they *want*. Nature, in her wisdom, rarely gives a rascal what he wants. Instead, she gives him what he deserves. What then, do the feds deserve? We know their crime . . . what will be their punishment?

Ah ha! Maybe they deserve the doldrums . . . locked in irons, with no wind at all!

They want to lower the debt burden by instigating inflation. They want to increase the velocity of money—by lightening it up a little so people are eager to get rid of it. They want to get lenders lending, and consumers consuming—all eager to turn over their dollars as fast as possible. They want to shift the burden of losses from the people who made them to the people who didn't. Well, what if the dollar doesn't cooperate? What if it grows heavier? What if it seems more solid? And what if dollar-denominated debts stick like tar to the people who incurred it?

Seems impossible, doesn't it? And yet, that is what happened in the Land of the Rising Sun.

Our hypothesis seemed so sure . . . so airtight. The feds have no alternative but to try to inflate the currency. Because it will reduce the debt load on consumers . . . and, not coincidentally, on the government too. It will also induce people to spend money rather than save it. This will increase the velocity of money, which will have a further inspiring effect on animal spirits.

If at first they don't succeed, the feds will try, try again. And sooner or later, they'll get the inflation they desire—first in moderation, then in exaggeration.

But what if it doesn't happen that way? What if the feds—and the entire debtor class—were tortured before they were finally killed? And what if we—those who think we know what is going on . . . and who are stacking up gold coins in our home safes in anticipation—are driven mad by deep corrections in the gold market? What if gold sinks to $600 . . . and stays there for years?

What if the markets stay irrational for longer than any of us can stay solvent . . . first wiping out the bulls in a major new break in the stock market . . . then wiping out the bears with a major new break in the gold market?

And then, when we have all given up hope . . . and sold all our stocks . . . and all our gold . . . and are curled up in a corner, whimpering, clutching a handful of crumpled dollar bills, maybe then Mr. Market will feel sorry for us. Maybe he'll finally come over and put us out of our misery . . . delivering the coup de grace of blow out inflation . . . à la Weimar or Harare?

Anything is possible.

## "QE" MARTINIS

Greenspan's EZ credit terms created a worldwide boom. In the spring of 2009, we paid for it with a worldwide bust.

Isn't that the way it always works? For every action there is an equal and opposite reaction. For every bubble, there's a pin. And for every politician, there's an envelope with $100 bills in it.

But Greenspan's successor wants to get his picture on the cover of *Time* just as much as his former boss did. He's determined to beat the bust. If he can do it, *Time* will probably give him the Man of the Year award. If he can't, he'll probably get the "Schmuck of the Year" award from us.

He's tried cutting rates. In fact, he cut them more than Greenspan, who stopped at a nominal rate of 1%. Bernanke didn't stop. Once he had his chainsaw in gear, he just kept cutting . . . down to zero.

Greenspan didn't put the Fed's own balance sheet in jeopardy either. When he was running things, the Fed held only a bare minimum of Wall Street's junk assets. Now, it has got trillions' worth of them.

Nor did Greenspan resort so nakedly to printing money. And now, the Bernanke Fed found a new superdrug: "quantitative easing." What is quantitative easing, you may want to know? It describes the Fed's latest ploy, in which it buys toxic assets from banks. The banks thus increase their reserves. If they were to maintain the same loan-to-reserve ratio, they would have to lend out more money. But when the Fed buys assets from the banks, it does not borrow the money; it creates it out of thin air. In other words, between quantitative easing and printing money, there is not enough space to wedge a subway ticket.

So far, this new treatment has produced no signs of recovery. But don't worry; the quacks won't give up. They'll give larger and larger doses—until the patient dies.

Soon, they will embark on "inflation targeting" too. No kidding. That's what it says in the paper. Bernanke is going to set a target for inflation . . . say 3%. . . and keep the printing presses running hot until prices are rising by at least that much.

Inflation is now only a problem because there isn't any. In the United States, the consumer price index crested at nearly 6% last year. Now, it appears to be headed down to zero . . . and perhaps below. That is what the feds are desperate to avoid. When consumer prices fall, consumers become obsessively frugal. They know that if they just wait, they'll be able to get what they want at a lower price. And then, why not wait a little longer . . . and get the item even cheaper still? This "propensity to save," as economists call it, becomes self-reinforcing. As consumers stop spending, lower demand causes prices to fall further . . . which incites consumers to dilly dally even more . . . which causes prices to sink again.

That is the Japanese-style deflationary cycle that gives Bernanke a nightmare. But, there's not much he can do about it—at least nothing honest. Rupert Murdoch says the financial crisis has caused $50 trillion in wealth to vanish. The feds have put back only $3 trillion (arguably) so far. Just looking at the numbers, it doesn't seem as though prices will be rising anytime soon. For every dollar the feds put into the system, $17 disappears.

What's a fellow to do? The only way out, as near as we can see, is the road taken by Gideon Gono. "Monetizing the debt" . . . "quantitative easing" . . . "printing press money"—it will no doubt go by a number of different euphemisms and code words. It's what happens when the Fed buys US Treasury debt directly. For this purpose, it simply creates a ledger transaction . . . effectively adding to the money supply.

But even printing money does not automatically and immediately cause consumer price inflation. According to classical economic theory, the shelves must be cleared, and the excess capacity must be reabsorbed before prices will rise. That could take a long time. But we're not sure it works like that. If money were suddenly dropped from helicopters, merchants probably wouldn't wait for their inventory to disappear before raising prices. They'd be concerned that they were giving away something that was valuable in exchange for something that was not.

When this kind of inflation happens—perhaps worthy of the adjectival modifier "hyper"—it can happen suddenly and violently.

We never thought central bank management was a science. It certainly isn't. The theories that guide it are unproven in practice . . . and unbelievable in theory. Instead, it's all guesswork, bunkum, and dead reckoning. Which is to say, the Fed will hit its target, or we reckon the economy will be dead.

Maybe Bernanke is a champion marksman . . . and maybe he isn't. We don't know, but if we were you, dear reader, we wouldn't stand too close to the target . . . if you know what we mean.

## WHEN GENIUS FAILS

Over the last 30 years, Americans believed they were on top of the world. Everybody said so. And, logically, they should have been. It was the post–Reagan Revolution, with the most modern, most capitalistic economy in the world . . . with the latest technology, with the world's best brains, with the top schools, and with Wall Street to "allocate capital" in the best possible way. If workers couldn't get ahead in this economy, they couldn't get ahead anywhere. At least, that was what people believed.

But capitalism is a jungle, not a zoo. It lets animals get fat, but only so they can be eaten by hungrier beasts.

To us, it was fun listening to the conceits and pretensions of the zookeepers. At the end of the 1980s, they announced their triumph over communism, apparently unaware that their biggest potential rivals had just cut themselves loose from a ball and chain. It is not even 20 years later, and both Russia and China are already formidable competitors. China's reserves of foreign currency, for example, are nearly 20 times those of the United States. And now, if the Red Giant decides to dump dollars, America's economy will be hit by a major crisis . . . and possibly paralyzed.

Then, near the end of the 1990s, the dreamers thought they had found some magic formula. The United States no longer needs savings, said the pundits, because now our information technology allows us to create wealth using virtual capital . . . brain capital.

"We think; they sweat" said one genius, as if the Chinese and Russians or the Brazilians and Indians couldn't think too.

After the dot-coms blew up, another hallucination developed. One that sophisticated financial engineering, combined with enlightened macroeconomic management, had made market crashes and recessions obsolete. The geniuses went to work with computers, proving that those fancy derivative contracts (which they were selling) were completely foolproof. They were supposed to run into problems only once in a blue moon. "You're talking about sigma 25 events," they said, as if they had a clue. Scarcely 3 years later, the moon was blue.

It was all great fun. Watching the show, that is. And it's not over.

In our years of reporting on the goings on of the economic world, we can say one thing for certain: people make the same mistakes over and over again, unaware that with each new movement comes a new set of delusions. The principle difference from one age to the next is the line of flimflam each falls for.

We end with a brief rehearsal of what went wrong: the economy as it was before the spring of 2007 was too wonderful for words; whenever you tried to describe it, it sounded ridiculous. For example, "the richest get richer by borrowing from the poorest."

"We think; they sweat" sums up the relationship between the East and the West. The West was just recycling the East's "savings glut," added the new Federal Reserve Chairman Ben Bernanke.[3] Meanwhile, derivatives—based on mortgage debt from people who couldn't pay—"helped to make the banking and overall financial system more resilient," said the International Monetary Fund in 2006.[4]

Each sentence must have made the gods choke . . . groan . . . and then laugh. But beginning with revelations that all was not well at the investment bank Bear Stearns in early 2007, came a correction. Suddenly, the big spenders saw their houses fall in value. Lenders watched their collateral collapse. Though, at first, the problem was pronounced "largely contained" by then US Treasury Secretary Hank Paulson on April 7, 2007;[5] just 3 months later, Fed Chairman Bernanke admitted the crisis could bring losses "up to $100 billion."[6]

But there was no container large enough to hold the subprime losses. Each time one was set out, it quickly overflowed. Reports in March of 2009 told us the bilge was now 500 times deeper than the Fed had forecast . . . and still rising. And this comes after $11.7 trillion has been committed in the United States alone to pumping it out. Whether the plumbers are plain idiots or clever rogues, we can't say, but it should be obvious after 2 years of watching them that their pumps don't work.

# PART THREE

# EXTRAORDINARY POPULAR DELUSIONS

*No man ever had a point of pride that wasn't injurious to him.*
—Ralph Waldo Emerson

# CHAPTER 8

# JOHN LAW AND THE ORIGINS OF A BAD IDEA

Throughout history, many different items have served as money—seashells, cows, beer, salt, copper bracelets, horses, chickens, amber, coral, dried fish, furs, tobacco, grain, sugar, playing cards, nails, rice . . . even paper.

The world's first experiment with paper money—China, AD 910—was abandoned after a few hundred years because it was susceptible to inflation.

John Law, a Scottish economist, brought the idea of paper money to Europe in 1716, knowing full well neither he nor anyone else had ever succeeded in curing its most dangerous defect. That said, Law profited tremendously from paper money's inherently speculative nature; he knew full well what he was doing.

The story of Law and his incredibly bad ideas reveals that the fever for profits in the United States circa Y2K—and the manias we suffer from today—absurd as they may seem to us now, were not the first time individuals got sucked into acting irrationally *en masse*. Nor is it likely to be the last.

"Men it has been well said, think in herds," Charles Mackay famously observed in his tome, *Extraordinary Popular Delusions*. He continued, "It will be seen that they go mad in herds, while they recover their senses slowly, and one by one."


## THE GENTLEMAN GAMBLER

Law's life reads like the stuff of legends: murder, sex, political intrigue, wealth, power. . . despair.

In a duel in Bloomsbury Square in London, Law fatally wounded a man named Edward Beau Wilson. Law was caught, convicted, and sentenced to death, but then escaped.

He spent the next 20 years on the run in Europe, gambling for a living and making a public nuisance of himself. In a biography of Law, Trinity College Dublin professor, Antoin Murphy, has suggested that the legendary Law—the rake, the womanizer, and the escaped convict—may, in fact, have been a calculated image to gain an advantage at the gaming tables of Europe's high society.[1]

After the escape, Law made his way to Amsterdam. Until resurfacing in Edinburgh 3 years later, he is reported to have spent his mornings studying finance and trade and nights at the local gaming houses, gambling and toying with the local aristocracy.

During this time, he began laying the intellectual foundations for what could be described as a prototype for modern central banking. He had a natural talent for figures, a willingness to take risks, and a deep interest in the way things work . . . particularly money. Plus, he was a gambler at heart.

In 1703, Law took advantage of the fact that English death warrants were not honored north of the Scottish border and returned to his hometown. There, at the age of 32, he became involved in the establishment of one of Europe's first "land banks."

Scotland at the time was reeling from the failed Darien Venture. The venture was an attempt to establish a Scottish colony in Panama, on the new continent of North America. The project fell through, draining much of the country's available capital.

Reacting to what he saw as a dearth of physical specie, Law began promoting the idea that if Scotland were to recover from the Darien Venture and prosper, it needed paper money.

Having studied banking systems in his travels in the New World, Law had come to believe that paper money, because of its portability—and availability—would facilitate trade in the country far better than gold and silver, the traditional specie.

He suggested the land bank should issue paper notes backed by, and never exceeding, the value of the total state holdings of land—hence the name "land bank."

Holders of the notes could redeem their paper for an equal value in land. "Just how the land would be redeemed by noteholders was uncertain," John K. Galbraith said of a land bank already established in Holland during the time.

Critics panned it as a "sand bank," suggesting that it would run the ship of state aground. In a second essay, *Money and Trade Considered* (1705), Law retorted: "What is important about the 'specie,' is not how much of it one had . . . but how it got used."

Spending, Law believed, is how a nation gets wealthy.

Fortune soon smirked in Law's direction. Louis XIV died in 1715, leaving the largest, most powerful nation in Europe to his successor Louis XV—aged seven. Because of the new king's tender age, custom allowed his uncle—Philip II, the Duc d'Orleans—to take control of the royal finances. Philip II became the Regent of France.

The royal finances were a mess.

After years of war and the building of extravagant palaces, such as Versailles, the French state was 3,000 million livres in debt. Annual revenues from taxes were only 145 million livres. Annual expenses before interest payments were 142 million livres.

The bag of tricks used by finance ministers of the time included declaring national bankruptcy (not exactly a good option for a new government), raising taxes, "clipping" coins (replacing the coins in existence with new coinage made up of a smaller percentage of precious metals), and selling monopoly trade privileges of the state's colonies or confiscating the possessions of corrupt state employees.

The new regent chose a combination of clipping and confiscation. Through the next year, he managed to scrimp, steal, and inflate his way to 150 million livres more in state revenue: barely 6% of the government's outstanding debt.

Philip II sent out word that he was looking for an astute financier to assist in saving the French state before it was forced to declare bankruptcy. Law answered the call.

The gentleman gambler with fanciful ideas about a "paper" currency, who was now 44 years of age and quite wealthy, would finally get a shot at playing the game with the highest stakes of all: the creation of money itself.

On May 5, 1716, the Banque Générale was founded with 6 million livres in capital and was assured success from the beginning. The Duc declared all taxes must henceforth be paid with notes issued by Law's bank. For the first time in modern history, paper money was being introduced and officially sanctioned by a government.

Law declared his notes were redeemable "at sight" at the bank for the full amount of coins. Then Law declared that any banker printing more notes than he could back up with coins "deserved death."

The paper notes—backed as they were by gold—traded at a premium. Investors had so much confidence in the paper and so little in the clipped coins that they began to pay 101 livres worth of coins for a 100-livre note. Law was able to expand his operation quickly. He opened branches of his bank in Lyons, La Rochelle, Tours, Amiens, and Orleans. The paper notes of the Banque Générale quickly became a national obsession.

Finally Law issued the final part of his plan to recoup all of France's outstanding debt. While it was perhaps the most ingenious move of Law's scheme, it also signaled the beginning of the end.

Law convinced Philip II to back a trading company with monopoly trading rights over the Mississippi River and France's land claim in Louisiana. Shares in the new company would be offered to the public, and investors would only be allowed to buy them with the remaining paper *billets d'etat* on the market. So begins the famed Mississippi Scheme.

## THE MISSISSIPPI SCHEME

Law's new venture, which would come to be known as the Compagnie des Indes, was granted all the possessions of its competitors—the Senegal Company, the China Company, and the French East India company—giving it exclusive French trading rights for the Mississippi River, Louisiana, China, East India, and South America.

Law's enterprise also received the sole right to mint royal coins for 9 years, it was allowed to act as the royal tax collector for the same amount of time, and it was granted a monopoly on all tobacco trade under French rule.

Immediately after the initial public offering, applications for shares in the Compagnie des Indes started coming in from all levels of society.

So many, in fact, that it took the staff at the bank weeks to sort through all the applications. Traders, merchants, dukes, counts, and marquises crowded into the little rue Quincampoix and waited for hours to find out if their subscriptions had been granted.

When the final list of subscribers was announced, Law and his awaiting public learned that the shares had been oversubscribed by a factor of six. The immediate result? Shares in the Compagnie des Indes skyrocketed in value.

The rue Quincampoix was transformed overnight into an open-air trading pit. Rents along the street shot up. Enterprising shop-keepers began renting out their storefronts at exorbitant rates to equally enterprising people who set themselves up as impromptu stockbrokers.

At roughly the same time, the Duc was beginning to notice that the paper banknotes acted like an elixir on the public. Law's theories were no longer an experiment—they were a sensational success.

And as he had predicted in his essays 15 years before, the people gained an unimaginable confidence in paper as a means for exchange. This new money began rapidly changing hands; trade and commerce flourished.

Using the flawless logic of politicians throughout the ages, Philip II must have thought: *People have gained confidence in the paper bank-notes; the notes appear to have provided a convenient way for the government to borrow (despite the outstanding debt still on the books); the paper money both traded at a premium and appeared to be reviving France's stalled economy. Why not print more?*

The Duc, previously reluctant to involve the government directly in the bank, renamed the bank the *Banque Royale*, bestowed on it the monopoly right to refine gold and silver, and by the end of 1719, issued 1,000 million new banknotes, effectively increasing the money supply by 16 times its previous amount. Coupled with the rage for shares in the Compagnie des Indes, this new money had the effect of putting firecrackers on the family's hearth fire. The crazy phase began. Shares traded in the free market on the rue Quincampoix shot to 10 times the issue price, and higher.

Speculators swooped in, believing they were going to make a killing on new issues. Law and the Duc were only too willing to oblige them, again and again. In moves worthy of the Federal Reserve circa 2001, by May 1720, five official proclamations from the Duc's office were issued, allowing the creation of 2,696 million new banknotes. The money supply was soaring!

Like America's baby boomers preparing for retirement in the 1990s, investors in Law's Mississippi Scheme probably should have been concerned. They were buying shares in the new company with junk paper issued by the government. No new capital was being injected nor were any trade proceeds actually coming out of Louisiana. But the crowd in front of Law's banque had its own ideas, its own logic—and its own imagination. An extraordinary popular delusion, indeed.

## OUT OF THIN AIR

By all counts, it looked as if the French economy had recovered.

In just 4 short years, the country had cast off despair and was brimming with excitement. Paris, the epicenter of the boom, bustled. Goods, luxury items, and people began pouring in from all over Europe. The population of the capital increased. Prices began to rise. Luxury fabrics—silks, laces, and velvet—came into vogue. Art and furniture were being imported from all over the world and not just by the aristocracy. For the first time in France's history, the middle class was getting in on the act. It looked like a new era: wages for artisans quadrupled, unemployment fell, and new homes were built at a blistering pace—everyone was going to get rich!

Shares issued in early August 1719 quickly rose to an exchange value of 2,830 livres. But by mid-September, they were fetching twice that figure. After a short correction back to 4,800 in late September, the shares broke through all resistance levels and skyrocketed higher and higher—6,463 on October 26; 7,463 on November 18; and 8,975 just a day later!

Up and up until on January 8, 1720, a single share of the Compagnie des Indes traded at 10,100 livres (see Figure 8.1).

Ordinary folk, buying shares on margin, made unimaginable fortunes: A waiter made 30 million livres, a beggar made 70 million, a shopkeeper made 127 million. A new word was even coined by the aristocracy to describe these people: they were referred to disdainfully as "millionaires." Richard Cantillon, a 23-year-old Irish banker who was working in Paris at the time, made a pile of money estimated at 20% of the annual French tax receipts. The stories became legend. The legends fueled the speculative fever even more. One speculator, who had gotten sick, sent a servant of his to unload 250 shares at the market price of 8,000 livres. By the time the servant got to the market, the price had risen to 10,000. He sold, delivered the 4,000,000 to his master as expected, and pocketed a nice bonus of 500,000 livres; then he packed his bags and was gone. In a similar way, Law's own assistant made a fortune.

Law, himself, became the most celebrated foreigner in France. To the French, he was a hero greater than any king, a financial genius who had restored prosperity to the land. His carriage had to be escorted by royal troops as throngs of admirers fought for a glimpse of him as he passed. The memoirs of Saint-Simeon recall: "Law, besieged by applicants and aspirants, saw his door forced, his windows entered from his garden, while some of them came tumbling from the chimney of his office."

Women from all levels of society plotted to gain his attention. "Law is so run after that he has no rest, night or day," wrote the Duchess d'Orleans. "A duchess kissed his hands before everyone, and if a duchess kissed his hands, what parts of him would ordinary ladies kiss?"

Owing to the "success" of his scheme, by 1720, Law became the richest man on earth.

To get away from the madness and mayhem stirred up by the trading on rue Quincampoix, Law bought a whole block of buildings on the present-day site of the fashionable Place Vendome. He opened offices in the Hotel Soissons and began to acquire chateaux around the country. By the time he was invited to leave France, he owned

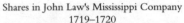

Shares in John Law's Mississippi Company
1719–1720

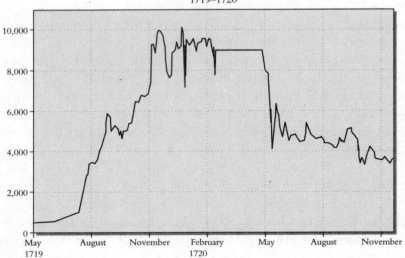

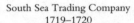

South Sea Trading Company
1719–1720

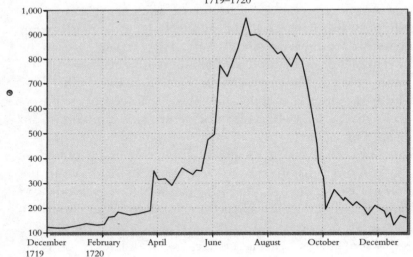

**FIGURE 8.1** Spread the Wealth

The "Bubble" Money Finds Its Way into the Economy. Much of the money employed by speculators in John Law's Mississippi Scheme (top) slipped across the border to participate in London's South Sea Bubble (bottom) just 6 months later. It also drove up prices of luxury goods and real estate in France—a pattern repeated three centuries later in Japan and the United States.

more than a dozen chateaux. At the height of his popularity and wealth, Law's possessions included the French central bank and the entire Louisiana Territory, which stretched from the Gulf of Mexico to the Great Lakes, from the Appalachians through the Midwest to the Rocky Mountains. His company had a monopoly on French trade with the Americas, India, and the Far East. Law, a Scottish commoner, was granted the title of Duc d'Arkansas—and became the first American duke.

Alas, all things get corrected—even men's reputations.

## THE TRUTH AT LAST

As Frederic Bastiat noted about a hundred years later, in economics there are things that are seen and things that are unseen. And it is often the unseen that counts.

The French in general—Parisians in particular—appeared, for all the world, to be getting rich at a pace never before seen in human history. The Duc d'Orleans was firmly convinced that Law's paper money was the elixir the country needed, so he printed more. "Why shouldn't he?" Tvede asks, "wasn't it evident that the money-printing had made the country prosper? And if so, why not print more? Money was simply like oil to the economic machinery, wasn't it? The more oil, the better the machinery worked!"

Unfortunately, for Law, the fabulous success of his ideas and his popularity incited the envy of more than a few political enemies.

Early in 1720, a well-known aristocrat, Prince de Conti, wanted to get in on a new issue of Compagnie des Indes shares, but Law did not permit the sale. De Conti's response? He rounded up all the Banque Royale notes he had previously earned—an amount large enough to fill two carriages—and presented them to the bank. "Voilà, monsieurs!" he is reported to have said. "[Here are] your notes, which are 'payable at sight.' Now, do you see them? Well then, hand over the coins."

The bank complied. When the Duc learned of the Prince's request, he was furious and ordered two-thirds of the metal coins to be returned to the bank. But the damage was done. A small fissure in the facade of confidence had opened. Richard Cantillon, well aware that nothing was propping up the notes, sold out his entire portfolio, netting some 20 million livres. Cantillon closed up his banking office and left France, never to return. Two other heavy hitters in the Paris banking scene, Bourdon and La Richardiere, began presenting their notes in small quantities so as not to attract attention. They secretly started to secure silver and jewelry and had it all—coins included— squirreled away in Amsterdam and England.

Before long, mobs of regular, everyday investors were trying to break down the doors of the Banque Royale en masse, in an attempt to redeem their plunging banknotes and shares of Law's monopoly holding firm, the Mississippi Company.

Average investors of the day began hoarding gold coins, stuffing them under their mattresses or shipping them secretly out of the country. The money supply, which had previously been expanding exponentially, reversed direction.

In the end, nothing could save Law's company or the worthless scrip issued by the Banque Royale.

The collapse of the Mississippi Company in 1720 ruined thousands of middle-upper class French citizens and destabilized the French currency.

Only months before, France had the outward appearance of the richest, most populated and confident nation in Europe. Now she was bankrupt.

From the king's court downward, the citizenry was traumatized by the very idea of stock companies. To this day, the French are reluctant stock market investors. Until recently, they even eschewed the term *banque*, preferring instead names such as *Credit National, Credit Lyonnais,* and *Caisse D'Épargne* for their savings institutions.

Once thought to be greater than the king himself, Law was forced, under protection of the royal guards, to live in the Palais Royale. At one point, when a mob saw his carriage pass, instead of trying to get a glimpse of the man, it attacked the carriage and smashed it to bits. Luckily for Law, he was not inside.

Later, Law was given permission by Philip II to leave France altogether—disgraced and in debt to the tune of 6.7 million livres. By the time of his death in Venice in 1729, Law, the man "of cool calculation and dazzling innovative ideas" would, by outward appearance, be "but a shadow of his former self . . . reduced to an aging trembler with a pro-nounced tic."[2]

Not surprisingly, following the collapse of the Mississippi Scheme, Law was the target of enough satirical engravings to fill a popular collection—published in 1720 in Holland, under the title, *The Great Mirror of Folly*. One famous engraving—a frontispiece for a short play about the mania—depicts a crowd of share speculators surrounding Law on the rue Quincampoix. The caricature of Law in the scene shows him ingesting gold and silver coins fed to him by the Duc D'Orleans, con-verting them into paper internally, shall we say, and a frenzied group of investors collecting the bills that fall from his backside.

Montesquieu wrote a satirical allegory based on the Law story, lampooning the idea that gold and silver—the pillars of the contem-porary monetary system—could be replaced by anything so light and airy as bank credit. And Daniel Defoe made light of Law's scheme with this colorful verse:

> Some in clandestine companies combine;
> Erect new stocks to trade beyond the line;
> With air and empty names beguile the town,
> And raise new credits first, then cry' em down;
> Divide the empty nothing into shares,
> And set the crowd together by the ears.[3]

Economic historians have been, if anything, less kind. Karl Marx suggested Law had a "pleasant character mixture of swindler and prophet." Alfred Marshal dismisses Law as "that reckless, and unbal-anced, but most fascinating genius."

Yet, on the other hand, serious economists in the twentieth cen-tury regarded Law's ideas with respect. "John Law, I have always felt is in a class by himself," Joseph Schumpeter wrote in his opus *The History of Economic Analysis*. "He worked out the economics of his projects with a brilliance, and yes, profundity, which places him in the front ranks of monetary theorists of all time." Meanwhile, the writer, J. Shield Nicholson suggested that, despite the catastrophe, John Law may have been an excellent financier, just as Napoleon was a great soldier despite Waterloo.

## SO WHAT?

"The saga of the Mississippi scheme is historically relevant," writes Marc Faber. He continues:

> . . . It contains all the major features of subsequent manias: shady characters, corruption, fraud, dubious practices, the creation of money and the extension of risky loans in order to keep the speculative orgy going, the catalyst, which leads to the initial collapse—usually the revelation of some fraud, the inability of a large speculator to come up with the money to meet a margin call, the revelation that insiders had cashed out, or some adverse economic or political news—and then panic during which greed and euphoria are replaced by fear and the speculators' desire to get out at any price.[4]

Time after time, generation after generation, ordinary people become convinced that they are seeing the dawn of a new era that will bring unimaginable riches and prosperity to all.

New era thinking comes in many packages, but is usually inspired by some sort of discovery: gold deposits in California in 1849, for instance, or outside of Sydney and Melbourne in 1851; the application of new inventions, such as canals, railroads, the automobile, radio, personal computers, the internet, and wireless communications; or even the opening up of new territories, such as India, South America, and the Mississippi Territory.

Each of these events has given rise to a spell of speculation. We'll see it again with the dramatic rise and fall of the cryptocurrency trading platform FTX. We also expect to see a speculative explosion in artificial intelligence (AI) companies, with Open AI's ChatGPT manhandling the imaginations of old and new tech investors alike. To say nothing of the fact that Nvidia, a maker of semiconductors necessary for AI technology to flourish, became the fifth American company to crest a $1 trillion market cap behind Alphabet, Microsoft, Amazon, and Apple.

## WHAT DOES A GOOD MANIA TAKE?

Spells of "irrational exuberance" grip entire populations from time to time, and spread from place to place like an infectious disease.

Gaseous fortunes made in the Paris of early 1720 found their way to the speculative halls of London only 6 months later, where they inflated the South Sea bubble. Richard Cantillon resurfaced there several years later too, where he wrote one of the first known books on economics. More recently, following the collapse of the Japanese market in 1989 and subsequent central bank rate cuts throughout the 1990s, money flowed from Japan to the US markets. In what had become known as the "yen carry trade," money was borrowed at interest rates approaching zero in Japan and was used to purchase US Treasury coupons yielding 8.16%.

Minor manias have occurred with regularity in the past century but have caused little damage. In the United States, stocks in bowling rallied irrationally in 1961, gaming stocks flew off the shelves in 1978, and the first personal computer companies, such as Commodore, Atari, and Coleco (whose original business was above-ground swimming pools), soared in 1983. Likewise, dubious companies such as Presstek, Diana, and Iomega reached nosebleed valuations in 1995. But these minor bubbles are like border wars or revolutions in small countries. They attract little attention and are over before most people become aware of them.

Also recently, there have been larger, but still harmless, speculative manias, confined to individual sectors. Ray Devoe lists at least four: the Great Garbage Market of 1968 involving any stock that appeared to be related to technology, reminiscent of the dot-com frenzy of 1999; manias in uranium, airlines, and color television also occurred—but these did not infect other areas of the market.[5] When these bubbles burst, the participating stocks incurred most of the damage. However, there is always some spillover, as many of the former high-flying stocks are virtually unsellable when a bubble bursts. Liquidity disappears, and large-capitalization stocks with good markets are sold instead.

But major manias, like wars, are another matter. When these major bubbles—1873 and 1929 in the United States, 1989 in Japan, 1997 in the emerging economies—are pricked, the impact on the economy is usually serious and often global. Bubbles usually begin in a low-inflation environment, thus allowing the expanding credit to feed directly into asset prices instead of consumer prices. Consumer price inflation was low in the 1920s, very low in the 1980s in Japan, and low and falling in 1990s America.

Faber again:

The bubble model always involves a "displacement," which leads to extraordinary profit opportunities, overtrading, over-borrowings, speculative excesses, swindles and catchpenny schemes, followed by a crisis during which fraud on a massive scale comes to light, then by the closing act during which the outraged public calls for the culprits to be taken to account. In each case, excessive monetary stimulus and the use of credit fuels the flames of irrational speculation and public participation, which involves a larger and larger group of people seeking to become rich without any understanding of the object of speculation.

Investors never squawk when their assets are rising in price, so the money and credit inflation is allowed to continue—and is even encouraged—until it finally reaches such grotesque levels that the smart money cannot help but notice and begins looking for a way out. Likewise, a major boom is almost always accompanied by some technological or business excitement. In the 1920s, people believed that new machines, radios, and appliances were the source of the apparent boom. In the 1980s, people believed in the quality of Japanese management and Japan's whole enterprise system.

As Hyman Minsky has shown, booms actually play an important economic role—they focus resources on an up-and-coming sector and speed its development. Investors are not crazy to put money into a boom at the beginning; they are crazy to do so at the end, when prices have become absurd.

The bust phase of an investment mania comes about when reality begins to nag, profits are not realized, and confidence turns to trepidation . . . and then fear. A big bust is often accompanied by rapid reductions in the money supply and a contraction of credit, as creditors fear lending to riskier and riskier clientele. Following the deflation of the Mississippi bubble in 1720, despite the aggressive efforts of Philip II to stop it, the money supply in France decreased rapidly. The savviest investors physically removed the gold and silver coins from the country. Having lost confidence in the paper money, spooked merchants and traders engaged in widespread hoarding of the coins, stuffing them in mattresses and burying them in holes in the ground. And bank credit shrank.

Another edict stating that all notes bearing a value between 1,000 and 10,000 livres could only be used to buy government bonds, Compagnie des Indes shares, or be placed in bank accounts further reduced the money supply. One of the central tenets of Law's theory had been proven wrong. Once confidence is shot, a central bank cannot manage the money supply. Still, the idea persists.

Law died in disgrace, but central banking was as big a hit as income tax. The first modern central bank with any staying power, the Bank of France, was set up less than a century later following another financial disaster: the French Revolution. The rest of Europe soon followed suit.

The strong, centralized governments of the nineteenth and twentieth centuries wanted control over money. Central banks gave it to them. But they had learned their lessons—at least for a while. According to Ferdinand Lips of Lion Capital Group in Zurich, Switzerland, the gold standard of the nineteenth century represented "the highest achievement of the civilized world. The gold standard was neither conceived at a monetary conference, nor was it the brainchild of some genius. It was the result of centuries of experience."[6]

When you enter the Bank of England museum today, you are greeted by animatronic seventeenth-century members of Parliament having an argument about money.

"The use of paper money must always be secondary to the precious metals and must flow from credit," says one. "And credit must, of its nature, rise out of the opinion that the paper money was issued in due proportion to the quantity of coins."

"Rubbish," says the other.

Our wigged, latter-day hard money enthusiast is not to be deterred. He concludes, "The value of paper money must always be dependent on the possibility of converting it into silver and gold."

"The Bank of England is famous for the gold (it used to have) in its vaults," writes colleague Dan Denning, "but the Bank itself was capitalized by government debt, not gold. Private creditors pooled their resources in 1694 and made the government a loan of 1.2 million pounds at 8%. The loan was secured by customs and excise revenues, which the state commands of course, upon pain of death.

"There were times," Dan says, "when England was not at war, that the Bank notes were convertible for gold. But war and gold standards are mutually exclusive. And so the gold standard was abandoned."[7]

The economic debacle of the 1930s spelled the end of the gold standard for domestic economies. And ever so gradually, the dangers of paper money faded from memory. Little by little, economists, central bankers, and politicians alike came to accept fiat paper currencies and began to argue about how they could use them to promote greater prosperity than Nature herself allowed—the very same idea once put forward by John Law (see Table 8.1).

**TABLE 8.1**   A short history of speculative excess.*

| Mania | Era | Country | Object of Desire |
|---|---|---|---|
| Tulip Mania | 1636–1637 | Dutch Republic | Exotic tulip bulbs, real estate, canals, shares of the Dutch East India Trading Company |
| Mississippi Scheme | 1719–1720 | France | Shares of the Mississippi Company, banknotes from the Banque Générale and the Banque Royale |
| South Sea Bubble | 1720 | England | Shares of the South Sea Trading Company, government debt |
| Treasury Bond Bubble | 1792 | United States | U.S. Bonds (on acceptance of the U.S. Constitution) |
| Waterloo Speculation | 1815–1816 | England | Speculation in commodities and trade with the United States |
| Wildcat Bank Bubble | 1837 | United States | Cotton, land, silver, banks in the Wild West that printed their own money |
| Railroad Mania | 1847–1857 1873 | England, European Continent, United States | Shares in railroad companies, real estate, wheat, building supplies |
| Precious Metal Mania | 1893 | Australia, United States | Silver, gold, gold mines, land |
| Money Panic | 1907 | France, Italy, United States | Coffee, railroads, bank lending |
| Postwar Boom and Bust | 1920–1921 | England, United States | Stocks, commodities, ships |
| The Great Crash | 1929 | United States | Stocks bought on margin |
| Collapse of Bretton Woods | 1974–1975 | United States, worldwide | Stocks, REITs, office buildings, tankers, Boeing 747s |

| Mania | Era | Country | Object of Desire |
|---|---|---|---|
| **Black Monday Collapse** | 1987 | United States, worldwide | Stocks, luxury real estate, office buildings, the dollar |
| **Japan Inc.** | 1990 | Japan | Nikkei shares, real estate |
| **The Great Tech Wreck** | 1996–2000 | United States, worldwide | Stocks, especially Internet and telecom companies |
| **The World Wide Crack Up Boom** | 2007–20?? | United States, worldwide | Stocks, Bonds, Commodities, Real Estate, Fine Art . . . you name it |

*In the 1990s, investors in U.S. equities markets had come to believe that booms and busts were no longer a part of the investment landscape. Au contraire, the 1996–2000 bubble attracted—and consumed—a larger amount of capital than any other speculative bubble in history. Speculative manias often accompany the opening of a new territory, the introduction of a new technology, or the end of a war.

# CHAPTER 9

# THE DIGITAL AGE OF CROWDS

Professor Joseph Lawrence of Princeton University earnestly declared: "The consensus of the millions of people whose judgments decide the price levels in the stock market tells us that these stocks are not overpriced."

"Who then are these men," he continued, "with such a universal wisdom that it gives them the right to veto the judgment of this intelligent multitude?"[1]

There is little doubt what the intelligent multitude thought. They had priced stocks at 20 . . . 30 . . . 40 times earnings. Who could question the judgment of so many?

In large groups of people, complex and even elegant ideas get mashed down to a fermenting syrup of empty jingles, slogans, and campaign folderol.

From time to time, Mr. John Q. Public takes up the brew and quaffs it like an alcoholic on an empty stomach. In practically no time at all, it has gone to his head. Professor Lawrence gave us his opinion.

Writing in the summer of 1929, his timing was unfortunate: he was right about what the multitudes thought at the time; but a few months later, the multitudes changed their minds.

"That enormous profits should have turned into still more colossal losses," wrote Graham and Dodd in their review of the 1929 crash and the aftermath, "that new theories have been developed and later discredited, that unlimited optimism should have been succeeded by the deepest despair are all in strict accord with age-old tradition."[2]

Traditions are not created in the course of a single generation. What makes them valuable is that they develop little by little, wrought by heat and cold, beaten into a serviceable shape by countless pounding over many generations, through many complete cycles.

Knowledge costs time and effort. Like the difference between real profits and virtual ones, the transformation of data or information into knowledge requires time and effort.

The more important the knowledge acquired, the more time and effort it takes to get it. Wisdom can take decades. Rules and principles—such as "love thy neighbor" or "buy low, sell high"—can take centuries to evolve.

## BABOONS AT THE DINNER TABLE

One evening, in the heat of the tech frenzy in 2000, we overheard a conversation in car number 8 of the Eurostar. We were traveling en route from London to Paris, reading Alan Abelson in *Barron's*, when two men entered the car and sat down nearby. They were dressed casually. Mid-40s. Americans. The sort of men you might find managing an electronics store or enjoying the Super Bowl with friends. One took out a Swiss Army knife the size of a chain saw and opened a package. Out of this, he drew a new watch and put it on—a monstrous thing, it looked like a flying saucer had landed on his wrist. Soon they were joined by a third man whose belt was too tight.

"Whoa," said one, looking at the stock pages of *USA Today*, "look at this . . . I bought this company at 30 two days ago. It's up to 47."

"I got a friend who knows someone at the company. They're going to announce a merger or something. The stock is supposed to go to between 70 and 75."

"What's the name of the company?" asked the one whose belt was too tight.

"It's called e-Plus, I think. Yeah, I think there's a hyphen in there. E-Plus. The stock symbol is PLUS."

"What's it do?"

"I don't know . . . computers or something high tech. But I've already made $1,700 on this stock."

"Why didn't you tell me about it? I don't like to miss a move like that. What d'you say was the symbol?"

"P–L–U–S."

A moment later (and we are not making this up), he had his cell phone out.

"Lenny? Hi, I'm calling you from France." [Note: We were still in England.] "Yeah, I'm on the train. Can you hear me okay? Look, I want you to check out a stock for me. It's called e-Plus . . . No, I don't know what it does . . . technology or something." Then, turning to his friend, "He says he's never heard of it!" Then, back to Lenny on the phone, "Okay . . . look, my buddy says they're going to make an announcement or something. Buy me 20 shares. The price should be about $47. It's going to $75. Okay . . . No, I'm in France . . . so I can't send you a check until next week. Just 20 shares, okay?"

Oscar Wilde complained of people who knew "the price of everything and the value of nothing." In this age of information, these guys were ignorant of everything except the price. The company's numbers, its business plan, its position in the industry, its management, its record of the past, and hopes for the future—all were as unknown as the contents of a sausage or the voter registration rules of a distant galaxy.

These fellows were not investing. They were having a lark. They were like baboons at a Buckingham Palace dinner party. Throwing the food around. Laughing. Playing. Getting rich. They had no idea of the rules. No concept of the history. No clue about the risks. Investing was a game to them. And thanks to their ignorance, they were winning.

Did e-Plus have earnings? Did it really have a solid business? Do not bother to check the fundamentals. Most likely, there were none. If you had to ask, it was not for you. The more you knew, the less likely you were to want to buy it. And if you didn't buy it, it couldn't make you rich.

This kind of stock play was not one you should approach with information . . . and certainly not with knowledge, or with its distilled derivative—wisdom. It was the kind of speculation that needed to be made in near-complete ignorance. With reckless abandon even.

The prevailing formula of the New Era was that Information equals Wealth. Information was thought to be the capital of the age. The reciprocal of this algebra was that Ignorance equals Poverty. But the investment markets of the late 1990s seemed to show that the exact contrary was also true: at least a certain kind of ignorance was producing spectacular stock market profits. Ignorance equals Wealth . . . and at the same time Information equals Wealth . . . ergo, we had the proof of what we had guessed: Information equals Ignorance.

Swamped with facts, blinded by details, overwhelmed by an infinity of data, and paralyzed by endless analysis—information was making us all dumber.

And maybe poorer too. The inflation of the information supply rendered it as worthless as Weimar deutschmarks. Like any inflation, we were impoverished by it. And like currency during inflation, the information, knowledge, wisdom, and judgment that had been saved up for so many years and used to guide our investment decisions was devalued.

## THE MADNESS OF CROWDS

Crowds of people can "know" things. But it is abstract public knowledge, not direct personal experience, which determines how crowds understand events. Public knowledge has its own peculiar character, for it must be dumbed down to a level that can be absorbed by a mob.

A learned and thoughtful man may speak before a crowd and get no positive reaction whatsoever. A real demagogue, on the other hand, will distill his thoughts into a few simpleminded expressions and soon have enough admirers to run for public office. Readers who have wondered why politicians all seem to be such simpletons now have their answer: it is a requirement for the job. For en masse, mankind can neither understand complex or ambiguous thoughts nor remember them.

That is why crowds can only remember history in its most intellectually vulgar form. Like everything else, history must be reduced to its lowest common denominator for mass consumption, usually ending up as pure myth. Take this simple matter "of fact": France and the rest of the Allies were victorious in World War I; Germany was the loser. As every schoolchild knows, it is true. It is *wissen*, as Nietzsche termed it, or public knowledge. No one has ever actually seen or experienced it—because it is purely an abstraction—but it is nevertheless considered true.

And yet, if you were to tell a French woman—whose two sons were killed in the war and whose husband was blinded by a grenade—that she should celebrate the victory, she would take you for a fool. A third of France's capital had been used up. Millions were dead. An important part of the country was in ruins. What kind of victory is that?

Ah . . . but France recovered its territories of Alsace and Lorraine! For whom was this an advantage? Did the surviving men in Lorraine find their petite new *femmes* more beautiful than their hefty old *fraus*? Was their *choucroute* tastier than their *sauerkraut* had been? Could they drink more of their local hooch, now that it was called *vin blanc* and not *weiss wein*? Not likely. Instead, they toiled the soil as they had before the war. And for years afterward, they would occasionally discover unexploded bombs from World War I—which often blew up when scraped by a plow.

And in the years following, were the victors of World War I better off than the vanquished? Alas, no. By the 1930s, France, Britain, and America were still in a slump—while Germany boomed. Whereas the Allies seemed tired, worn-out, and aimless—Germany entered a period of remarkable grit, pride, and energy.

Was France more secure, now that it had control over the west bank of the Rhine? Not at all. Germany quickly rearmed and, as subsequent events were to show, became a far bigger threat in 1934 than it had been 20 years earlier.

If France was the winner, what had she won? You might just as well say the French had lost the war as won it.

What kind of strange knowledge is this, dear reader? The process of *lumpen denken* tells you a "fact" is true, and yet, the exact opposite is also true. And what kind of thought process makes sense of it . . . what kind of reasoning can bring you to two conclusions at the same time, each one separated from the other as day is from night?

This is how the thinking process of a mob differs from an individual. The mob can come to believe almost anything because the knowledge it builds on is as unsound as its conclusions. An individual's knowledge is much more direct and immediate. A man knows what will happen if he holds a burning match too long or insults his wife; he is rarely mistaken.

Yet even for an individual, reason is less sure than most people think. We humans flatter ourselves. We believe we are reasonable people, and we almost are. So successful are we at applying reason to the things close at hand that we cannot resist applying the same process to things far afield, about which we haven't a clue. We try to make sense of the events around us by describing the "reasons" they happen . . . and then we extrapolate, looking logically forward to what those reasons will produce next.

Unlike the tsetse fly or the wallaby, a human can put two and two together. A man working up close, with things that make sense to him, comes up with four more often than not. But when he applies these same reasoning abilities to other people's business—such as how to achieve peace in the Mideast or profit from a boom on Wall Street—the facts turn to mush, and the whole equation soon degrades into complete nonsense.

Reason, as it turns out, is our greatest strength. Alas, it is also our greatest conceit. Simple statements of fact, such as "I am a liar," confound us all. If this statement is true, it disproves itself. If it is untrue, well. . . .

Even in mathematics, the most rational of all pursuits, reason is not as clean as it looks. Bertrand Russell's *Principia Mathematica* tried to establish the logical foundations of all mathematics. Kurt Godel, a brilliant mathematician, pointed out the inescapable contradiction in Russell's work in 1931. Years later, Russell, who had moved from one dubious proposition to another over the years, recalled, "I realized, of course, that Godel's work is of fundamental importance, but I was puzzled by it. It made me glad that I was no longer working at mathematical logic."[3]

Godel, one of the world's most gifted mathematicians, died in 1978. He starved himself to death, crouched in a fetal position, refusing to allow nurses to enter his room because he feared that they were trying to poison him.

Poor Kurt. All he had left were his powers of reason. The Cartesian logic that made his career sparkle tarnished his death: he thought people were trying to poison him; therefore, they were.

The problem with this silly old ball we live on, as we have tried to elaborate in this book, is that life is infinitely complex. The closer you look, the more you see. What seems simple from a distance—say, the disciplining of a teenager or the politics of South Africa—becomes alarmingly complicated up close. The whole truth, being infinite, is unknowable. And for every tiny piece of it, there is a revolver in some poor fool's mouth . . . and a special corner of hell waiting for him.

"Nobody knows anything," they say in Hollywood, recognizing the complexity of the film business. A studio might spend $100 million on a blockbuster movie, and the thing might be a complete dud. Or a young guy with $20,000 might produce a big hit. The old-timers know that even a lifetime of experience is still no guarantee. Even the pros often guess wrong about which films will be box-office hits.

But walk up to a man on the street, and he is likely to have an opinion. He may have even bought stock in an entertainment company after hearing about the blockbuster films planned for the summer. He has not read the scripts, met the actors, or ever earned a dime in the cinema business—not even worked as an usher. Yet, he has an opinion based on what he has read in the paper or heard on TV.

People have opinions on everything—especially things they know nothing about. Voters in Baltimore during the 1980s could hardly figure out how to get their own municipal government to pick up the trash or fill in potholes. Yet though very few had ever been to South Africa—and almost none spoke the languages or could identify the major ethnic groups of the country—they nevertheless had strong opinions about how to reorganize its government.

The more people knew about the situation in South Africa, the harder it was for them to have a simple opinion. A knowledgeable man, asked to comment on the situation, prefaced his thoughts with "I don't know . . . ."

Thanks to Information Age communications, people grow more ignorant every day. Tall weeds of groupthink and common knowledge crowd out the few pullulating shoots of real wisdom and truth. Collective dumbness spreads like kudzu. Soon there will be nothing else alive; we will know nothing at all.

## WHEN A CROWD TURNS INTO A MOB

The twentieth century would be the era of crowds, Gustave Le Bon predicted in his 1896 book, *The Crowd*. Crowds had taken over almost all Western governments. There were still monarchs and emperors in their palaces, but popular assemblies were gaining ground everywhere. Modern communications provided the means. Cheap newspapers, trains, and the telegraph made it possible for an entire nation to think almost the same thing at almost the same time. Mobs, which had formerly been limited to fairly small groups in urban areas, became national, even international. Soon, the vast crowds would be interested in politics . . . and in getting rich.

Crowds tend to amplify whatever emotion an individual may feel. People who are normally sensible—drive on the right-hand side of the road, can figure out how to use the electronic controls of their home sound system, have no trouble picking out the lowest price at the supermarket—put them in a crowd, and they become raving maniacs. In markets, greed and fear are loosed. Prices are bid up to levels that no sane man would pay if you put it to him on his own, or they are driven down to levels that no sane man could resist. But what does it matter? Sanity has gone out the window. During the last stages of a bull market, like the opening stages of a war, the crowd gets very brave. In the final stages of a war or a bear market, on the other hand, people give up all hope; they become desperate and flee to safety. Reason does not merely sleep . . . it drops on the floor unconscious.

As technology progressed, modern communications enabled more and more people to feel and act as though they were physically together. Ideas were quickly spread—instantaneously, in fact—so that a man watching CNN in Dubuque was in direct and immediate contact with events that happened all over the world. Television, radio, newspapers, magazines—all helped shape the masses' thoughts, and ensure that all were thinking more or less the same thing at more or less the same moment.

The rise in TV coverage of Wall Street during the 1990s, for example, greatly amplified and exaggerated popular awareness and involvement in stock markets. Without leaving his office or bedroom, an investor could get caught up in the current excitement just as though he were on the trading floor.

The great achievement of the internet was that it allowed people to get stirred up with mob sentiments . . . and to do something about them immediately. In the mid-1990s, thousands of people became convinced that they could get rich by day-trading stocks via their home or office computers. The 24-hour-a-day online chatter available on the internet also allowed people to take part in rabble-rousing demagoguery—no matter where they were. At the outset, users learned they could get riled up about the Monica Lewinsky affair, about Enron, or about any number of things and feel as though they were right there in the Tuileries garden during the French Revolution. They could join the mob without leaving home!

It was widely said that the internet would make people smarter by giving them access to much more information. What it really did was make people more in tune with mob thinking—for now their own thoughts were crowded out by the constant noise of the World Wide Web.

A man on his own may have had his own experience, good or bad, with the internet. But once connected, he was likely to have an opinion of the new medium formed not by his own experience but by the collective rattle of sentiment over the e-waves. Once caught up in groupthink, the judgment of the group, even when absurd, is hard to resist.

"Love afar is spite at home," wrote Emerson. A man neglects his wife but takes a keen interest in the plight of women in the Sudan.

Or perhaps he worries about public sanitation in New Delhi but forgets to take out the trash.

Groupthink is popular because it is easier than private thinking and the stakes are lower. A man's public attitudes are buttressed by others, held up by the media, and reinforced by constant repetition. His private thoughts, on the other hand, are fragile, lonely, and often desolate. He cannot even get his own children to clean up their rooms or his wife to agree to his family budget. Who can blame him for wanting to tell others what to do?

Masses of people do not go to war because it will make their private lives richer, longer, or better but for abstract principles that few can explain or justify. Lebensraum . . . Preserving the Union . . . Driving the Infidel from the Holy Land . . . Making the World Safe for Democracy . . . the Domino Theory . . . the jingo hardly matters. But it must be simple if the masses are to understand it and bright enough to lure them to their own destruction.

Before the development of the modern state following the American and French Revolutions, wars engaged relatively few people. They tended to be small-scale, seasonal affairs . . . though combatants were often very nasty to each other and anyone who got in their path.

But in 1793, after the French monarchy had been pushed aside by the Convention, France was menaced on all sides. At every border was a foreign army, many of them bulging with aristocratic French émigrés, eager to invade, topple the popular new government, and restore the monarchy. Thus, threatened, the Convention began the first *levée en masse* of conscripts to fight for *la patrie*. Many of the officers (Lafayette, the great hero of the American Revolution, was one of them) had gone over to France's enemies, which left the way clear for talented young officers from modest backgrounds to rise quickly. Thus, it was that Napoleon Bonaparte assumed command of French forces in Italy and promptly rose to become the nation's greatest hero.

That Bonaparte was a military genius, few would dispute. But what made his campaigns so historically puissant was as much a product of demography and collective involvement as it was of the man's talents for war. As we see in the next chapter, France had enjoyed a baby boom in the eighteenth century. These young and restless citizens pushed the monarchy out of the way of history. They made it possible for Napoleon to bring his many "big battalions" to bear in wars thousands of miles apart—and to replace his fallen soldiers when he put them in harm's way.

## INFORMATION COMMODIFIED

Part of the challenge we perceived, then and now, is information itself. Once online, it gets dehumanized. Specifically, digitized information was thought to be a more valuable resource than oil or farmland. And yet look as this recent experiment with the artificial intelligence app ChatGPT, which is an appendage of and also being integrated into Microsoft products.

The new information technologies were supposed to have the power to bring about a number of improvements, including healing the sick, raising prosperity levels, eliminating the business cycle, and ending war forever.

But what has been the actual result? Fraud, manipulation, and deception are more efficient now. Sprinkle a little artificial intelligence on the menu, and things are going to get wild. Booms, busts, and bear markets are not new. But at the root they result from imperfect information. The dot-com bubble of the early 2000s set the tone for the new millennia. Businesses produced too much and borrowed too much when times were good. Soon there were too many products on the market and too much debt. "Information," the market believed, would eliminate these problems, as businesses would have more accurate and timely data on which to base their projections.

Business owners, speculators, and economists alike believed there would be no more down cycles in business. There would be no more falloffs in earnings and no more reasons for bear markets. A pull of a lever here . . . a push of a button there . . . and the economy would just function perfectly, without friction, as it's meant to.

And war? Well, forget about that. We've already seen the end of history, correct?

Now that people could connect to the internet and communicate in this one, vast, new, free market—wouldn't war be a thing of the past too? For the entire world would now have access to the undeniable superiority of the US model of free elections and a free economy. Surely all nations would put down their weapons, take up computers, and get on with the serious business of life—making money! We're writing in 2023, after a boom and bust in the technology sector, then another debt-fueled bubble burst in housing in the first decade, followed in the second by a spate of aggressive speculation, a global pandemic, and a new war in Europe. The Promethean light of the New Era now seems antiquated, bygone, and forgotten. Hope has given way to inflation, political divisiveness, and mistrust at every level of society. Social media amplifies these anxieties, but it rarely edifies.

Imaginations at the turn of the millennium had already begun to run wild. In their fantasies, they pictured the little ones and zeroes of the digital age marching forward forever in a world of eternal peace, ever-increasing prosperity, and constantly expanding contentment. That is what people wanted; surely the latest information technology would help them get it.

There were, of course, theoretical problems. You could have set down the most powerful computer ever made—with the most complete database of information ever assembled—in front of the smartest man in Plato's Athens. What good would it have done him? Would he have any idea what he had in his hands? Imagine Napoleon shivering in his tent. Give him the price of grain in New York or the number of atoms in a cubic centimeter of cognac, and you do him no favor. You might as well ship him a crate of sunscreen. Information out of context is useless.

Information is useless not only when it is unwanted or out of context, but also when it is in too great a supply, for then it has to be sorted, rerouted, or thrown away. "Paralysis by analysis" is the popular expression. In any given situation, an infinite amount of information might be brought to bear. Any of it might be relevant and useful. But time is limited.

Napoleon knew full well he could not wait for every possible message to make its way to him. Nor did he have the luxury of weighing every bit of information just in case the optimum course of action should reveal itself. Like every general and every other human on the planet, he had to act based on imperfect information—guessing what was really important and hoping he had the information he needed.

Every bit of information beyond what he actually needed was a cost—and potentially an expensive one. Every bit of extra information slowed him down; he had to evaluate it for relevance and authenticity and, ultimately, absorb it into his view of things or reject it.

## "SH★TPOSTING," OR GRAFFITI ON THE INTERNET

While we first made this observation many years ago, little has changed. With TikTok and Instagram, LinkedIn and Facebook, the fact has only become more pronounced: information is just that, facts and details.

Recently, there has been some hope that artificial intelligence (AI) is going to help us search for meaning. The fervor for AI stocks and chipmakers has spawned a bubble of its own on Wall Street. But what does AI really do? It makes the search for facts and details more efficient. Even with efficiency, it takes human insight . . . and a lot of work . . . to find any idea worth its weight in, uh, electrons.

If we step back and explore, we'll find many examples from military history illustrate perfectly how the quality and integrity of information—if used correctly—can be decisive.

In the middle of World War II, the Allies dressed a dead man in a British officer's uniform. They then fastened a set of plans to the body for their counterattack on Hitler's army in Europe. The plans were, of course, intended to mislead Hitler about Allied intentions. The body was then dumped into the sea, so it would wash ashore where the Germans could find it. Hitler also believed he had a network of spies in England who would be able to fill him in on the coming landings. But these spies had almost all been discovered and "turned," so they were feeding false information reports to the Nazi high command. Thus, the information that Hitler was receiving was worse than no information at all. It lacked integrity. The more of it he had, the worse off he was.

Solzhenitsyn tells us how the Russian army in World War I was commanded by German-speaking officers from Prussia, who would transmit their orders and battle plans in the German language. The enemy often intercepted and read these messages, whereas Russian troops, for whom the plans were intended, found them incomprehensible. In our own War Between the States, Lee's plans at Antietam were betrayed to the Yankees when a Southern officer used them to wrap a cigar—and left them by mistake to be discovered by Union troops.

In the military, the units charged with gathering information and separating fact from fiction are called "intelligence" units. This screening process is tough work, and it gets tougher the more facts and fictions there are to sift through. Today the internet, though ultimately just a means of communication, delivers an almost infinite number of facts and fictions. The tough part—the "intelligence" work—is sorting them out.

Social media has added an extra degree of complexity. Any knucklehead with a computer or smartphone can post or share his or her opinion anonymously, hiding behind a screen and a hip screen name. Data points and media stories are regularly as disfigured as a fresh victim on the *Walking Dead*. What social media has really done is liberate us to disregard any idea with which we don't already agree—regardless of the facts. If we don't agree, well it's obviously "fake news." Attention spans dissipate, evaporate. Patience and empathy? Gone.

At the turn of the century, George W. Bush was promising a more "compassionate" conservatism. What happened to civilized discourse in the past two decades? Our ability to agree to disagree, even at the neighborhood or family level, has dissipated into the air like gas from a stovetop burner the owner forgot to light. Rather than increased freedom, prosperity, and a bright future, the Information Age has given us tribalism, discord, extremism, and violence. We leave aside Big Data censorship of ideas that run counter to "community standards" of the platforms, the heated debate over the veracity of the 2000 election or government policy during the lockdowns, and the shrill protests over COVID-19 vaccines. One presumes more knowledgeable, well-researched, and legitimate analyses of these and other controversial topics are out there. Or given our topic, maybe not. Either way, we prefer to stick to our guns and look at the impact of a world awash in "information" and its impact on the economy and the financial markets.

Although information is free on the internet, free information turns out to be worth a lot less than you pay for it, even if ChatGPT serves it up quickly.

## THE ETERNAL PROMISE OF THE NEXT "NEW ERA"

The surfeit of information available to us—through cable TV, cell phones, email, texting, Facebook, and Twitter—now makes people dumber in another curious way. People become numb to the subtle details and nuances that they actually observe. Because processing information takes time and effort, the more of it you have to deal with, the more likely you are to seek shortcuts. Popular interpretations offer a substitute for careful reflection or observation. In other words, instead of actually figuring things out for themselves, people become more susceptible to collective thinking.

You only need observe our slash-and-burn political tribalism to see politics are a wasteland for anyone with a modicum of self-respect. That's true whether you're running for office or are simply an armchair critic of those who don't share your point of view. Once you engage in the ideas of others, whether you agree or disagree with them, you surrender your independence to the whims of the mob. Never has that been easier to do than in 2023 with our access to so many ways to complain about or attack the "other." Likewise, the financial markets are, as we've seen, equally susceptible to groupthink. The last thing you want to do when trying to manage your own money is surrender your ability to think for yourself.

Public thinking replaces individual thinking—simply because there is too much information to process. Unable to keep up with all the data from Wall Street, for example, people are forced to rely on summaries from CNBC or TheStreet.com.

The pretense of the Information Age was that the introduction of the silicon chip and the World Wide Web had suddenly revealed the value of information. In fact, the amount of information available to people has steadily increased over the past 200 years with new technology and new material: the telegraph, telephone, teletype, radio, television, fax, Minitel, and cheap printing processes. An individual in the twentieth century had vastly more information than an individual in the eighteenth century.

During the early tech boom, we saw first-hand how people were being lured into believing that the stock market would never fail them. During the real estate bubble, otherwise average Americans believed above-average things to be true of their humble homes.

In the decade following, we saw a rapturous belief develop in crypto-currencies and even in marijuana stocks. Now, in 2023, Americans are only just beginning to realize the end of history—the eternal promise we began the epoch with—ain't what it was cracked up to be.

## ROBBIN' DA HOOD

Still one can dream, right? An anecdote from our personal life illustrates one facet of booms and busts in the digital era. When you hear stories like this one, the Promethean light gets fired up all over again.

A friend and business associate, Frank Holmes, told me during one of our interviews on the *Wiggin Sessions* that he'd started an airline ETF in February 2020. If that doesn't make you wince, recall that was nary a month before the COVID-19 pandemic and subsequent lockdown of the global economy . . . including all airline travel, domestic and foreign.

Through his firm, US Global Investors, Frank had raised $100 million dollars to deploy in the fund. Immediately following the lockdowns in March of that year, the fund plummeted. The value of the capital dropped by two-thirds down to $30 million. What were the fund managers to do? Months earlier, who could have predicted the entire global economy would be mandatorily shut? Well, no one.

Then a curious thing happened. Without any forward guidance on how airline stocks were going to process, the fund started gaining new interest. Down to $30 million at one point, suddenly the fund climbed to $50 million, then $80 million and so on . . . upward. Frank and his team investigated and learned that a group of investors using Robinhood, a trading platform popular with millennials, were involved. Robinhood boasts a user-friendly interface, commission-free trading, and accessibility through mobile apps . . . all features ready made for a generation of kids who grew up with phones iGlued to their hands. The platform allows individual investors to trade stocks, exchange-traded funds (ETFs), options, and cryptocurrencies from the palm of their hands.

In the ensuing six weeks, Frank's ETF was not only back to par at $100 million but $20 million higher. The fund sucked up $90 million dollars from small time investors playing a momentum trend. It didn't matter whether the planes were still grounded or not. The crowd had spoken.

Robinhood played a role in another widely ogled market event: the GameStop (GME) frenzy of 2021 and the advent of "meme" stocks.

In January and February of that year, investors piled into the flailing stock of a moribund brick and mortar gaming retailer. As with Frank's ETF, the frenzy was driven by small individual retail investors who were sharing their insights and coordinating buying sprees through online communities, particularly on Reddit.

Members of "Reddit Nation" united over a simple premise. One of the individual investors lurking about the subreddit "r/WallStreetBets" noted GameStop stock had a majority "short" interest, mainly by institutional investors. Several big Wall Street firms had borrowed and sold shares of GameStop in anticipation of the stock's price declining.

Retail investors on r/WallStreetBets began buying shares of GameStop, collectively, driving up the stock price rapidly. Their buying created what's known as a "short squeeze." As the price rose, institutional investors who had shorted the stock were forced to cover their positions by buying back shares at higher prices again (and again) in an effort to limit their losses. The squeeze created even more demand for the stock, which pushed the price even higher. It didn't take long for the event to become mainstream news in the financial media. Which, in turn, created even more interest in the stock.

Did it matter that GameStop was a dinosaur with a business strategy formed back in antiquity? Not at all. The mob of retail investors, on whispers and collusion alone, effectively challenged and disrupted the traditional strategy of evaluating a stock on its fundamentals. By rights, the institutional investors were correct in shorting the stock. GameStop should have gone out of business. And fast. Once the mob got wind the squeeze was on, the exact opposite happened.

Eventually, after a brief appearance in the nose-bleed seats, GME stock got pummeled all over again. The higher price was pure puffery, smoke and air. Even members of Reddit Nation got caught in the sell-off.

In the spring of 2021, a similar fate befell other so-called "meme stocks" like AMC Entertainment (AMC), BlackBerry (BB), Overstock (OSTK), and Nokia (NOK). Tesla (TSLA) for a time was among the bunch, but since the rapid rise in its stock price in 2021, it has maintained a margin somewhere near its high.

In all these cases, the information was imperfect, but that made no difference to the crowd. The euphoria of watching these meme stocks, and the specious idea they were sticking it to the man, drove the prices up . . . and helped them deflate unceremoniously.

## BITCOIN EVANGELISM

We remember one day in our office in early 2009, sitting alongside the inimitable Jeffrey Tucker. He was then writing a newsletter for us called *Laissez Faire*. Tucker had been going on for months about a new form of money based on "block chain" technology. It was secure, private, untraceable. The perfect antidote for the fiat currency system we'd been critiquing ourselves for over a decade. Frankly, the man was obsessed.

To prove to me the benefits of this new money, Tucker opened a "wallet" for me and placed a single Bitcoin in it. At the time, Tucker spent one dollar.[4] "You'll see," he promised. As I'm a late adopter of new technology—I didn't get my first cell phone until after the iPhone had already debuted—I promptly forgot about the wallet, the coin itself, or the key to retrieve it. Ha! You know where this is going. If I knew where that key was today . . . that single dollar would be worth $30,083. If I'd really been smart, I would have cashed it out at $64,000 on November 12, 2021.

Alas, I'm not that smart.

We've observed that every revolution, every innovation, comes with its share of prophets, evangelists, zealots, . . . and frauds. Bitcoin and the 22,392 other cryptocurrencies are no different.

Michael Saylor, you'll remember him from our chapter on dreamers and schemers, famously shocked the financial press in August 2020 when he announced he'd converted nearly $4 billion of Microstrategy's cash into 129,699 Bitcoin at roughly $30,664 per coin. "Bitcoin is a swarm of cyber hornets serving the goddess of wisdom," Saylor has said, imbuing god-like qualities to the digital method of exchange. He continues, it is "feeding on the fire of truth, exponentially growing ever smarter, faster, and stronger behind a wall of encrypted energy."[5] Indeed. We admire the zeal.

As we write, Elon Musk, the on-again off-again richest man in the world, stands accused of insider trading following a transaction in the crypto Dogecoin. Musk allegedly raked in $124 million from Dogecoin sales by temporarily changing the Twitter logo to a Shiba Inu, then pumping the price of Dogecoin through Twitter.[6]

No current, or perhaps ever, crypto fraud takes the cake more than Sam Bankman-Fried, however. Imagine our giddiness when, after several decades of studying booms, busts, delusions, and manias, we get a front row seat to what could be the biggest financial scheme in history.

Mind you, the jury's still out . . . quite literally . . . on cryptocurrencies. Sam Bankman-Fried, or SBF as the media has come to truncate the charlatan's name to, was arrested on December 12, 2022, in the Bahamas following the collapse of his ubiquitous crypto exchange FTX. SBF stands accused of lying to investors and committing fraud. He was later also accused of bribing a foreign official. While arraigned on March 30, 2023, in New York City, the trial in his case was postponed to begin on October 2, 2023, well after the manuscript for this book is due to the publisher.

## FTX and Alameda Research

The saga of FTX draws in public figures from sports, news, and entertainment to finance and politics. If you're an American football fan, you'll remember the Super Bowl commercials touting FTX featuring quarterback Tom Brady and supermodel Gisele Bundchen trying to make up their minds about a crypto trade. Or Larry David, co-creator of *Seinfeld*, as a chronic skeptic eschewing crypto as a gimmick. Super Bowl LVI had so many splashy crypto advertisements that it was dubbed the "Crypto Bowl."

FTX, Crypto.com, Coinbase—competitive exchanges in the crypto space—all shelled out major simoleons to get their celebrity endorsements in front of an unsuspecting national audience. Brady, Bundchen, and David are all facing litigation for their roles in promoting the exchange, as are NBA superstar Stephen Curry, tennis phenom Naomi Osaka, former baseball superstar David "Big Papi" Ortiz, and *Shark Tank's* Kevin O'Leary.[7]

So what happened? The story is explained clearly in a Bloomberg Big Take expose entitled "From Math Camp to Handcuffs."[8] We recount it here, briefly, knowing the parties involved are innocent until proven guilty.

By any high school jock's account, Sam Bankman-Fried was a nerd. The son of two Stanford professors, SBF met his future business partner, Gary Wang, at math camp at Reed College in Oregon. Later they'd become frat brothers at MIT. Following their college experience, Wang landed a job at Google as a software engineer. The more outgoing SBF started his career as a quant trader at the Wall Street firm Jane Street. There, he grew restless and reached out to his old friend, Wang.

"By now," Ava Benny-Morrison and Annie Massa wrote in Bloomberg, "the broad outlines of what followed are well known: the early days in Berkeley, where the two founded Alameda, in a three-bedroom apartment; their move to Hong Kong, where FTX took flight; and their shift to Nassau, where FTX raced to giddy heights, with a value of $32 billion, its name emblazoned on a Miami sports stadium and the comedian Larry David starring in its Super Bowl ad."

Alameda Research, with CEO Caroline Ellison, SBF's girlfriend, served as the trading arm. FTX was the platform. The principal assets being traded in Alameda were two "stable coins"—Terra and Luna—whose values were determined by a peg to the US dollar. Unfortunately for the future of FTX and its millions of customers, two traders in Hong Kong disregarded the dollar peg. Terra and Luna were no longer stable. Once word got out, traders and investors hit the "exit" button in a hurry. Alameda started hemorrhaging profits.

Here's where the trouble comes in for SBF, Garry Wang, and Caroline Ellison. To cover their losses in Alameda, SBF commingled funds from customer accounts at FTX. He is alleged to have ordered changes to the core computer code at FTX, giving Ellison's Alameda access to trade money from those accounts without disclosure. The result, prosecutors will argue in October, allowed FTX to embezzle billions.

We've had a saying for years that goes something like this: "Investors don't get what they expect; they get what they deserve." The frenzy for cryptocurrencies between 2019 and 2022—when

FTX was founded to its ultimate demise—was fueled by classic, delusional enthusiasm we've seen time and again throughout history dating back to John Law and the Mississippi scheme . . . and the tulip mania a decade before.

As with all bubbles, the consequences ripple their way through the broader economy. Two banks friendly to cryptocurrency traders, Silvergate and Signature, were both directly impacted by the billions in losses endured by FTX account holders. Not long after, Silicon Valley Bank (SVB) had to sell assets at a loss to cover depositors, most of whom were tech entrepreneurs, as they withdrew money to cover their own crypto speculations. When SVB announced they were under water on the accounts, an historic bank run like we haven't seen since 2008 ensued. The bank collapsed in 48 hours.

In the weeks and months ahead, more banks would fall. In the spring of 2023, three of the largest five bank failures happened in rapid succession. The combined assets of those banks—Silicon Valley, Signature, and First Republican—were greater in magnitude than the first 25 banks that failed in 2008.

# CHAPTER 10

## THE CRACK-UP BOOM

Early in the twentieth century, Albert Einstein upset the world with his theory of relativity.

All of a sudden, there were no fixed positions; everything seemed unhinged . . . loose. It's all relative, people said. Nothing was absolutely this or that, right or wrong, here nor there.

And then Heisenberg's indeterminacy principle came along, and even Einstein had had enough. Not only are there no absolutes, said Heisenberg, but you could not know it even if there were. Everything is in motion, he pointed out; you can figure out where an object is, or its speed, but not both. And the process of trying to figure it out cannot help but change the readings!

"God does not play dice," Einstein protested. After Einstein and Heisenberg, the world had begun to look like a giant game of craps. A gamble, you throw the dice and hope for the best. What else can you do?

The idea of an uncertain, unknowable universe did not please Einstein; he spent the rest of his life trying to prove it was not so.

But Einstein and Heisenberg proved the latter's point. Trying to describe the world, they changed it. "A kind of madness gained hold . . . " wrote Stefan Zweig of Germany in the 1930s. The whole nation seemed to come unhinged by the realization that nothing was quite what they thought it was.

Today, we hear the rattle of dice everywhere. People blow the dice for another throw. What are the odds of this . . . or that . . . they wonder.

The odds of a huge meteorite destroying lower Manhattan, we assume, are fairly low—as remote as the odds of Osama bin Laden winning a Nobel Peace Prize.

Anything can happen, yes, but some things are more likely than others. As Heisenberg warns us, however, as soon as we try to figure these things out, we distort the odds.

That is the strange perversity of the marketplace.

As people come to believe that something will happen, the odds of making any money at it go down. Herein lies the difference between hard science and a more human science of exchange. When people realize that a market event is forthcoming, likely as not, it has probably already happened.

As people come to believe they can get rich by buying stocks, for example, they disturb the universe—they buy stocks and run up prices. Then, the higher the stock prices go, the more people believe in them, and prices go still higher. At some point, because this cannot go on forever, stocks eventually reach their peaks—at almost precisely the point when people are most sure they can get rich by buying them.

This point was reached in the United States somewhere between fall 1999 and March 2000. A kind of madness had taken hold.

Almost all market forecasters were wrong over the next 3 years; they overwhelmingly thought stocks would go up, not down—especially in 2002, as stocks "almost never go down 3 years in a row." Abby Cohen, Ed Yardeni, Louis Rukeyser, James Glassman, Jeremy Siegel, Peter Lynch—all the big names from the 1990s—still believed that stocks would go up, if not last year or this year, certainly the next.

They seemed completely unaware that their own bullishness had tilted the odds against them. Talking up the bull market year after year, they had helped convince Mom and Pop that stocks for the long run were an almost foolproof investment.

Now, the fools were having their way.


## ROLLING THE DICE

In the last quarter of the twentieth century, nothing seemed to succeed better than US consumer capitalism. Stocks began rising in 1975 and continued, more or less, until March 2000. By then, all doubt had been removed. Americans had become believers in the stock market.

"To believe that stocks will be rotten again in 2002," wrote James Glassman, the unashamed author of *Dow 36,000*, "is to believe that they will buck a strong tide that has been running in the same direction for more than 60 years."[1]

Glassman did not seem to notice that tides do not run in a single direction forever. Rather, they ebb and flow in equal amounts and opposite directions.

Glassman was like a weather forecaster who never looked out the window. "It rains, but the sun comes out again. Stocks fall, but they always recover to a higher ground," he wrote. And then, he failed to mention, it rains again!

And if the sun shines long enough, people stop noticing clouds on the horizon. Who noticed, on those perfect days of early 2000, that the odds had changed; that the stock market had become very different from the stock market of 1975; and that the few investors who bought shares in 1975 were very different from the many Moms and Pops who put their money into stocks in 2000?

Who noticed, as Buffett put it, that these people might have bought for the right reason in 1975—but that they bought for the wrong ones in 2000?

Millions of new investors entered the stock market in the last 25 years of the twentieth century, lured by Buffett's example, Rukeyser's spiel, and the appeal of getting something for nothing. Hardly a single one of them carried an umbrella.

When the market crashed, the little guys got wet, but they did not panic. They still believed—at least at the beginning of 2003—in the promise of US consumer capitalism and its gurus. They believed the reasons given for why stocks were likely to rise . . . because they hardly ever go down 4 years in a row!

Stocks rarely go down 4 years in a row because, usually, after 36 months, they have almost always hit bottom. But at the beginning of 2003, stocks were still selling at prices more typical of a top than a bottom. Based on core earnings, S&P stocks were priced at 40 times earnings. Or as *Barron's* calculated it, based on reported earnings in 2002, they sold at a P/E of 28. Either way, they were expensive.

While earnings were subject to interpretation, dividend yields were not; stocks yielded only 1.82% in dividends at the end of 2002. The number is important, partly because dividends do not lie, and partly because so much of the promise of the stock market actually reposes on earnings. For a hundred years, according to popular interpretation, stocks gained ground at a rate of 7% per year—beating bonds, real estate, old masters' paintings, everything. Little noticed was the fact that five of those seven percentage points came from compounded earnings, not stock market appreciation. Take that away, and stocks would have underperformed several other asset classes, including bonds.

Dividends depend on earnings. As noted, earnings have been falling for the entire consumer capitalist period—since the 1960s. With falling earnings, it became more and more difficult for companies to maintain their dividend payments. As a percentage of earnings, dividends actually increased in the boom years, from about 35% in 1981 to more than 50% in 2001. And after 1997, profits took their worst dive since the Great Depression. How could investors reasonably expect dividends to increase? And without higher dividend payouts, how could they expect to match the returns of the past 100 years, let alone the returns of the last 25 years of the twentieth century? A retiree looking to live on 1.82% dividends would need $2 million invested in stocks to give him a $36,000 income. Yet, at the end of 2002, the average baby boomer had a grand total of $50,000 to invest.

The patsies hardly considered the issue. And who knows, maybe they will get lucky. Maybe stocks will go up. Maybe it is just luck, after all. Imagine the roar of laughter when Einstein arrived in heaven and God explained, "I don't have any plan . . . I just roll the damned dice!"

God can do what He wants, of course. We do not presume to know God's plan or His method.

But so what? As the existentialists tell us, we still have to get up in the morning and make decisions. Recognizing that we cannot know whether stocks will go up or down in the year ahead, what do we do?

We take a guess . . . and try to do the right thing. We might try to do the smart thing, but we are not that smart. All we can do is to try to protect ourselves from madness by following the most ancient and venerable traditions: the distilled wisdom of previous generations.

We guess that stocks are a bad investment for very simple reasons: "The place to find a safe and remunerative investment is usually where others aren't looking for it," writes James Grant.[2] Everybody is looking on Wall Street. So we will look elsewhere.

"Buy low, sell high," the old chestnut practically pops out of the pan toward us; the rule tells us the right thing to do. For the past 100 years or so, the average stock has sold for less than 15 times earnings (which used to be calculated more honestly). Almost any measure you take puts them at about twice that price today.

"A bear market continues until it comes to its end—at real values," says long-time observer Richard Russell. Stocks are at real values when they sell for 8 to 10 times earnings, not 28 to 40 times. If stocks are destined to sell for 10 times earnings at some time in the future, why would we want to buy them today?

Of course, stocks could go up. And maybe they will. But we are not smart enough to know. So rather than roll the dice, we will follow the rule. And cross our fingers.

## OCCASIONAL CATASTROPHES

At the *Wiggin Sessions*, the warnings of the gods don't fall on deaf ears. "A hard rain's gon' fall," we keep saying . . . and saying . . . and saying . . . But there is a very important difference between the weather and the markets. A broken clock is right twice a day.

In nature, you get occasional catastrophes. But despite the climate change theorists, these episodes of wind and water, heat and cold are not the fault of the human race. At least, not since the Flood. It was not man who caused Vesuvius to erupt or swamped Galveston or caused the creeping freeze of the "Little Ice Age" in Europe at the end of the Middle Ages. No, man is innocent. Nature herself is the culprit.

But who caused the Crash of 1929? What made the tech bubble blow up in 2000? Who's behind the huge run-up in prices in Shanghai in 2007?

Ah, there's the difference. Nature acts more or less independently of mankind. She may be cruel, but she is not perverse. She does not conspire to bring down a shower only when most people have left their umbrellas at home. Nor does she collude to cause temperatures to drop just when people have forgotten to cut firewood. No, she can be tough, but she is not malicious.

Markets, on the other hand, have a malevolent streak. They get together and cause storms precisely when they will do the most damage—just take a look at the housing market.

The crash of the Nasdaq, for example, was caused by the people who bid up prices in the years preceding. In the 5 years ahead of the 2000 crash, prices rose six times. Had buyers not been so bullish, sellers would not have had so much to sell. In the event, prices fell in half . . . and then in half again.

The crash did not just happen; it happened because of the bubble in tech shares. A bubble is a natural market phenomenon. But bubbles are created by man; all bubbles are destroyed by men too. And then, investors are underwater.

By the end of the twentieth century, America was riding so high, it could only come down. But how? Let us take a moment to review: we have seen that man is rational, but not always and never completely. In fact, he makes his most important decisions with little resort to reason. That is, he chooses his mate, his career, and his lifestyle on the basis of what appeals to him, using his heart, not his head.

And no matter how reasonable he thinks he is, he still gets carried away by emotion from time to time. In markets as in politics, he is a fool as often as not—driven by whatever emotion that has taken hold at that moment—fear, greed, wanton confidence, disgust, the desire for revenge, bonhomie. . . . But markets and politics are even more subject to delirium because they involve large groups of people. And one of the major achievements of modern technology was that it made the mobs larger than ever before.

The madness of crowds has two important features. First, crowds can only know things in their crudest, most dumbed-down form. Since the truth is infinitely complex, it follows that what a crowd thinks is almost always reduced to a point where it is more lie than truth. Second, though the same emotions beset individuals as well as crowds, a man on his own rarely causes much trouble. He is restrained by family, friends, and the physical circumstances. A crowd, on the other hand, so magnifies his emotions and so corrupts his ideas that soon the whole society is on its way to hell.

The particular road to hell on which Americans were embarked at the debut of the twenty-first century was a feature of their own unique situation. A half century of economic progress and a 25-year bull market had led them to believe things that were not true and to expect things that they were not likely to get. Never in the history of man had any people been able to get rich by spending money . . . nor had investment markets ever made the average buy-and-hold investor rich . . . nor had paper money, unbacked by gold, ever retained its value for very long.

In the late 1990s, however, all these things seemed not only possible, but inevitable. Everything seemed to be going in Americans' favor. Then, suddenly, at the beginning of this new century, everything seemed to be going against them.

How could US consumer capitalism, which had been phenomenally successful for so long, fail them now? It can't, they will say to themselves. Why should they have to accept a decline in their standards of living, when everybody knew that they were getting richer and richer? It cannot be.

Besides, said Americans to themselves in early 2003, if there were problems, they must be the fault of others: terrorists, greedy CEOs, or policy errors at the Fed. There was nothing wrong with the system, they assured themselves.

Americans cannot turn back from the promise of something for nothing. It would be too reasonable . . . too sensible . . . too humble. Yes, the administration could cut expenses. It could renounce its worldwide gendarme role, for example, and return to defending the nation. Large spending cuts would enable the government to balance the budget and still give citizens a tax cut. And yes, people could cut their own expenses and begin saving 10% of their earnings, as they did in the 1950s and 1960s. The trade deficit would be eliminated, and debts could be paid off. And yes, the dollar could probably be saved too. Maybe it would be marked down a bit, but a stern "strong dollar" policy (perhaps bringing Paul Volcker out of retirement to give it credibility) might arrest its decline.

After a difficult recession—in which stocks have been marked down and living standards reduced—the US economy might recover and rest on a firmer foundation of domestic savings.

As we will see, that is why Americans' borrowing actually went up after the first recession began in 2001; as joblessness increased, Americans mortgaged more and more of their houses and bought new cars at a record rate. And it is why the US federal government actually increased its spending—and its deficits (enormously)—after its tax revenues began to collapse early in the new century. And it is why the trade deficit grew larger and larger—even as the dollar fell. By the beginning of 2003, the entire nation—its stocks, its currency, its military, and its consumers—seemed hell-bent.

## THE INFLATIONARY PROCESS

"This one will be no exception," we remember thinking before the carnage got underway. But of course, it's not the certainties that make life interesting; it's the uncertainties—the known unknowns and the unknown unknowns, as Rumsfeld said. We are all born of woman and end up where all men born of women end up—dead. But that doesn't mean we can't have some fun between baptism and last rites.

The worldwide financial bubble we faced was both worldlier and more financial than any in history.

And in the summer of 2007, it was still very much alive. So much alive that the media could hardly keep up with it. *Forbes* magazine, for example, tried to estimate the wealth of the world's richest people. But the rich don't typically give out their balance sheets, telephone numbers, and home addresses. So, there's a fair amount of guesswork in the calculations.

When it came to guesstimating the net worth of Stephen Schwarzman, founder of Blackstone, the Forbes crew wandered off into fiction. They put his wealth at about $2 billion. Recent filings in connection with the new Blackstone IPO show he earned that much in a single year!

In that phase of the bubble, it is as if your neighbors were throwing a wild party and you weren't invited. You detest them . . . envy them . . . and want to join them, all at once. A very small part of the population is having a ball; everyone else is getting restless and wondering when the noise will stop.

Meanwhile, the experts, commentators, kibitzers, and analysts were saying that there is a whole new phase of the giant bubble about to unfold; things could get a whole lot crazier. Even many of our respected colleagues were pointing to a text by the great Austrian economist, Ludwig von Mises, for a clue. What we have here, they say, is what Mises described as a "crack-up boom."

Before we go on, readers should be aware that the "Austrian school" of economics is probably the best theory about the way the world works. Like our newsletter, *The Daily Reckoning*, it is suspicious of efforts to control the natural workings of an economy in general and suspicious of central banking in particular. The fact that he was a one-time "Austrian," Greenspan, who became the most celebrated central banker in history, only increases our suspicions. He was able to master central banking, we imagine, because he understood what it really is—a swindle.

Von Mises described a "crack-up boom" as follows:

This first stage of the inflationary process may last for many years. While it lasts, the prices of many goods and services are not yet adjusted to the altered money relation. There are still people in the country who have not yet become aware of the fact that they are confronted with a price revolution which will finally result in a considerable rise of all prices, although the extent of this rise will not be the same in the various commodities and services. These people still believe that prices one day will drop. Waiting for this day, they restrict their purchases and concomitantly increase their cash holdings. As long as such ideas are still held by public opinion, it is not yet too late for the government to abandon its inflationary policy.[3]

But then, finally, the masses wake up. They become suddenly aware of the fact that inflation is a deliberate policy and will go on endlessly. A breakdown occurs. The crack-up boom appears. Everybody is anxious to swap his money against "real" goods, no matter whether he needs them or not, no matter how much money he has to pay for them. Within a very short time, within a few weeks or even days, the things which were used as money are no longer used as media of exchange. They become scrap paper. Nobody wants to give away anything against them.

This is what happened with the Continental currency in America in 1781, with the French mandats territoriaux in 1796, and with the German mark in 1923. It will happen again whenever the same conditions appear. If a thing has to be used as a medium of exchange, public opinion must not believe that the quantity of this thing will increase beyond all bounds. Inflation is a policy that cannot last.[4]

Mises is describing the lunatic phases of a classic inflationary cycle.

At first, no one can tell the difference between a real dollar—one that is earned, saved, invested, or spent—and one that just came off the printing presses. They figure that the new dollar is as good as the old one. And then prices rise . . . and people don't know what to make of it. Later, they begin to catch on . . . and all hell breaks loose.

If you could really get rich by printing more currency, Zimbabweans would all be as rich as Midas, since the Mugabe government ran the presses full tilt from 1980–2009, ending in a severe bouts with hyperinflation. When Zim dollar began in 1980, it traded one to one with its predecessor the Rhodesian dollar making in slightly above par than the US dollar at the time. By the time the currency was abandoned in 2009, the central bank of Zimbabwe was printing trillion dollar notes. During the height of its hyperinflationary period, prices for basic goods and services were doubling every day. Instead of getting rich, Dr. Gono Gideon, then president of the central bank, was printing as fast as he could just to feed the people.

Von Mises died in 1973—long before this boom really got going—let alone cracked up. He may have never heard of a hedge fund . . . or even a derivative, for that matter. A world money system without gold? He probably couldn't have imagined it. People spending millions of dollars for a Warhol? Twenty million for a house in Mayfair? Chinese stocks at 40 times earnings? He would have chuckled in disbelief. He understood how national currency bubbles expand and how they pop, but he probably never would have imagined how insane things could get when you have a whole world monetary system in bubble mode.

He'd have recognized the beginning of this bubble, and he'd have recognized the end, but the middle—or the beginning of the end—that would have dumbfounded him. During his lifetime he saw a crack-up boom in Germany in the 1920s . . . and a few more here . . . but he never saw a worldwide crack-up boom.

No, dear reader, no one, anywhere, has ever seen a worldwide crack-up boom. We're the first, ever. Pretty exciting, huh?

## EXPANSION AND CONTRACTION

Nothing fails like success we remind readers. In the fall of 2002, foreign investors looked down at the grenade in their hands and began to wonder. What would happen if other foreigners decided they had enough US dollar assets? Or worse, what would happen if they suddenly decided that they had too many?

There is a neat symmetry to all things natural—and markets are natural. No one designs them. No one controls them. Nor can they ever be fully understood or predicted. All we have is intuition . . . and experience. Success is followed by failure as things normally regress to the mean. But investors who have been very successful begin to think that their success knows no limits. They begin to think they deserve outsized success because they are smarter or luckier, or because their economy, their central bankers, or their government is superior.

But nature in her magisterial simplicity goes about her business no matter what people think: the warm, sunny weather of summer gives way to the cold, gray days of winter. Somehow the mean, the average, the long-term trend must be reestablished. People cannot be super-confident forever. They cannot be super-bullish all the time. They cannot be super-anything in perpetuity. Instead, they have to balance out their good days with their bad ones . . . their sense of adventure with their fearfulness . . . and their yin with their yang, so that they come to the happy medium that we know as "real life."

A long time ago, economists noticed that commerce had a certain natural rhythm to it. They illustrated this by describing the pattern of hog farmers.

When the price of pigs rose, rational profit-optimizers that they were, farmers increased production. But it took time to raise the new pigs. About 18 months later, the new hogs arrived on the market. The new supplies caused prices to fall—whereupon, the farmers decided to cut back, which caused prices to rise again.

This pattern of expansion and reduction, magnified across an entire economy, is what economists refer to when they talk of cyclical booms and busts. Since World War II, the Fed has managed these cyclical ups and downs, attempting to control and soften them. Indeed, the Fed appeared so successful at managing these cycles that it began to look as though it had mastered the science of central banking—eliminating the downward part of the cycle altogether.

However, there is another type of downward motion that is not merely cyclical, but "structural." It occurs when there is something fundamentally wrong with the structure of the economy. Since 1945, the US economy has suffered many ups and downs. All were cyclical. All downturns, save two, were intentional. These "planned recessions" were deliberately brought about by the Fed in an effort to cool down the economy and lower inflation rates.

"None of the postwar expansions died of old age; they were all murdered by the Fed," or at least that's what professor Rudi Dornbush of the Massachusetts Institute of Technology used to say. The first exception was the downturn of 1973 to 1974, in which an oil embargo played the Fed's role. The second was the slump of 2001.

## HELL OR HIGH WATER

There are good booms . . . and then there are bad booms.

A good boom is like the one following World War II. Real money was invested. Production increased. Real savings were spent. Wages increased. Profits increased. At the end of the boom, people were wealthier than they were at the beginning of it.

A bad boom is based on bad money. When the Fed (by way of the Treasury) prints up an extra dollar bill, the gesture lacks sincerity, like a duelist who first smiles and shakes your hand, then walks back 20 paces and pulls a trigger. You know he didn't really mean it. Instead of being built on real savings, the faux boom is built on monetary inflation and credit. And when it comes to an end, people are no better off. Their money is worth less than it used to be. And the average fellow has dug himself deeper into debt in order to enjoy the boom years.

"But many people really have gotten much richer during this boom, haven't they?" you might ask.

Yes, a crack-up boom is fundamentally a financial boom. Money comes into the system—a lot of it. People don't know it's phony money; they can't tell the difference. This money hangs around the financial industry, and everyone there has a good time. But society, as a whole, is not any richer because Monet paintings are more expensive . . . or because stocks are more expensive . . . or because a hedge fund manager makes a billion dollars. Society is richer when people generally earn higher wages, stash away more savings, and pay down debt. That is not what is happening.

"Well, okay, maybe in the end, a lot of people regret it . . . in the meantime, why not join the fun?" Be our guest. Buy a Warhol. Put some money into China. Get a parking space in New York for $225,000. Better yet, start a hedge fund. That's the best way . . . make "2 and 20" on other people's money. Take big risks, the bigger the better. Heck, the bigger the risk, the more you'll make . . . right up until the end. Then, of course, the hedge fund will get wiped out. But what do you care? The investors will take the loss.

Which, of course, raises a key question: when will this boom end?

## WISDOM AND TRADITION

In the early 1920s, age-old tradition had told investors to watch out for stocks—they were dangerous. In 1921, the great mass of investors judged a dollar's worth of corporate earnings to be worth only $5 of stock price. But something happened in the late 1920s that changed the stock-buying public's view. There was a "new era" in the 1920s, complete with a number of important new innovations such as the automobile, electrical appliances, radio broadcasting, and so on. By 1929, lightheaded investors were willing to pay $33 for every dollar of earnings—and they still considered it a fair trade. Then, of course, came the crash.

By the end of the year, investors asked themselves: "Whatever made me think General Electric was worth so much?" Mr. John Q. Public never had a clue—then or now.

Groups of people neither think nor act as individuals do. As mad as individuals can be, groups of individuals can be even madder. Not only do they act differently, they think differently too—usually in a manner that is simpleminded and often moronic or delusional.

Gustave Le Bon wrote:

A crowd thinks in images, and the image itself immediately calls up a series of other images, having no logical connection with the first. Our reasoning shows us the incoherence there is in these images, but a crowd is almost blind to this truth, and confuses with the real event what the deforming action of its imagination has superimposed thereon.[5]

Before St. George appeared on the walls of Jerusalem to all the Crusaders, he was certainly perceived in the first instance by one of those present. By dint of suggestion and contagion, the miracle signalized by a single person was immediately accepted by all.

Such is always the mechanism of the collective hallucinations so frequent in history—hallucinations that seem to have all the recognized characteristics of authenticity, since they are phenomena observed by thousands of persons.

In the freewheeling play of mobs—whether conducting a battle, watching CNBC, or listening to a campaign speech—the frontier between fact and fiction comes unstuck. Crowds cannot tell the difference. If a man says to the crowd that Martians are about to attack a planet or that they are being victimized by the International Monetary Fund, each member of the crowd has no personal experience or knowledge to contradict him. In fact, a crowd cannot be certain about anything; its knowledge is of an entirely different kind than that of an individual. A group takes up events or facts only in the crudest and most elemental way. The individual experiences of group members—infinitely varied and nuanced—count for almost nothing.

A generation that has lived through the Great Depression, for example, or the Great War, is likely to remember the event itself, but to *understand* it only as anecdotal evidence of the public knowledge. A man could have lived happily through the 1930s with no idea that he was part of a great anything. But once informed that he had experienced the Great Depression, his particular experiences take on new meaning and are reinterpreted to support the collective sentiment.

## HEADING FOR THE EXITS

In economics, the problem is known as the *fallacy of composition*. In short, what may work for a single person may not work for a group. Looking back at the cavalry charge, an individual soldier could rein in his horse as he approached the enemy . . . letting his comrades make the initial contact with bayonets and musket balls. The cavalryman may increase his own chance of survival. But if all the horsemen did the same, they would almost certainly fail and probably be shot to bits as they hesitated before the enemy lines.

The paradox arises over and over again in economics and elsewhere. The owner of a business may be better off firing employees, cutting expenses, and improving the profit margin. But if all business owners suddenly fired workers, consumer spending would fall. Soon, businesses would notice falling sales and profits.

Charles Kindleberger mentions the phenomenon of spectators standing up at sporting events. When a few stand up, they get a better view. But when all stand up, the advantage disappears. A man may sell an overpriced stock and reap a tidy profit. But if other stockholders all attempt to do the same thing at the same time, the price will plummet. Instead of making a profit, they may all end up with a loss.

The great mass of citizens in a participatory system believe things so degraded by the crowd that they are mostly untrue. They may believe that the king has a "divine right" to tell them what to do, for example . . . or that the majority of their elected representatives does. Or that they are racially superior, have a "manifest destiny," or are in danger of being knocked down by a falling domino. In politics, lies, nonsense, and foolishness run their own course—often sordid, sometimes pathetic, and occasionally entertaining. But in markets, the outcome is always the same: maddened by a lie, participants run right into the fallacy of composition like a panicked mob into a theater exit. They may believe that they can all get rich by buying stocks, but getting rich is relative. Only a few can do it. Compared with most people in history, almost all US investors are rich already. But it is only the comparison to other living investors—their friends and neighbors—that matters to them. Can they all be richer than their friends and neighbors? It is no more possible than that all their children will have above-average intelligence.

At the end of 2002, for example, America's baby boomers believed they could retire by selling their houses at appreciated prices. But to whom? The first to sell may do well, but what would happen to real estate prices if all 78 million boomers decided to sell at the same time?

As mass participation in markets increases, it brings in more and more capital and more and more people who do not know what they are doing. Prices rise, which confuses even many of the old-timers who should know better. Thus, the stage is set for the final, disappointing act. Ultimately, the common myth of the masses fails them for it is fanciful or physically impossible.

## THE REVOLUTION WILL BE TELEVISED

Recently sitting at a café in the heart of the Latin Quarter in Paris, and listening to the conversations at neighboring tables, not once did your authors hear anyone mention the credos of Marx, Lenin, Freud, Foucault, or Sartre. They might as well all be dead.

Thirty years ago, this street corner was so smitten by politics that the revolutionaries of the era pried up the paving stones and built barricades. "Come the revolution," they would say to each other, "things will be different." Cafés and restaurants were crowded then too, but not with tourists. Instead, they were full of ideologues—greasy-haired youths who smoked, drank, and squabbled about the fine points of Marxism until the wee hours. Che was not on their T-shirts, but on their lips and in their brains, such as they were.

Probably the scene was not much different 219 years ago. The French Revolution was "the source of all the present communist, anarchist, and socialist conceptions," wrote Prince Peter Kropotkin.[6]

At the end of the eighteenth century, France enjoyed an exaltation not too different from that of the United States at the end of the twentieth century. It was the biggest country with the biggest economy and Europe's dominant military power. (It was French intervention that had allowed the American colonies to escape British rule a decade earlier.) France could even lecture other countries on the benefits of free enterprise!

But success is self-correcting. Turgot and the Physiocrats had been applying their "laissez-faire" principles to the French economy, to great effect. In doing so, they disturbed powerful interests close to the monarchy who were concerned with protecting their privileges and their markets—much like the West Virginia steel mills and Kansas farmers of the Bush years. In 1776, the same year in which the American War for Independence began and Adam Smith published his *Wealth of Nations*, Turgot was ousted.

"The dismissal of this great man," wrote Voltaire, "crushed me . . . Since that fatal day, I have not followed anything . . . and am waiting patiently for someone to cut our throats."[7]

Someone came along with a knife just a few years later. On July 14, 1789, a Paris mob attacked the old fortress at the Bastille. There, they liberated "two fools, four forgers, and a debaucher," wrote an observer at the time.[8] The prison guards were promised safe conduct in return for surrender, but once they laid down their arms, the mob cut them to pieces and was soon marching through the streets of Paris with the guards' heads, torsos, and other body parts on the ends of pikes.

For the next 25 years, France rocked and reeled from one collective madness to another. The Marquis de Sade was released from prison, while thousands of decent people took his place. Paper money replaced gold and silver. Identity cards were required of every citizen, called "Certificates of Good Citizenship." Permits were required for nearly everything. And travel was strictly controlled.

## ASSAULT ON TRADITION

Every revolution is an assault against tradition—whether it is a new era on Wall Street or in Paris. The church was plundered. Local languages, schools, and legal jurisdictions were dismantled. Even the old forms of address were tossed out—henceforth, everyone would be called "citizen."

Finally, the French could stand no more. Napoleon Bonaparte brought order to Paris with "a whiff of grapeshot" at a critical moment.

But today, the only revolutions one talks about in the Latin Quarter are in technology and fashion. There are lesbians on every street corner, but you can search an entire city and find only a few moth-eaten communists who lost their minds 30 years ago. There are Che T-shirts, but who cares what Che said, except a few tenured relics of the 1960s? There are no Republicans either. For how was Bush's agenda different from Clinton's, Chirac's, Blair's, or Louis XVI's? They all do the same things—tax, spend, and regulate as much as they can get away with.

What is this strange intersection that we have come to? All major governments seem to have come together in some unholy socialism, but where are the socialists? Few politicians will even admit to the creed they all share. And what voter really cares?

"We lived through the Reagan revolution . . . mainly rhetorical . . ." wrote economist Gary North. "After Reagan, we lived through the Bush-Clinton counter-revolution. Now we are getting more of the same under the present administration: more controls on our lives, more government spending, larger federal deficits."[9]

"The Reagan victory did not shrink the State," North continued. "We are not going to see lower taxes, reduced government regulation of business, a lower federal budget, the repayment of the national debt, better schools, safer cities, and smaller welfare rolls . . . ."

The revolution, begun in Paris more than 200 years ago, continues, but in the mid-1900s, the crowd turned its attention from tragedy to farce—that is, from politics to economics, from war to commercial competition, and from ideology to consumerism.

## THE GREAT MODERATION

This most recent slump was not a normal, garden-variety postwar downturn. It was more like the structural, post-bubble depression of the 1930s. Examples are few. The only other structural downturn in a major economy in the postwar period can be found in Japan beginning in the 1990s. Japan's hysterical boom was followed by a long period of false recovery, bear market, and on-again, off-again recession. America's post-bubble slump, too, might reasonably be expected to resemble Japan's—since both are structural and both have happened amid the mass capitalism of the late twentieth century.

The structural problem is not the same, but the effects may be similar. Japan thought it could export its way to permanent financial growth and prosperity. The United States thought it could do the same with imports. Thanks largely to mass participation, both economies exaggerated their advantages during the boom years . . . and then resisted the inevitable structural adjustments.

"This is no traditional business cycle," explained an *Economist* article from autumn 2002, "but the bursting of the biggest bubble in America's history. Never before have shares been so overvalued. Never before have so many people owned shares. And never before has every part of the economy invested (indeed, overinvested) in new technology with such gusto. All this makes it likely that the hangover from the binge will last longer and be more widespread than is generally expected."[10]

Part of the blame for these long hangovers must be the magnitude of the hullabaloo that preceded them. The world had never seen anything on quite the same scale as Japan's bubble, or the United States'. So many participants exaggerated typical bubble excesses. These people—and institutions—had a keen interest in keeping the good times rolling. Many of them also had the power to influence the economy in a major way.

In the United States, the effects of the collapsing stock market bubble were visible almost immediately on government budgets at every level. The federal government swung from running a surplus of about $94 billion in the first 11 months of fiscal year 2001, to a deficit of $159 billion in 2002, and a projected loss of nearly $500 billion the following year. California announced a budget deficit, at the beginning of 2003, equal to $1,000 for every man, woman, and child in the state; New York said it was looking at a $10 billion shortfall; and the Texas deficit was close to $12 billion.

Panics were virtually eliminated—like polio—following the Roosevelt era changes. There was no reason to panic—because banks were now insured! Indeed, although there were major panics in 1890, 1893, 1899, 1901, 1903, and 1907, none occurred after World War II.

"The business cycle is unlikely to be as disturbing or as troublesome to our children as it once was to our fathers," announced Arthur Burns in his 1959 address to the American Economic Association.

Skewed somewhat by the outsized expansion of the 1990s, the average postwar period of growth exceeded the typical prewar expansion by 65%, Romer discovered. "The bottom line," she concludes, is that "expansions are noticeably longer after World War II than before World War I, indicating that recession happens less often today than in the past."

Before the Great Depression, there was little public pressure to do something to interrupt the natural course of boom and bust. Those notably busted were usually rich people, entrepreneurs, and speculators . . . and who cared about them? Politically, capitalists in the late nineteenth century were no more popular than smokers in the late twentieth. They were too few to elect even a city councilman.

During and following the Great Depression, however, central banks and governments undertook to soften the busts that had vexed mankind since the beginning of time. Keynes had a theory that told them what to do. Prices fail to adjust quickly enough, he said, because they are "sticky." The government should step in, he said, and provide the economy with a boost, by cutting taxes and spending money. Keynes's idea was simple: government would run surpluses in the good years and deficits in bad ones. This action would offset the ups and downs of the business cycle.

Years later, Milton Friedman and Anna Schwartz added their own theory. Depressions were caused by too little money in circulation, they said. The Great Depression resulted from the failure of so many banks, which reduced the money supply suddenly. The Fed should have stepped in and replaced the money quickly. Its failure to do so was the biggest policy mistake of the entire era, say the monetarist duo.

The monetarists say a slump can be corrected by printing more money. The Keynesians say the problem can be solved by spending it. Investors do not know one from the other, but they are sure something can be done.

Since our approach is literary and historical, we will not attempt a detailed critique of either of these schools. Instead, we will return to Japan and let the facts speak for themselves.

Offering an explanation for the strange events of the new century, economist Paul Krugman suggested the following, "The world became vulnerable to its current travails, not because economic policies had not been reformed, but because they had. That is, around the world, countries responded to the very real flaws in the policy regimes that had evolved in response to the Depression by moving back toward a regime with many of the virtues of pre-Depression, free-market capitalism. However, in bringing back the virtues of old-fashioned capitalism we also brought back some of its vices, most notably a vulnerability both to instability and to sustained economic slumps."

Krugman imagined a kind of social contract after the Great Depression in which voters agreed to tolerate capitalism, but only with safety nets and regulations to make sure no one got hurt. In his mind only, these restraints produced a stable prosperity in which the benefits were shared out among the population during the 1950s, 1960s, and 1970s.

"The America I grew up in—the America of the 1950s and 1960s," he said, "was middle class. . . . Yes, of course, there were still some rich people," he admits, "but [thank God!] there weren't that many of them. The days when plutocrats were a force to be reckoning with in American society, economically or politically, seemed long past."

Krugman was writing to an appreciative audience in the *New York Times* magazine in October 2002. Typically, he let himself get distracted by envy, worrying that the rich might be making a comeback. The average compensation for the nation's top 100 CEOs rose from just $1.3 million in 1970 (in 1998 dollars) to $37.5 million in 2000. There are not enough of these super-rich Americans to fill a zoning department in a mid-size town, yet Krugman was so indignant about it that he missed the important point altogether: the triumph of American laissez-faire capitalism, which conservatives celebrate and Krugman rues, was a sham. By the close of the twentieth century, true capitalists had almost disappeared from the face of the earth. *Capitalism* is a pejorative invented by Marx to describe a system in which the rich owned the means of production and exploited the masses. The system Marx described never really existed the way Marx imagined, though a casual observer with a chip on his shoulder may have been tempted to see it that way.

Marx's economics were as fanciful as his history. But at least one of his predictions proved correct . . . though not at all in the way he thought. As the champagne glasses were hoisted and the new millennium was rung in, the Marxist vision had triumphed at least as much as the laissez-faire vision of Smith and Turgot; the means of production were owned by the workers. (Curiously, the most laissez-faire economy in the world in 2002 was in Hong Kong—a city under the direct control of still-communist China. And the world's fastest-growing—and in many ways freest—economy was on the Chinese mainland.)

## COLLECTIVIZED RISKS

Both in the United States and Japan, the freewheeling laissez-faire capitalism of the nineteenth century gave way to a consensual, collectivized capitalism of the twentieth century, with massive state involvement and mass participation by people who would not know a balance sheet from a bed pan. The very rich CEOs that galled Krugman were only hired guns—not genuine capitalists. Their extravagant pay levels were testimony not to the victory of raw capitalism, but to its defeat. Real capitalists would never allow so much of their money to get into the hands of managers.

If there were any real capitalists around, they must have been sleeping. For they had let their managers practically steal away their businesses and ruin their investments. Corporate debt rose 382% in the 1990s, more than 30% faster than GDP growth. Nor were the borrowings used for capital improvements that might make the capitalists more money. Instead, much of the borrowed money was frittered away on mergers, acquisitions, and stock buy backs. These maneuvers were not designed to enrich real capitalists, but merely to drive up the share price by impressing the new class of citizen-shareholder, the *lumpeninvestoriat*.

Likewise, what capitalist would stand still for such generous stock options—given away to employees in the heyday of the boom years as if they were turkeys at Thanksgiving?

Modern corporations are owned by small shareholders, not big ones—often through collectivized holdings in pension funds, mutual funds, and so forth. These small holders have neither the gumption nor the power nor incentive to resist absurdly high executive salaries. In the late 1990s, even CEOs of companies whose earnings were falling or approaching bankruptcy were paid as if they were star quarterbacks in the Super Bowl. Maybe they were especially talented, and maybe they were not. But the mere fact that they were paid so much and appeared on magazine covers seemed to awe small shareholders and impress analysts. The great mob of investors took up the stock of these celebrity managers with no serious thought about them and too little interest to justify a serious investigation.

Stock market investors had come to act like voters!

Mass capitalism produced mass delusions—and a new shareholder arithmetic. It might have made sense for Warren Buffett to object to stock options and look carefully at executive compensation: as a substantial shareholder, much of the money that went to overcompensate key employees would have otherwise gone to him. But the two or three cents a small stockholder might have had at stake made serious investigation not worth the trouble.

## THE GREAT BARGAIN

Krugman believed that a grand bargain was struck following the Great Depression of the 1930s. Capitalism would remain the economic system of the West, but it would submit to the control of government to avoid future debacles. In a sense, this was true. Capitalism in the United States was not the same after the Roosevelt administration finished with it. But this was merely part of the bigger trend toward a mass capitalism directed by government for its own purposes. Share ownership became increasingly widespread. By the end of the century, enough Americans owned shares to elect a president. Share ownership rose from just 5% of the population at the beginning of the twentieth century to fully 56% of its households at its end.

Like any large group of people removed from the facts or from direct experience, shareholders were as subject to mass emotions as a group of voters or a lynch mob. With only public knowledge to go by, they could be readily whipped up by the financial media and were ready to amplify any fad to the point of absurdity.

The first large movement of mass capitalism took place in the United States in the 1920s. Share ownership was uncommon in 1900. The whole country only had about 4,000 stockbrokers. Thirty years later, the number of brokers had increased more than 500%. Stocks became such a popular subject that even shoeshine boys had an opinion on them.

The Dow shot up from 120 on the first day of business in 1925 to 381 at the peak in 1929.

Then, after the bubble burst, the United States experienced its first bout of mass depression. Unlike previous busts, the 1930s brought suffering to the entire nation, not just a handful of rich capitalists. A quarter of the workforce became unemployed. In 1931 and 1932, more than 5,000 banks failed. The bear market on Wall Street dragged on and on, with the Dow not returning to its 1929 high until 1954.

For the first time too, voters demanded that their government "do something." The Roosevelt administration did something. It arrived on the scene with a program of monetary and fiscal stimulus, following the most recent fads in macroeconomics. Never before had a government attempted such forceful intervention. And never before was an economy so unimpressed. Instead of bouncing back as it had following the Panic of 1873 or the Bust of 1907, the nation lay down in a gutter of recession, bankruptcy, and sluggish growth. And it stayed there for the next decade. Even then, it seemed to take the biggest war in world history to pry the poor fellow up again.

"Too little, too late," was the professional opinion of the leading economists. Government had made a good attempt, but not massive enough or fast enough.

## SHAREHOLDER NATION: FOR BETTER . . . OR WORSE

Another interpretation, out of step with the fashions of the day, was that the government's own efforts to help the economy out of its funk had actually made the situation worse—by stretching out the painful readjustments that needed to be made over a long period and at much greater cost.

Either way, it was a New Era in capitalism. For now, government—often acting through its bureaucrats at the Federal Reserve—promised to soften capitalism's rough edges. It would put into place safety nets to protect people from serious injury, on or off the job, and it would manage the nation's monetary and fiscal policies so as to ease the pain of the downward slope of the business cycle. Henceforth, budget deficits would become an economic tool, not merely a convenience for pusillanimous politicians, unwilling to raise taxes to pay for their programs. And henceforth, the market would not determine interest rates based on the supply of savings and the demand for it. Instead, interest rates—at least at the short end of the interest-rate curve—would be set by the central bank for the good of the economy.

But Krugman believed that in the 1980s a neoconservative push for deregulation reinstated the rough-and-tumble capitalism of the pre-Roosevelt era, and that a return to pre-Depression policies inevitably led to Depression-era economies that explained Japan in the 1990s and the United States in the early 2000s.

If anyone can figure out how the shallow deregulations in the United States in the 1980s produced the long malaise in Japan in the 1990s or the current slump in the States, he is not working on this book. The Japanese adopted capitalism following the war. But Japan's capitalism never bore much resemblance to the raw capitalism of Krugman's imagination. The essential feature—the disposition of capital—was never in the hands of freewheeling capitalists. Instead, groups of bankers, large corporate combines, and government made major capital decisions.

And even in the United States, the Reagan-era reforms hardly changed the nature of late-twenty-first-century capitalism. Barely a single thread in the massive public safety net was unraveled. Government spending went up by every measure—as a percentage of personal income, in nominal dollars, and in real ones. The fundamental trend toward mass consumer capitalism accelerated. While only 23% of households owned shares in 1989, by the end of the century fully half of all US households were little pseudo-capitalists. And of them, nearly half counted the majority of their wealth in the form of shares in public companies!

The United States had become the Shareholder Nation—every bit as obsessed with stock prices as Japan had been 10 years earlier.

Risk had been collectivized—so that hardly anyone felt immune from a slump.

Scarcely noticed by economists of any persuasion was the way in which government became a partner in the managed, risk-averse capitalist systems of the late twentieth century. Governments throughout the developed world had increased their shares of GDP during the entire century. In the United States, from an estimated 8.2% of GDP in 1900, by the century's end the government spent about 30% of GDP. Taxes soared too. At the dawn of the twentieth century, there were still no federal income taxes in the United States. They would not arrive until more than a decade later. And even then, the first federal income taxes applied only to the richest citizens. Conservative politicians argued against the imposition of the tax, warning that the rate could eventually rise as high as 10%. But the threat seemed so preposterous that the constitutional amendment was passed over their objections.

By the end of the century in the United States, the average federal income tax rate had reached 13.2% with a top marginal rate of 39.6% (2001 figures). Meanwhile, as taxes of all kinds multiplied and rose, the total tax burden on the average American was much higher—between 30% and 40%. Taken together, across the spectrum of developed Organisation for Economic Co-operation and Development (OECD) nations, the top personal income tax rates averaged about 47% and the top corporate income tax rates 34% by the year 2000, with total government spending among the leading developed nations consuming an average of 38.8% of GDP (OECD figures for 2000).

This left politicians and central bankers even more keenly concerned about the economy and its markets. Not only were voters demanding that the government "do something" to promote prosperity, the government's own revenues depended on it. To its citizens, government was no longer an incidental expense—but a major one, their largest single expense item. For the economy, government was no longer a minor parasite—but, likewise, the biggest one.

Reagan administration economists had realized that parasites depend on the health of their hosts. The stronger the host economy, they reasoned, the larger the parasite could become. The genius of supply-side economist Art Laffer's curve (said to have been drawn out on a napkin at lunch) was that reducing marginal tax rates would actually increase gross revenues to the state. Reagan, in his first term, took advantage of this insight, cutting the top marginal rate from 70% to just 50%. The result was the same as with the Kennedy cuts of 20 years before—government revenues increased along with economic activity.

In short, democratic government was no longer a spectator, or even a disinterested referee. It had become the biggest participant in the supposedly free markets of the Western world. It was the biggest spender in consumer economies. It was the biggest borrower. It controlled money and credit. It was the watchdog on the capital markets, its chief observer, and its chief beneficiary. Is it any wonder George W. Bush rushed to "do something" to protect its revenues? Is it any wonder that Barack Obama—the man who would be FDR—superseded him in every way and promised to rout and stifle bubbles wherever they may be detected?

Barely had the internet begun working than fraudsters were using it to mislead investors. A typical scheme, such as the one perpetrated by a student at Georgetown Law School early in 2001, involved buying the shares of some marginal company and then going on the internet, spreading rumors or outright lies to ramp up the price.[11] You only had to announce some new breakthrough, some new contract, a rumored buyout, new technology . . . whatever. The whole idea was to create the kind of buzz that got people talking about it. Then supposedly reasonable "investors" would jump at the chance to buy a stock they knew nothing about, on the basis of a recommendation from someone they did not know, founded on information whose accuracy could not be affirmed, and whose source could not be traced.

A lawyer defending one of the alleged Georgetown manipulators responded that it was impossible to mislead people on the internet: according to him, internet postings were nothing but "graffiti," with no more informational content than graffiti has artistic content. The lawyer's argument was that his client had just used the internet as a graffiti artist uses the wall of a public building . . . or perhaps as a dog uses a tree. He pollutes it, perhaps vandalizes it, but no serious person would mistake it for useful information. But here, junk life imitates junk art. Pumping and dumping stocks on the internet did in fact work. In just a few hours, the graffiti artists of the internet were able to sell their shares at a profit.

The Georgetown episode was a primitive example of the pandemic-era fixation of millennial age speculators with "meme stocks"—moribund brick and mortar stocks like movie theater chain AMC Entertainment and the video game retailer GameStop that got pumped up on the social media site Reddit then bought and sold on the trading platform Robinhood.

Elon Musk's electric car company, Tesla, even became the object of meme traders' desire in 2022. To make the point, the "information" used by serious investors for generations, price to earnings ratios, expected ROI for existing inventory or a new product launch, costs of rental or office space, and employee benefit and pension obligations didn't matter. Only the internet mob and the price of the stock mattered.

While information may be cheap, knowledge is dear. It takes time to learn how to do anything. It can take a lifetime to master a trade—even one that is as rudimentary and analog as woodworking or gardening. And the internet did nothing to expand the supply of time. On the contrary, it made time more dear. Herbert Simon, winner of the 1978 Nobel Prize in Economics, gave the following reason for this: "In a world where attention is a major scarce resource, information may be an expensive luxury, for it may turn our attention from what is important to what is unimportant."[12] Spend any time at all with a teenager obsessed with TikTok videos and Simon's observation will be self-evident.

In the first wave of the Information Revolution, internet investors treated every digit as if it had value. In fact, few had any worth whatsoever. Many were not only valueless, but had antivalue, reducing the sum of knowledge or wisdom in whomever took them seriously.

By the mid-2000s, America was already suffering from information overload. As one commentator put it, "Americans today are literally drowning in information . . . we find ourselves awash in a vast ocean of data, what with the internet, nonstop cable TV news, email, voicemail, faxes, pagers with stock quotes, cellular phones and an explosion of newspapers, magazines and books and well, you get the idea." Add now, gadgets and services that didn't even exist then: streaming services and a plethora of social media platforms like

Facebook, YouTube, Instagram, Twitter, TikTok, LinkedIn, Zoom, Google Meet, and more. We marvel at the fact none of these existed when we began writing about the value of information two decades ago. Heck, the iPhone wasn't introduced to the market until the year the second edition of *Financial Reckoning Day* was written.

In a phrase, "data glut" has become a noxious issue in the American workplace. Like a traffic cop in a busy intersection, the average worker now spends more than half his or her day processing documents. And that was before the American middle class all began working from home online during COVID-19. Meanwhile, in a twist of irony, paper use per employee rose to 10,000 sheets in 2022. Nationwide, offices use 12.1 trillion sheets of paper, on average, per year.[13] Remember the information age dream of the paperless office? After peaking in 2006 at 213 billion units, rising at 13 times the population rate, "third-class mail" was still humming along at 128 billion pieces in 2022.[14]

In the early years of the third decade of the 2000s, office workers and those working from home often spend hours reading and answering email, sending texts, and chatting it up on Slack and other apps meant to cultivate efficiency and increase productivity. Initially a blessing, email is now a curse to those whose inboxes are inundated with "FYI" messages, random forwards, free marketing services, and other "information" on a daily basis.[15] Perhaps they make the day more productive for a segment of the disciplined world, but has it really made our work life better, more gratifying? You're now on the hook 24/7, especially if you are still working from home. One concern we have had consistently, both as a colleague and an employer, is people confuse all those conversations held by the myriad of apps and devices as actual work.

As early as 1997, author David Shenk found that "information overload fuels stress and promotes faulty thinking." The data glut we all slog through every day at work simply "reduces our attention span" and "makes us numb to anything that doesn't lurch out and grab us by the throat" Shenk concluded.

Having two mistresses is not necessarily better than having one. Nor is eating two lunches an improvement over a single one. But information was supposed to be different, wasn't it? The more you had, the richer and smarter you were supposed to be. Yet, people seem no brighter than they had been before the Information Age began lo those many years ago. Movies don't seem any better than those of the 1950s and 1960s; art is becoming more grotesque, perverted, and digital. Blockchain, the technology behind cryptocurrencies, has given rise to a new form of oddity, the non-fungible token (NFT) through which modern art has taken an even more ephemeral, if less comprehensible turn. Like "meme stocks" the value of NFTs is judged by the mob, not by any intrinsic value.

In our office in Paris back in the tech boom, we often started the day with the editorials in the *International Herald Tribune,* as collected from the *New York Times* and the *Washington Post* were already as absurd as ever. . . now they don't even seem to correspond to reality. Investors appear to have made it a mission to make ever-increasingly ridiculous decisions. And that was before a decade of below-market interest rates encouraged rash speculation. While everyone proclaimed the benefits of the Information Age, it was, ironically, the most ignorant who seemed to reap its greatest rewards.

## REAL WEALTH AND POVERTY

Wouldn't it be nice if people really could cure their financial troubles by spending more money? Who wouldn't jump at the chance to fix an overdrawn account by going out and buying a new car . . . or salve the pain of bumping into credit card limits by charging a European vacation? If only the world worked that way!

Our intuition tells us it does not. Nothing comes from nothing; adding zeros produces no positive number. We know that in our private lives spending money does not make us wealthy. Forbearance and thrift, not profligacy, lead to prosperity. How could it be any different for an entire economy?

As Adam Smith explains in *An Inquiry into the Nature and Causes of the Wealth of Nations:*

> Capitals are increased by parsimony and diminished by prodigality and misconduct.

Whatever a person saves from his revenue, he adds to his capital, and either employs it himself in maintaining an additional number of productive hands, or enables some other person to do so, by lending it to him for an interest, that is, for a share of the profits. As the capital of an individual can be increased only by what he saves from his annual revenue or his annual gains, so the capital of a society, which is the same with that of all the individuals who compose it, can be increased only in the same manner.

Parsimony, and not industry, is the immediate cause of the increase of capital. Industry, indeed, provides the subject which parsimony accumulates.

But that is the marvelous chimera of collective thinking; things we know would not work in our private lives, magnified a million times, suddenly seem possible.

A man could certainly improve his standard of living—at least in the short term. He could just go out and borrow a million dollars and spend it. A nice new car . . . a beach house . . . a new home entertainment system. And, oh yes, take a luxury trip around the world. His standard of living would go up dramatically. Soon, people unaware of the source of his new wealth, would be asking him for financial advice!

If only he did not have to pay the money back! You do not have to be an economist to figure out what happens when he has to repay. Not only does the new spending have to go, but he must also cut expenses below what they were before he borrowed the money.

For an individual, it is obvious that borrowing and spending will not produce enduring wealth. But for an economy, it almost seems possible. Besides, if a hundred million people believe it—it must be true!

Let us imagine a man who is naked and alone on a tropical island. If he spends all his time just trying to get enough to eat, his condition can scarcely be expected to improve; he will live in that savage state until he drops dead. But if he is able to save a little time from his daily maintenance, he may prosper. He might, for example, apply an hour a day to building a shelter, planting a garden, or making better hunting tools. Little by little, he might greatly improve his living standard, for each incremental improvement releases more time with which to make even more progress. Once he has completed his home, he might turn to his garden, which would provide more food in a fraction of the time. Or better fishing hooks might also produce more fish in less time.

If, however, he were merely to dig holes and then fill them in, or pile up rocks pointlessly, how would he be any better off? Or imagine that there are two such men on an island and that the two of them go to war. Instead of planting papayas, they build catapults to throw rocks at each other's gardens, thereby reducing yields. They would each be fully employed, no doubt, and each richer in defense capability, but the idea that war would make their economies more prosperous is preposterous.

It is obvious that two elements are essential to material progress— saving and applying the savings to some useful enterprise. Classical economists knew the importance of these things and focused their efforts on how to encourage savings and improve profits. Yet, the corpus of modern economic thinking gives little attention to them. Instead, modern economists focus their intellectual efforts on a fantasy. They imagine that they can "stimulate demand" by decree . . . and that money created out of thin air is as good as the real thing.

Let us return to our island. After a time, a third man washes up on shore. The three decide to specialize, to divide the labor between them so that they will be more efficient and more productive. One gathers coconuts. The other fishes. The third plants banana trees. The coconut gatherer and the fisherman exchange their products with each other.

But what about the banana planter? It will take a couple of years before his bananas are ready to eat. How will he survive?

The other two men recognize the benefit of what he is doing and look forward to eating bananas. They decide to give him coconuts and fish . . . with the understanding that they will get paid back in bananas when they are ready. To effect this transaction, the banana planter issues "money" equal to his entire crop. It is understood that these little shells may be exchanged against his bananas, and thus the other two men begin amassing their fortunes, feeling wealthier each time they acquire another shell.

But what if the banana planter decided to double the supply of money? What would be the point of it? The fish and coconut suppliers might think they were getting richer—but there would still be only so many bananas, no more.

And yet, most modern economists seem to think that they can create more fish, more coconuts, and more bananas—just by putting more money in circulation at critical times. The point of it is very simple: the extra money makes people feel as though they have more to spend. They then increase their consumption—which encourages producers to increase output.

The old economists knew that this was too simpleminded to be true. "The encouragement of mere consumption is no benefit to commerce," wrote Jean–Baptiste Say in 1803, "for the difficulty lies in supplying the means, not in stimulating the desire of consumption; and we have seen that production alone furnishes those means. Thus, it is the aim of good government to stimulate production, of bad government to encourage consumption."[16]

The Greenspan Fed and the Bush White House moved faster than the Japanese—but in the same direction. Greenspan began cutting rates in January 2001. Fiscal policy cranked up a little later—the Bush administration announced a $675 billion stimulus plan, stretched out over 10 years. The smell of sushi hung over the entire effort, but no one seemed to notice or care. If US consumers stopped spending—as the Japanese had—the government stimulus efforts would do nothing, except waste valuable savings.

When savings rates fall, less money is available for capital investment. Other things being equal, lower savings rates lead to higher interest rates—because there is less money available to borrow. Higher interest rates suppress economic activity because fewer new projects can make it over the "hurdle rate." If an innovation would produce a 10% profit, but the cost of the capital to build it is 11%, the project will be shelved. At 2%, the hurdle may be low enough to make the project worthwhile, for it will still produce an 8% profit after the cost of capital.

There is no magic to it, but real savings must be involved . . . and the savings must be used in ways that make people better off. A man cannot lend another what he does not have. It seems obvious enough to two men on an island. But in the hot smoke of public thinking, additional credit from the central bank looks as good as the real thing.

During both bubbles—in Japan as well as the United States—savings rates generally fell, but interest rates fell too. Interest rates should have gone up—reflecting the fact that there was less capital available and, at least in the boom years, more borrowers who wanted it. Where did the additional capital come from to force down rates? Economists hardly bothered to ask the question, for they had long since given up wondering about how savings worked or where they came from. They knew that central bankers could make as much new credit available as they wanted—creating savings "out of thin air."

But what was this strange money that the central authorities had created out of nowhere? It looked real. You could hold one of the new Federal Reserve notes up to the light and study it carefully; it was indistinguishable from the other notes and bills ginned out by the Bureau of Printing and Engraving. You could take it to the bank and deposit it. You could take it to the grocery store . . . or the haberdasher. You could even take it on a European vacation. All over the world, the new money was as sound as the dollar.

But what really happened when central bankers gave the economy additional credit at a time when actual savings were going down? How was it possible to provide extra savings when there were actually fewer to be had?

Again, modern economists hardly stopped to ask the question, let alone answer it. One Federal Reserve note was as good as another, they believed. Lucre was lucre. Phony savings were as good as real ones. But therein hangs a tale. For what increases production and output is not make-believe savings, but real ones. After all, there are only so many real savings in an economy. Like the man on a deserted island, a hundred million men cannot really increase the amount of free time, or of available capital, just by wishing it were so. Cement factories only produce so much cement. Only so many bricks are held in inventory. Gas tanks and pipelines only hold so much energy—and no more. Of course, they can be increased—but not without the investment of real resources!

Neither the Federal Reserve nor the Bank of Japan have the power to increase the length of time in a day. They might, by decree, increase the number of hours or minutes, but the time it takes for the earth to make its daily rotation remains a constant. Likewise, neither central bank has the power to increase—by proclamation nor by legerdemain—the amount of real savings in a society. All they can do is make believe: Issue new credit and new notes that look for all the world like the real thing.

Milton Friedman said, in response to how to avoid a Japan-like slump, "just print money."[17]

"Don't ask where the money would come from," adds Paul Krugman, "it could and should simply be created . . . the situation offers a perfect opportunity to effect a salutary expansion of the monetary base."[18]

The trouble with these new credits was that they had no real resources behind them—no extra time, no extra materials . . . no nothing. Businessmen, investors, and consumers mistakenly took up the well-made counterfeits because no one could tell the difference. The consumer thought he had more money—didn't his house just go up in value? Weren't his stocks rising every day? He asked few questions and spent more money. The businessman mistook the new spending for more real demand rather than the temporary fraud it was. He hired extra workers and built new facilities to meet the new demand. And the investor thought he saw a boom. Eager to participate, he bid up the prices of capital assets and thought he had gone to heaven without dying.

It is all too wonderful—while it lasts. But it is a boom built on deceit and cannot continue forever. The trouble is, it can last so long that it begins to look eternal. And the more successful the central bankers are at keeping it going, the greater the embarrassment and dislocation when it eventually falls apart. To keep the whole thing rolling, the central bank provides even more credit at even lower prices. Interest rates come down, inducing even further indebtedness among an already spendthrift population. After stocks collapsed in the United States, beginning in March 2000, borrowing for business expansion, IPOs, mergers and acquisitions, and stock market margin accounts gradually trailed off. But borrowing on real estate—particularly, home refinancing—soared.

Rising real estate prices, lower monthly payments, and cash-out refinancing made homeowners feel as if they were coming out ahead. But even with increasing real estate values, they were getting poorer.

Astonishingly, the net worth of most US households had gone down during the biggest boom in the nation's history. A University of Michigan study released in February 2000 determined that "the net worth of households headed by Americans under the age of 60 actually declined . . ." during the previous 10 years.

Households headed by older Americans got wealthier because those were the people who held most of the stocks and real estate. If the decade of the 1990s did anything, it boosted stock prices. But the next 3 years knocked down stock prices, which affected the over-60 households more than any others.

Americans did not make nearly as much from the bull market as they thought, either.[19] John Bogle, founder of the Vanguard group, interviewed in *Fortune* magazine at the end of 2002, explained that frequent trading by fund managers and high fees had reduced the average rate of return during the biggest bull market in history—1984 to 2001—to just 4.2% per year. This was a period in which the S&P rose 14.5% a year. If the results from 2002 had been included, he estimated that the average return from equity funds would have fallen to less than 3% per year—or lower than the inflation rate!

If they had bothered to look hard, Americans might have noticed that their economy was not making them as rich as they thought. This, too, was not a cyclical or accidental problem; it was a structural feature of their late, collective capitalism—the consequence of a half century of rising consumption. Instead of saving and investing in profitable new projects, Americans had chosen to live beyond their means. Now, the day of reckoning had come.

## ECONOMIC DEAD END

In America, a disturbing feature of the credit-led economy showed itself in the early 1960s: profits as a percentage of GDP had started heading down, and the current account deficit began heading up. Pretax profits, which were more than 9% of GDP in 1963, fell to less than 3% by the century's end. Why? Because there had been little capital investing that might actually create profits for investors or pay increases for workers. This partly explains why wages for manufacturing workers have gone nowhere in the past 30 years and why the average American has enjoyed only minimal increases in his income. The problem lies at the very deepest structure of the consumerist economy. Spending beyond your means does not produce economic perfection but an economic dead end, just as might have been predicted by a moral philosopher but missed by an economist.

But wasn't there a huge increase in capital spending in the late 1990s? It was widely thought that large amounts of money were being invested in new businesses and new technologies. And they were. But the investments took the peculiar direction dictated by US mass capitalism. Instead of investing in real projects that might produce real profits over the long haul, companies concentrated on financial engineering in order to produce short-term profits that would wow the *lumpeninvestoriat.* "A penny more than forecast" was the ideal earnings report of the last half of the last decade of the twentieth century. It did not seem to matter what was behind the numbers—no one bothered to look. Analysts rarely issued a "sell" signal or even questioned the companies' pro forma footnotes. Wall Street strategists rarely expected prices to go anywhere but up. Economists told investors that whatever price the market assigned to a stock must be the right price—the perfect price. And everyone was too busy making money to worry about it.

After the Nasdaq plummeted and the dust cleared, it became apparent that little actual money had been invested in new plants and equipment after all. Besides the investments in acquisitions, buybacks, IPOs, and mergers and so on . . . much of the money actually invested in technology was for projects that would never make a dime of profit. Offices were full of young programmers and dealmakers working for dot-com businesses. On paper, billions had been invested in the new technology—but it was largely worthless.

Also, the Bureau of Labor Statistics came up with an ingenious way of crunching the numbers that distorted them so badly even their own mothers never would have recognized them. As described earlier, the theory was that the Bureau should measure real output rather than nominal output. But when the concept was applied to information technology, where dramatic advances in computer processing were taking place, these hedonic measurements made it look as if huge amounts of money were being invested.

## JUST IN TIME

Actual business investment in plants and equipment was sinking, but one of the many conceits of the New Era was that it needed less capital than traditional business. The new economy was supposed to produce wealth with minimal investment. Businesses had discovered that "just-in time" inventory systems could reduce their capital requirements. They needed faith, of course. Supplies had to be there when they needed them or their factories would shut down.

Likewise, US consumers discovered that just in time worked for other things. They no longer needed to carry much cash in their wallets because ATM machines delivered currency whenever they needed it. Nor did they need to save money because what really mattered was cash flow. What point was there in having idle cash earning low rates of interest when the money could be working, either invested in the stock market or spent on something that you could enjoy? There was always cash available . . . from paychecks that came along just in time to pay the bills.

Besides, everybody knew that savings lost value over time. Better to take the money off the shelves and put it to use.

The just-in-time mentality seemed to work for everything. Jobs were plentiful. There would always be one when you needed it. Food too—who stocked food at home when the supermarkets and convenience stores would do it for you? Even stacks of wood seemed to go out of fashion in the late 1990s: there would always be someone who would deliver wood . . . or oil, gas, or electricity . . . just in time for when you needed it.

Just-in-time thinking encouraged a close look at a person's operating budget, but it neglected the balance sheet. It did not seem to matter how much of his house he had mortgaged, or how much he owed, as long as the cash was there to pay the bills. Of course, Americans did not save; there was no need to. Savings rates in the United States declined, not cyclically, but structurally. From a high of 10.9% in 1982, Americans stocked fewer and fewer dollar bills on their shelves, until, by the end of the 1990s, the savings rate had declined to less than 3%.

This just-in-time economy, at the end of 2001, was still widely saluted as the crown of economic creation. But its thorns were beginning to prick. Consumer debt as a percentage of GDP could not grow larger forever. Nor could a society expect to make economic progress without savings. Running down the savings rate had given the US economy the appearance of growth and prosperity, but how long could that go on? Deprived of real investment and saddled with relatively high labor costs, US businesses were becoming less profitable. How would they pay higher wages? Without higher wages, how could consumers continue spending?

The US economy, once famously rich in profits and growth, now depended on myths and lies—that the trends of the past half century would continue forever and that the US consumer (the consumer of last resort for the entire world) would continue going deeper and deeper into debt indefinitely.

When the slump began in 2001 and jobs were lost, little by little Americans began to ask themselves: will the cash really be there, just in time, when I need it? The baby boomers in particular, began to wonder if they would have enough money, just in time, to retire on. It was a trend hardly noticed at first, but while no one was looking, consumers began to set aside a little more money.

Against a backdrop of inducements to buy new cars at 0% financing or new homes with 100% mortgages and low monthly payments, savings rates began to rise ever so slightly (to 4% in the last quarter of 2002). Having leveraged themselves over a half century, Americans were beginning the long, slow, painful process of deleveraging themselves. "Just in time" was becoming "just in case."

## THE BALANCE SHEET RECESSION

As we forecasted in the first edition of this book, the recipe of tax cuts and low interest rates outlined by then-Governor Bernanke helped mutate a relatively harmless bubble in the market for tech stocks into a larger, all-encompassing bubble in housing, derivatives, and consumption. Unfortunately, the strategy merely postponed the day of reckoning for 6 years. Now, in the spring of 2009, the larger, all-encompassing housing and consumption bubble has popped. What's next? Look at Japan!

Richard C. Koo has prepared a remarkable report: "The Age of Balance Sheet Recessions: What Post-2008 US, Europe and China Can Learn from Japan 1990–2005."[20] His argument is not far from the one we made 6 years ago. In the 1980s, Japan ran up stock and property prices in a spree of debt and leverage. Then, when the bubble popped, the usual monetary stimulus didn't work. The Bank of Japan cut rates to almost zero . . . still, few people were willing to borrow.

The economy did not recover; instead, it got worse and worse until 2005—15 years later—when stocks had lost 72% of their value, land was down 81%, and golf course memberships had sunk 95% from their peak.

The problem, Koo explains, was that it was a "balance sheet recession," not a typical business cycle downturn. Companies, banks, and individuals had to pay down the debt that they had accumulated in the boom; they did not want to borrow more money, even at zero interest rates. For 7 years, from 1998 to 2005, net business borrowing went negative—meaning, businesses were paying off more debt than they were taking on.

This came as a shock to modern economists. Japanese officials were flummoxed. US economists accused them of not acting swiftly enough . . . or not having the stomach to let the big banks fail. But almost no one seemed to understand what was really going on. They should have. Irving Fisher described it back in 1933, observing that when people who are deeply in debt get into trouble they usually sell assets. Investors dump stocks and property for any price they can get—desperate to pay off their debts before they are dragged into bankruptcy.

This is the phenomenon known to economists as the "fallacy of composition." What is good for every individual investor—cutting expenses, paying off debt—turns out to be bad for the economy itself. Asset prices fall. Sales fall. Unemployment rises. The slump deepens.

In Japan's case, combined capital losses from land and stocks grew from 1990 until 2002, at which time they reached $15 trillion—or 3 years' worth of Japan's GDP.

You can do the math yourself, dear reader. The US GDP is about $14 trillion. Multiply that times three and you get $42 trillion. So far, the United States has lost about $4 or $5 trillion in housing prices . . . and maybe another $6 trillion in stocks, for a total of about $11 trillion, maximum. A long way to go . . .

Within the first few weeks of the election win, Obama was beginning to realize what he was up against. This was no ordinary cyclical downturn. Typically, a slump brings interest rates down. (Usually accompanied by central bank rate cuts.) Cheaper borrowing arouses business and speculative activity . . . which, in turn, tends to get the economy moving again.

That's not what was happening. In November 2008, authorities handed out money below the inflation rate and practically begged banks to lend. But who wants to lend when there's a danger you might not get your money back? And who wants to borrow when everyone is desperate to get out of debt?

The *Financial Times* announced that another 70,000 jobs could be lost on Wall Street.[21] Who needs so many employees when no one's doing any deals? No one's borrowing . . . no one's lending . . . investors are running scared . . . and private equity is curled up in a cave somewhere . . .

This is what happens in a balance sheet recession. It is not a regular, cyclical downturn. People have lost a lot of money . . . and they're afraid of losing more. So businesses begin cutting back as fast as they can. The job losses aren't limited to Wall Street. At the end of 2008, 10 million people were out of work—the most in 25 years . . . and unemployment was at a 14-year high.

Investors all over the planet were taking a beating. We point this out because in the spring of 2023, we have yet to see the true impacts of a recession spawned by inflation-fighting strategies conducted by central banks around the world.

In 2008–2009, Mr. Market had taken a cudgel to stocks, property, consumer spending, and the economy—just as he did in Japan during the "Lost Decade." People were afraid to lend and afraid to borrow; they worried that the money will be knocked senseless before it found its way home.

This time, the economy did not overheat . . . nor did labor rates go up. And when the bubble popped, the pin was not higher lending rates. This bust was caused by too much credit, not by too little. Now is the time when businesses, investors, and householders realize that if they don't cut back they could go broke.

And unlike the more typical recession, this is a slump the feds can't control and can't cure. They can offer easier credit, but more debt is just what both lenders and borrowers are most afraid of. The feds can offer more props, more handouts, and more public spending too, just like Japan. But all they are doing is retarding the correction. Mistakes of the bubble era need to be fixed. Balance sheets need to be brought back into balance. There's no way around it. Japan proved it.

Just a few months ago, investors reached for the highest yields they could get. Now, they fold their arms, clutching to their breasts the lowest-yielding paper on the planet. Once they believed in capitalism and its bonds. Now, they want nothing that does not have the seal of the US government on it. A few months ago, they saw no danger. Now, they see nothing else.

Everywhere, investment portfolios are being trimmed . . . cash is more than king; it has become a demi-god—this despite the fact that there are some great investment bargains around.

In 2009, stocks had been overpriced for 20 years. Suddenly, they weren't so overpriced. In fact, by almost any measure used, they became fairly reasonable. Compared to the yield from Treasury bonds, for example—a popular method of gauging the stock market—stocks look like a good deal. P/E ratios too were in the "normal" range.

But a balance sheet recession is an unforgiving, mean, and tenacious rascal. After such big losses, businesses, consumers, investors, and banks need to rebuild their balance sheets by paying off, defaulting on, or working out their debt. And then they need to rebuild their confidence . . . with rising asset prices and a growing economy. All that takes years . . . many years.

Worse, a balance sheet recession is like a straightjacket; the harder you fight against it, the tighter it gets. When government tries to prevent assets from being marked to market, for example, it delays and obstructs the process of adjustment. Rather than let the debts and mistakes be flushed out, they remain on balance sheets . . . blocking progress, frustrating change.

If "change is Nature's delight," as Marcus Aurelius put it, then trying to stop change—at least in a balance sheet recession—is Nature's horror. Balance sheets need to be corrected. Until they are corrected, future growth can't happen. So, the whole system is stymied, clogged, stopped up, constipated . . . like the US economy in the 1930s . . . or like Japan's economy in the 1990s.

## TOO SMALL TO BAIL

AIG was deemed "too big to fail," but Lehman Brothers investment bank was not so lucky.

In 1998, the New York Federal Reserve Bank called upon Lehman Bros. and a handful of other major players on Wall Street to rescue a high-flying hedge fund. The firms grumped and whined . . . but they came up with the money, $3.7 billion. The rescue was a success. LTCM's positions were unwound slowly; there was no panic; Wall Street soon went back to doing what it is supposed to do—separating customers from their money.

LTCM was run by a couple of Nobel Prize–winning economists who believed they could use past financial patterns to model the future, just as if price movements were the same as the weather. If a hurricane had hit Houston twice in the last century, they figured the odds that another hurricane would hit the city at 1 in 50. Likewise, if the price of Lehman stock traded between, say, $10 and $30 during its 158-year history, they figured—grosso modo—that it would stay between $10 and $30.

LTCM went bust when the future turned out to be different from the past. Anyone with his eyes open at the time could have told the Nobel laureates why: weather patterns were independent of human decisions; market patterns are not.

One of the big revelations of the 1990s—or was it the 1980s?—was that stocks were traditionally, historically underpriced. Compared to bonds, said a popular financial author, stocks were a better deal. Stock buyers earned a premium over bonds for the risk they undertook, he said. But if you held stocks "for the long run," the risk disappeared. Buying stocks seemed like a no-brainer.

Thus did the *lumpeninvestoriat* begin pumping money into stocks . . . cautiously in the beginning of the 1990s . . . and recklessly at the end of the decade. And by the year 2000, the stock market no longer reflected the "random" movement of prices as predicted by the previous hundred years of stock market history; instead, it reflected the recent and remarkable belief that stocks always went up . . . and that if an investor held stocks long enough, the risk disappeared.

From the peak of 2000 until 2009, stock market investors earned nothing for their trouble. In nominal terms, stocks dropped to a level they were 10 years before. Adjusted for inflation, they were down 25% to 80%, depending on how you measured it. That's a period of time we can learn from as the post-pandemic economy reels from inflation and consumers get tapped out. We can expect the return of a balance sheet recession. And a difficult decade for stocks.

In the first decade of the new millennium, Wall Street made a fortune selling stocks to naïve investors. When the stock marked topped out, the financial industry might have gone back to sleep. Instead, it got a double dose of caffeine. The Greenspan Fed cut rates in 2001–2002, while the Bush administration boosted spending and cut taxes. All of a sudden, every hand on Wall Street turned to pumping out credit—derivatives, SIVs, CDOs, MBS. They didn't really have to invent any new theories; they merely recycled the same numbskull ideas that sank LTCM—basically, that you could eliminate risk by modeling historic price movements. If Lehman Bros., for example, had never failed in more than a century and a half, the odds that it would fail were so close to zero as to be not worth discussing.

But in the fall of 2008, Lehman was failing. And no consortium of Wall Street banks were willing, or able, to bail it out. Lehman had some $80 billion of dubious credits. These were the products of its own—and many other—whiz kid financial engineers. Lehman hired some of the best talent on Wall Street. It had some of the world's top financial mathematicians on its payroll. It could compute the risk of loss down to 3 . . . 4 . . . heck . . . as many decimal places as you like. But it could do so only as LTCM did—based on past history.

And so, on September 16, 2008, Lehman filed the biggest bankruptcy in Wall Street history with $613 billion in debt.[22]

The handwriting has been on the wall for a long time. Once its collateral began to go down in 2007, the bubble in the financial industry couldn't last long.

But all good things must come to an end . . . especially things that are too good to be true. The great bubble in credit popped—and everyone began squawking. Lehman Bros. became the poster child for the Financial Panic of 2008. We learned even a venerable Wall Street firm with a sterling pedigree could crumble quickly. A year before it went bust, investors had an asset worth $45 billion. Now they have nothing. What happened to that $45 billion? It disappeared.

But what's really new? This is what always happens when boom turns to bust. Asset values disappear. And with them, the money supply itself contracts. People spend less freely. They lend less recklessly. More money stays tucked away for longer periods in pockets and bank accounts. Prices fall. Many assets turn out to be worthless, and many people go broke.

## Built on Bad Loans

But, of course, lessons are not learned until it is too late. As the housing bubble began to deflate, US financial institutions began to struggle. (See Figure 10.1.)

It looked like bankruptcy was imminent for Countrywide Financial. Flourishing only months before, the country's largest mortgage lender found itself in deep trouble—and lax lending standards were far and away to blame. The lender saw a spike in mortgage defaults and foreclosures especially in subprime mortgages, which was too much to shoulder.

Bank of America swooped in and bought Countrywide for $4.1 billion in stock in January 2008.[23]

More than a full year later, Countrywide was still making headlines. On June 4, 2009, word came that the Securities and Exchange Commission had filed fraud charges against former Countrywide CEO Angelo Mozilo and two other individuals. Turns out Mozilo et al. misled investors about the mortgage lender's health. Mozilo pocketed $140 million from insider trades.[24]

As the year went on, more and more lenders went the way of Countrywide, buckling under the burden of bad loans. IndyMac, an offshoot of Countrywide, was seized by federal regulators on July 11, 2008. The *New York Times* reported that the debacle could cost the FDIC as much as $8 billion—and shareholders were all but wiped out. What had happened was no big surprise: "Executives at IndyMac, like many people on both Wall Street and Main Street, apparently never dreamed home prices might fall. To the contrary, IndyMac made many loans on terms that implicitly assumed prices would keep rising," reports the *New York Times*.[25]

IndyMac would have been the biggest bank failure in history—that is, until Washington Mutual came along. WaMu is also a prime example of a bank built on bad loans. The bank fell victim to the

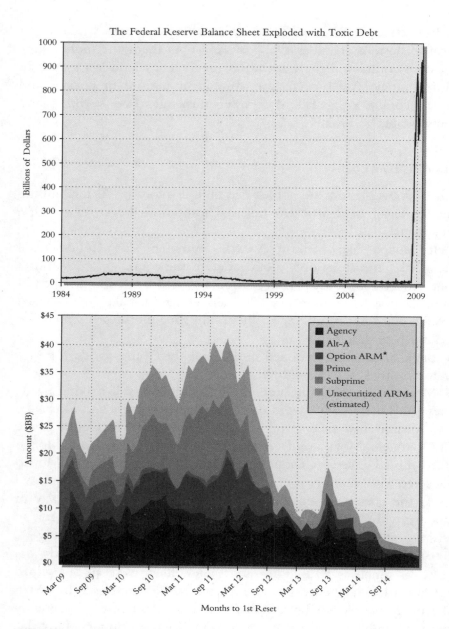

**FIGURE 10.1**   Lender of Last Resort

In the fall of 2008, the Federal Reserve responded to the banking crisis by buying up mortgage-backed securities, making its own balance sheet balloon with toxic debt. And yet the epicenter of the crisis—bad mortgages of all exotic varieties—were expected to continue defaulting at a breathtaking pace for another 4 years.

**\*Option ARMs show estimated recast schedule based on current neg-am rate.**

*Source:* Credit Suisse (US Mortgage Strategy), LoanPerformance, FH/FN/GN.

subprime fallout. With about $310 billion in assets, WaMu was seized by federal regulators and then acquired by J.P. Morgan Chase for $1.9 billion.[26]

Following the fall of Washington Mutual, there were 48 bank failures in the United States (as of June 1, 2009). By 2015, that number had climbed to more than 400.

Banks weren't the only American institutions staggering toward insolvency during the credit crisis. In June 2009, General Motors, once the backbone of US manufacturing, went officially bankrupt.[27] It was a shame, really. The company was set up in 1916. If it had been able to hold together for another 7 years, it would have gone 100 years without having to declare bankruptcy.

All people die. All companies die too. That's why "buy and hold" is wishful thinking. Buy and hold long enough and you are sure to go broke. And die.

Eventually the undertakers and bankruptcy lawyers get you. And business is good in Detroit. What cleared the way for the GM bankruptcy was a deal with the bondholders . . . in which they take equity in exchange for their debt and agree not to contest the bankruptcy filing. Still, the deal—and other deals relating to it . . . including the presence of one very big and very odd shareholder, the government of the United States—is so complicated, it's bound to give bankruptcy lawyers plenty of work for many years.

Lord knows GM couldn't just be a run-of-the-mill insolvency. The Obama administration had its hands deep in the thing . . . here's the fine print of the second largest industrial bankruptcy in US history:

- Uncle Sam got a 60% stake. The government pumped an additional $30 billion into GM (on top of the $20 billion already squandered). In exchange, the government became the largest shareholder. . . leverage it would use to usher GM through bankruptcy and convert it to a "leaner, stronger company."
- Half of the UAW's $20 billion healthcare fund was converted to GM stock, which gave it a 17.5% stake in the company; 12–20 factories were closed, at the cost of approximately 21,000 union workers. Of the 6,000 GM dealers, 40% were closed too.
- The Canadian government got a 12% stake, given all GM's design/manufacturing activity up north.

- Bondholders were bought (bullied?) out. They swapped their $27.1 billion in unsecured debt for 10% of GM, with warrants to own 15% more. Surely, they learned from Chrysler's bond-holders, who were publicly vilified by President Obama for demanding what was lawfully theirs . . . so much for that hall-mark of American capitalism.
- Existing shareholders got nada. At least that rule of bankruptcy is still intact. "If you were long GM," we advised at the time, "please consider letting someone else manage your money. Anyone."[28]

The French nationalized their auto companies after the war. Then, when the socialists took control of the government in the 1980s, they nationalized the banks too. "Silly frogs," said US economists. "Don't they know that a free market works best?" And so you see, dear reader, in all time zones and all languages, people are the same—always hus-tling up something for nothing, whenever they can get away with it.

## A CLASSIC SUCKER'S RALLY

After months of the markets in a free-fall, in the spring of 2009, something remarkable happened: the money began flowing again. People thought they saw a bottom.

"Cramer: The Depression is over," says a headline.[29] *Mad Money's* Jim Cramer says the bottom has come and gone. That's all we need to know. If Cramer thinks the worst is over . . . well, it must be so.

Even Nouriel Roubini, according to *Forbes,* saw a "light at the end of the tunnel."[30]

"Bernanke Sees Hopeful Signs," read the headline in the *New York Times.*

"Ben S. Bernanke, the chairman of the Federal Reserve, said the economic free fall of the last nine months was nearing an end and that the United States should begin a fragile recovery by the end of this year."[31]

Is this good news? Or what? "Or what" is our bet.

Can the feds now fix the trouble they never saw coming? Can the people who ran banks into the ground now run the banks that will help finance the recovery? Can the investors who bought trashy investments with borrowed money now recognize the good investments that are put in front of them?

Neither Ben Bernanke, Tim Geithner, Hank Paulson, nor Alan Greenspan could see it—but there was something clearly wrong with the Bubble Economy of 2001–2007. We said so many times.

"Good riddance," we celebrated, when it keeled over.

But now they struggle to revive it. Like a brain-dead codger on life support, they are bankrupting the next generation trying to keep it alive.

"We expect that the recovery will only gradually gain momentum," Bernanke forecast, trying to manage expectations, "and that the economic slack will diminish slowly."[32]

Really? Oh, the wonders of modern medicine. Now, with 20/20 vision, the Fed chief can look ahead and tell us what will happen next. If only he'd gone to the doctor 2 years ago!

Stocks are rallying all over the world. Economists are putting on their spectacles and looking to the future. Bankers are cashing their checks and laughing all the way home from work.

"That sense of unremitting free fall we had a month or two ago is not present today," says White House economic advisor Larry Summers.[33]

*Barron's* Big Money Poll showed professional portfolio managers were bullish again. They were looking for the Dow to gain 7% in 2009 . . . and 17% by the middle of 2010.[34]

This was good news for us. We were beginning to look around and notice that too many stupid people agreed with us. But now that we see the pros are in the opposite camp . . . we can sleep more soundly.

The proximate cause of all this optimism was the vigor with which the people who didn't see the problem coming have gone about fighting it. Mr. Market may taketh away . . . but Mr. Federal Official putteth back. At least, that's the logic of it. In the end, the United States alone earmarked a sum nearly three times the cost of fighting World War II. Not all of that was direct cash outlays. Much of it was in the form of financial "guarantees" and "investments" (such as buying up Wall Street's smelly derivatives). Even then, it was a lot of money.

In the years ahead, we'll see this rush to bailout become the norm. Funny, what we're willing to adapt to if the conditions are right.

Normally, in a correction, the supply of money—M1—falls. Asset values are destroyed . . . borrowers default . . . money disappears into vaults and mattresses. But this time, so vigorous had been the authorities' response that M1 actually increased at about a 14% annual rate. The money had got to go somewhere.

Japan announced another $100 billion stimulus program in April 2009.[35] That should do the trick. After 17 years of bailouts and stimulus programs, the Japanese should be getting good at them. But it's a little like a guy who's getting good at suicide—if he's so good at it, you'd think he'd be dead by now.

But no . . . the Japanese economy was still one of the worst performers in the world; their bailouts and stimuli did no good . . . maybe they've even made the situation worse.

No matter, there's a rally on . . . this is not the time to ask questions. Our instinct tells us this rally is going to carry the Dow back above 9,000 . . . possibly above 10,000. Why? Because people do not go directly from believing nothing can go wrong to believing that nothing can go right. (See Figure 10.2.)

The kind of delusional optimism that took stocks up over 14,000 on the Dow . . . and doubled property prices . . . and had sober bankers buying billions' worth of ticking debt bombs doesn't disappear overnight. It has to be killed like Rasputin—many times. Stab it. Shoot it. And then douse it with gasoline and set it on fire. Maybe then, it will finally die.

That's why this rally is just a trap for the unwary . . . a suckers' rally. Investors are getting back on their feet just so Mr. Market can whack them again. So, if you're playing this rally . . . be sure to keep those stops moving up behind your stocks.

This rally recovered less than 20% of the previous losses. Typically, at least one good rally in a bear market will recover more than half of the losses. Looking at the long term, the Dow rose from the low in the early 1930s of only 41 points to the high in 2007, when it was over 14,000 points. The bear market wiped out more than half of the capital gains made by investors during that whole 76-year period. A 50% bounce from the January 2009 low would put the Dow back up close to 10,000.

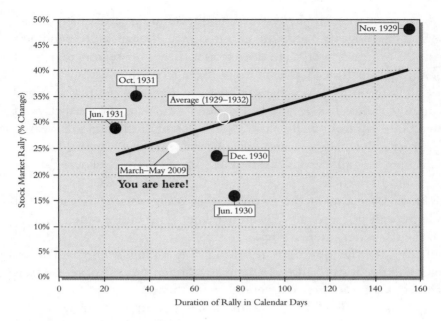

**FIGURE 10.2** A Classic Sucker's Rally

Markets don't go smoothly in any one direction—up or down. During the Great Depression the Dow rallied 15% or more at least five times. The rallies lasted as many as 180 days. Some even longer. After a long slow trudge—and a world war—the market finally began rising again in the 1950s.

*Source*: chartoftheday.com.

Bulls, bears, spenders, savers—in a sucker's rally Mr. Market paddles them all. And yet, with the feds on the case, investors came back into the market. The banks were flush with money again. What could go wrong?

Why . . . everything . . . of course!

## HEARTS AND MINDS

The sucker's rally itself is a part of a larger battle between two contradictory body parts—the heart and the mind. The heart wants to believe that the worst is over. It reacts sentimentally, remembering the glory days of the great bubble era and wishing they were back. For example, higher consumer confidence readings will send the stock market higher—in this case, the heart ruled.

But then comes the head's turn. The head looks at the facts: housing and employment are still going down. People will spend less money. Businesses will make less money. Ergo, no reason to expect stocks to go up. Instead, they're more likely to go down.

The head noticed too, that the Treasury market is getting slammed by higher yields. The long bond yielded 4.56% in the final days of May 2009—up from well below 3% at the end of the previous year.

"Treasury yields give cause for concern," says the *Financial Times*.[36]

"Rising Treasury yields threaten to stifle economic recovery," continues another article.[37]

But has the top of the bond market really passed? Is the credit cycle now in full retreat? Will homeowners and businessmen be tortured with higher interest rates?

Those are the questions the head was asking yesterday. And it didn't like the answers. If there were any "green shoots" of recovery, it reasoned, higher interest rates could crush them.

And then at least a few heads began thinking about what this meant to the big strategic issues . . . and how this all will turn out.

At the end of 2008, America's great buddy, China, changed its policy. Instead of buying long-dated US debt, China began buying the short stuff. China's top man openly wondered whether the United States would be able to protect the value of the dollar and keep its promises to foreign lenders.

"We have a huge amount of money in the United States," said China's premier. He reminded the United States that China had entrusted a lot of its wealth to US paper and went on to request that the United States respect its obligations to bond buyers. Obviously, the Chinese must wonder if the United States is capable of protecting its currency while still funding its war against deflation.[38]

Tim Geithner promptly responded. "Yes we can!" But the Chinese cogitated on the matter . . . "No they can't," they began to think.

Then, they switched to buying short-term US debt, leaving the longer-term bonds to other buyers. (See Figure 10.3.) Since the Chinese were the biggest buyers at US Treasury debt auctions, this switch in policy had a quick and noticeable effect. Bills rose. Bonds fell. The yield on bills fell to below zero, while the yield on the 30-year bond has gone steadily up. On June 1, 2009, when Mr. Geithner told a group of students at Peking University that the Chinese investment in

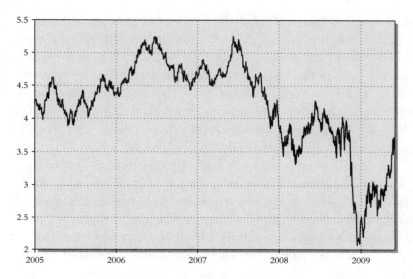

**FIGURE 10.3** A Bubble in Bonds

At one point during the fall of 2008, investors were willing to take a negative yield on US Treasuries, meaning they were willing to pay the government to keep their money safe from carnage in the stock market. This overinvestment in treasuries will unwind itself in as dramatic a fashion as it wound up.

US Treasuries was safe, the auditorium erupted in laughter. The event was barely mentioned in the US press.[39]

Still, if US supply lines to cheap credit have been cut, she is at a great strategic disadvantage. Or rather, her preexisting strategic disadvantage is becoming more apparent: she depends on foreigners just to be able to continue living in the style to which she has become accustomed. As Barack Obama acknowledged: "We're out of money now."[40]

In the fall of 2023, we're again experiencing a surge in Treasury yields as the government seeks to fund operations. The Fed's aggressive efforts to rein in inflation have resulted in a tenuous environment. Fears of a wider economic recession remain.

## AN AVALANCHE OF CLAPTRAP

Illusions pile up. They're sure to come down sooner or later.

Like snow at high altitudes, the central banks' new money is piling up. At the end of May 2009, all the world's major central banks turned on their snow machines. The Federal Reserve was authorized to "print" $1.75 trillion worth of new money in order to buy Treasury bonds. The Bank of England began its own program—worth 75 billion pounds, so far. Even Switzerland was printing money—so much that its money supply, as measured by M2, was growing at 30% per year. In addition, the European Central Bank announced that it too would begin creating money in order to buy corporate bonds.

This, you recall, is referred to as "quantitative easing"—how central banks describe what is essentially an act of counterfeiting. They buy bonds with money created—electronically—specifically for that purpose. Abracadabra—"money" comes into being.

The feds aim to provide liquidity for the cities and farms. But so far, only a trickle is coming down. Instead, chilly weather in the upper reaches of the financial sector holds it frozen in place. Hundreds of billions comes down from central banks, but there it stays . . . waiting for spring.

The feds' counterfeit money does such a good imitation of the real thing, you can't tell them apart. But the problem with all money is that it is as fickle and unreliable as a bad girlfriend. One minute she goes along with the flow. The next minute she turns silly and bubbly. And then, she gives you the cold shoulder.

According to theory, an increase in the supply of something leads directly to a decrease in the price of it . . . That is, if other things remain constant. Despite the credit crunch, the banking freeze-up, and the economic recession, the money supply in the United States as measured by M1 is actually rising at 14% per year. Yet consumer prices are not keeping pace. The latest report shows them actually going down slightly in the spring of 2009.

Turns out, causing inflation is not as easy as it looked; controlling it probably will be even harder. It's not enough to manage the quantity of money; you also need to be able to control its behavior. Money can be a solid, a liquid, or a gas depending upon the temperature of the economy. At normal temperatures, money runs freely, watering the economy. And when things really get hot, it vaporizes, creating gaseous bubbles such as those of the late Bubble Period. But when the temperature falls, money shivers in wallets and bank accounts—reluctant to go out into the cold. Economists refer to the "velocity of money" to describe the magnifying effects of motion. When the same dollar bill appears in three different places in the same day, it is as if the money supply had been multiplied threefold. In a freeze, on the other hand, it comes to a dead stop.

When the thaw will come, we don't know. But the authorities are ready for it. When consumer prices begin to rise, they'll stop adding to the money supply. Then, they'll withdraw liquidity, as need be, to keep it under control.

They know that runaway inflation would cause problems—the collapse of the dollar . . . and the US Treasury bond market, for example. So, at the first signs of inflation, they will move quickly to remove excess liquidity from the system. How? Their emergency plan is simple enough. Now, they are buying bonds. When their inflation targets are met, they will begin selling them.

We thought the Bubble Epoch was the peak in claptrap and illusions. But we were only in the foothills. The feds now pretend to bail out the economy by giving money to companies that pretend to be concerned, run by people who pretend to know what they are doing. And when they run short of money, they create more of it, pretend it is real . . . and pretend they can tell it what to do.

What is likely is that money will have a mind of its own. First, the markets will react . . . and the authorities will not. They will remember their own critiques of Japanese and Roosevelt-era monetary policy. In both cases, they believe central banks removed the punch bowl too early—before the party really got rolling. In both cases, the recovery was cut off.

Then, while they are hesitating, money will turn on them. Inflation rates will rise further. The velocity of money will pick up. And investors, including foreign governments, will become eager sellers of government debt. Suddenly, it will be too late. In order to remove the monetary inflation they previously added, central banks will have to sell bonds instead of buying them, trying to reabsorb money from the economy. The extra cash would then disappear back into the central banks. But in order to bring inflation under control, the biggest bond buyers in the world must turn into the world's biggest sellers. Bond prices, already falling as investors feared the worst, will collapse immediately. An avalanche of dollars will fall upon the world markets—as dollar holders all over the world become desperate to get rid of them.

We don't know what day it will happen. But we have a good idea as to what time of day central bankers will realize that they are doomed. About 4 a.m. is our guess. That is the moment when Bernanke and other central bankers begin to feel like members of the Donner Party. That is, like imbeciles.

And at no other time have we edged up to that precipice like we did a decade and a half ago. The affects could be felt and seen for years. Zero interest rate policies (ZIRP) and rounds of quantitative easing (QE) fundamentally changed the structure of Wall Street and policies enacted by central banks the world over. You can draw a straight line from the credit bubble bust in 2008 to the inflationary bonfire of 2021–2022.

# CHAPTER 11

# THE PARTY AT THE END OF THE WORLD

Of course, what the majority of people don't realize is that this is the way real capitalism works. It goes from crisis to crisis . . . from creative boom to creative destruction. From fully functioning, liquid markets to markets as frozen solid as the polar ice cap in the days before global warming. From boom to bust . . . from profit to loss . . . from wealth to poverty . . . By studying the creative and destructive booms and busts of the past, we have a greater chance of understanding how trends in the present will play out. "That is . . . until the central banks step in."

The boom is fine, they say, but we'll put a stop to those nasty busts. How? By providing more credit! By buying up the securities that free-market players didn't want—including subprime-backed mortgages. By injecting billions of dollars into the system.

Here, readers may already be suspicious.

"Now wait a minute," they may be saying to themselves. "Wasn't this whole problem caused by too much liquidity in the first place? Isn't more liquidity going to make the situation worse?"

Bingo!

What a joy it is to watch central bankers at work! They are charged with keeping this great modern, capitalist economy going. In practice, that means keeping the bubble in speculative finance from deflating too fast. Of course, the bubble is largely the central bankers own making—a direct consequence of the liquidity they injected after 9/11 . . . and the subsequent EZ credit conditions throughout the world economy.

But even so, Ben Bernanke and the whole company of central bankers from Tokyo to London to New York got to work making sure that the bubble got enough hot air.

The world as we have known it is coming to an end. But what do we care? We smile and vow to enjoy it. It took the Roman Empire hundreds of years to fall. During that time, most people did not even know their world was coming to an end. Most must have gone about their business, planting their crops, drinking their wine, and bouncing their children on their knees, as if the empire were eternal. Of course, the mobs in Rome may have reeled and wailed with every news flash: the barbarians had crossed the river Po and were headed South—soon, they would be at the gates!

But others lived quiet lives of desperation and amusement—as if nothing had happened. And what could they have done about it anyway . . . except get out of harm's way and tend to their own affairs?

Plenty of people enjoyed the Great Depression. If you had a well-paying job, it must have been paradise—no waiting in lines, no need for a reservation at good restaurants. Keeping up with the Joneses had never been easier—because the Joneses were in reverse. So much of the satisfaction in life comes from feeling superior to other people. What better time than a depression to enjoy it?

The secret to enjoying all mass movements is to be a spectator, not a participant. How much better it would have been to wave at the passing of the Grande Armée on its way to destruction in Russia than to march along with them. Perhaps you could have sold them ear-muffs and mittens!

Likewise, what better way to enjoy the great boom on Wall Street of the 1990s than by tuning in to CNBC from time to time just to see what absurd thing analysts would say next? And now that it is over, how better to enjoy it than from a safe distance, standing well clear of the exits?

Readers are urged to be suspicious of headlines in the news and opinions on the editorial pages. Almost all mass movements that they stir up will one day be regarded with regret and amazement.

But that is the way of the world; one madness leads to the next. A man feels excited and expansive because the economy is said to be in the midst of a New Era . . . and then he feels a little exhausted when he discovers that the New Era has been followed by a New Depression. And all the while, his life goes on exactly as it had before. His liquor is no better, his wife no prettier or uglier, his work every bit as insipid or inspiring as it was before. We have no complaint about it. Still, "the world is too much with us," wrote Emerson:

> Most men have bound their eyes with one or another handker-chief, and attached themselves to some one of these communities of opinion. This conformity makes them not false in a few particu-lars, authors of a few lies, but false in all particulars. Their every truth is not quite true. Their two is not the real two, their four not the real four; so that every word they say chagrins us, and we know not where to begin to set them right. Meantime nature is not slow to equip us in the prison-uniform of the party to which we adhere. We come to wear one cut of face and figure, and acquire by degrees the gentles' asinine expression . . .

What better time to shut out the world and wipe that silly grin off our face than now—when the world that we have known for at least three decades, the Dollar Standard period, is coming to an end?

US consumer capitalism is doomed, we think. If not, it ought to be. The trends that could not last forever seem to be coming to an end. Consumers cannot continue to go deeper into debt. Consumption cannot continue to take up more and more of the GDP. Capital investment and profits cannot go down much further. Foreigners will not continue to finance Americans' excess consumption until the Second Coming—at least not at the current dollar price. And fiat paper money will not continue to outperform the real thing—gold—forever.

The United States will have to find a new economic model, for it can no longer hope to spend and borrow its way to prosperity. This is not a cyclical change, but a structural one that will take a long time. Structural reforms—that is, changing the way an economy functions—do not happen overnight. The machinery of collectivized capitalism resists change of any sort. The Fed tries to buoy the old model with cheaper and cheaper money. Government comes forward with multibillion-dollar spending programs to try to simulate real demand. And the poor *lumpeninvestoriat*—bless their greedy little hearts—will never give up the dream of US consumer capitalism; it will have to be crushed out of them.

As Paul Volcker put it, "It will all have to be adjusted someday." Why not enjoy it?

## THE TRADE OF THE DECADE(S)

Investors do not need to make many decisions. Studies have shown that allocation decisions are what make or lose the most money. Individual choices—selecting individual stocks or bonds—do not seem to make much difference in the long run. But deciding which market to be in and when—makes all the difference in the world.

An investor would have done well, over the past 30 years, to pay attention to his investments on the first day of each decade . . . and otherwise ignore the whole subject. He could have made three simple decisions and turned an original grubstake of $10,000 into $268,300.

Think how his life would have been better! Instead of spending hours with CNBC, *Money*, the internet, and all the other enticements of the financial press, he could have gone fishing or read the classics. Think how much better off he would have been without the noise and information of the mass media.

All he had to do was recognize that in cutting the link to gold in the early 1970s, the Nixon administration practically guaranteed inflation and a higher gold price. Gold traded at an average of $36 per ounce in 1970. Ten years later, the same ounce of gold sold for $615. With no leverage, no stocks, no research, no headaches, and little risk, he would have made a profit of 1,708%. And he would have paid not a penny of tax on his investment during the entire period.

But then, on January 1, 1980, things changed. Our investor should have taken note that nothing lasts forever and that there was a new man at the Fed. Paul Volcker meant business. He would drive down inflation rates—and gold—one way or another. It was time to sell. But where to put the money?

He might not have noticed—they do not advertise these things—but Japan, Inc., was extremely energetic in the early 1980s. He could not have known at the time, but had he bought Japanese stocks, he would have seen his fortune multiply again. The Nikkei 225 index rose from 5,994 at the end of January 1980 to 38,916 at the end of 1989—an increase of 549%.

It was important not to open a paper to the financial section during the last years of the 1980s. The news from Japan was so absurd, a US investor would have wanted to sell too soon. But, if he had looked at the facts on New Year's Day, 1990, he would have seen it was time for a change.

On that day, he should have brought his money home to the United States and invested it in US stocks. At 12.4 times earnings, with the Dow at 2,586, American equities were a good deal. Besides, there were 78 million baby boomers ready to spend and invest as never before . . . and a friend at the Fed, Alan Greenspan, ready to make sure they had the money to do it with. Over the next 10 years, the Dow rose to 11,041, for another 426% profit.

By January 2000, that trend had run its course too. What would be the Trade of the Decade for the next 10 years? For all the reasons given in this book, we think it will be to sell the Dow and buy gold. In the first three years—2000 to 2003—gold rose from $282 to $342. The Dow, meanwhile, fell—from 11,522 on January 7, 2000, to 8,740 three years later. Our investor was already ahead 2,683%. (See Figure 11.1.)

As we pointed out earlier, the day of reckoning we thought was coming during "the recession that wasn't" in 2001–2002 was merely postponed 6 years. Should you stay with our trade of the decade? Should we go for two? We honestly don't know. But gold as it stands is more of an insurance policy against financial collapse.

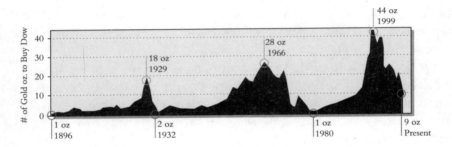

**FIGURE 11.1**   The Trade of the Decade

Priced in ounces of gold the Dow has historically reverted to the mean following periods of intense speculation in stocks. The trade of the decade—sell stocks, buy gold—still has some legs in it yet.

Gold continued its historic run, cresting at $2,499 in 2011. The zero interest rate years were not as good to the price of gold. By November 2015, it had lost nearly half of the 2011 high, dropping to $1,360. But as it turned out, that would have been a great time to buy. By 2020, during the shock and awe of pandemic lockdowns, gold regained its luster, shooting back up to $2,314. It has been trading at or above $2,000 ever since.

## ADVICE TO THE CLASS OF 2023

So far, not a single major university has asked us to make the commencement address. Nor a minor college. Not even a school of cosmetology or taxidermy. But as we write from London, protected by a broad ocean and a narrow reading of the First Amendment, we will give them advice no one asked for.

"Plastics" was the advice given to college graduates in Mike Nichols' 1967 film *The Graduate*. But that was when there was still hope for the US manufacturing sector. Even then, it was too late. The percentage of GDP from the manufacturing sector fell for the next four decades, from more than 20% at the end of the 1960s to barely 12% in 2008. Better advice would have been "derivatives." They stank just as bad, but they were much more profitable. Although only 8% of GDP, finance accounted for 40% of corporate profits in 2007. And derivatives grew from nothing to a face value of 16 times the GDP of the entire planet.

But your elders are always giving you bum advice.

"You cannot decline the burdens of empire and still expect to share its honors," said Pericles to the class of 430 B.C. He lived during a time not unlike your parents' era in the United States—when Athens was on top of the world. But vanity got the better of him. He launched an attack on Sparta that backfired badly. He soon died of plague, and Athens was not only ruined, but enslaved. Athens' "golden age" turned to lead. Young Athenians should have shrugged off the burden rather than accepted it. You should do the same.

When you were born 20-some years ago, the nation's total debt per person was less than $90,000—adjusted to 2009 dollars, of course. Although that was a lot of money, it was nothing compared to what was coming. Now it's $186,717 per person—more than twice as much, in real terms. Fortunately, private debt is not inheritable. But it comes to you as a lien against property. Instead of paying off their mortgages and leaving you a house, free and clear, the baby boomer generation spent the "equity" in their houses even faster than they got it. House prices rose. But mortgage debt rose faster. Although your grandparents owned 80% of their houses, by 2007, the typical homeowner only really owned four rooms of an eight-room house. And then, when house prices fell, so did his remaining equity . . . to the point where one out of six homeowners in the United States is now underwater. You could still eventually inherit a house, but you may have to scrape the barnacles off the front porch.

But that's not even the half of it. Although your parents had control of the US government, they allowed themselves a little larceny. Add the unfunded retirement and healthcare benefits they voted for themselves to the official national debt, and together they are scheduled to cost your generation four times the total annual output of the United States. This is over and above the private debt they accumulated.

Some of this debt can be carried. Some will have to be paid down. But as it stands, as much as $77 trillion of post-2009 earnings must be stolen from the future in order to pay for the liquor your parents drank . . . the bombs they dropped on god-forsaken foreigners . . . and the interest on their debts. So, forget about saving for a European vacation or a house of your own. Even if every penny of your savings—and every other American's savings—are put to the task you will still be paying for your parents' expenses all your life.

But wait, there's more! The burden is getting heavier. Federal budget projections show an additional $7 trillion in deficits over the next 10 years. Described as the cost of fighting recession, the present generation buries its own mistakes under cash that the next generation hasn't even earned yet. Today's bankers, businessmen, and speculators are being bankrolled by you—tomorrow's bankers, businessmen, and speculators. Today's homeowners get a helping hand . . . from whom? Tomorrow's homeowners—you. Today's employees get a boost too. Same story. Where do you think the money came from to pay Wall Street bonuses? How do you think GM stays in business . . . and Fannie Mae . . . and AIG? Who pays those salaries? Who pays to keep troops all over the world and keep old people supplied with new drugs? Who pays for hundreds of billions' worth of "shovel-ready" boondoggles? You will. At least, that's the plan.

## THE NEXT TRADE OF THE DECADE

We've been lucky with our "Big Bets" over the last three decades. Together, they would have multiplied your wealth about six times over the last 20 years. That doesn't seem like much, if you compare it to Tesla, Nvidia, or Bitcoin. But all of those are far more speculative bets based on growth, not value. Any of these could have gone to zero. There was no way, on the other hand, that gold or all Japanese stocks were going to zero.

And so, here it is again . . . a new decade. What to buy now? What to sell? We only do this once every 10 years, so we have to get it right. When we first started planning our big bet for the decade, we didn't account for a war started by one of the world's largest oil producing countries.

Before the war in Ukraine, Russia pumped out close to 11 million barrels of oil per day (mbpd). As global demand recovered from the financial crisis, oil prices stayed high until 2014—at which point the investment boom of the previous 10 years (especially in fracking) brought so much new supply on-line that prices fell.

Never say never, the saying goes. But it's unlikely you'll see negative oil prices again anytime soon. Over the next 10 years—and largely because of the underinvestment of the last 10 years—we expect prices to be high. Demand will grow. Supply will struggle to keep up. And renewable alternatives (or the much-vaunted "energy transition" to electric) will not live up to the marketing hype.

Here's the deal: we live in a culture in which all of our institutions—government, corporate, sports, entertainment, media—are increasingly politicized. It would be a mistake to underestimate just how difficult life could get for the oil and gas industry in the next few years, even with the current energy price spike and war-time conditions.

But in our big bet, we're willing to claim that markets are ahead of politics and that demand could surge as the tentacles of the pandemic finally recede. Value, emerging markets, and real asset plays will see a big rotation of investor money as growth, momentum, and renewables stocks fall off their highs.

This is not a complicated Trade of the Decade: Buy oil and gas. Sell the US dollar. Don't misunderstand us. Renewables will increase their share of electricity generation in the coming years. But they can't fully replace coal and gas anytime soon. This gap can only currently and immediately be filled by oil, gas, and coal.

The SPDR S&P Oil and Gas Exploration and Production ETF (XOP) is an ETF that tracks the underlying index of the same name. Its major holdings are companies like Phillips 66, Devon Energy, ExxonMobil, Valero Energy, ConocoPhillips, and Chevron.

There are other ways to play rising energy prices, even with exchange-traded funds. XOP has about $2.3 billion in assets under management. XLE, the Energy Select Sector SPDR ETF, has $13.6 billion. But 45% of its holdings are in just two companies, ExxonMobil and Chevron. XOP just spreads your risk around a bit more. Vanguard and iShares also have various ETF offerings around the energy sector. The goal here is simple: find something that tracks oil and gas producers without a big management fee or unnecessary exposure to smaller producers and explorers. XOP fits that bill.

As we know, for a Trade of the Decade you don't have to pay too much attention to the price action on a week-to-week or even month-to-month basis. You just have to decide if we're right about the long-term analysis.

We'll have to learn to use energy more efficiently or get used to much lower real growth, which makes sense for a world that's already "brought forward" so much growth through debt. It also makes sense

for a world that's aging and in which technology is inherently deflationary for most wages and prices.

Our Trade of the Decade isn't a bet that oil and gas are infinite
resources. But it is a bet that their economic scarcity is more important than their physical scarcity. Maybe it will be the last boom, using
technology and capital to squeeze out every last drop of the world's
high-density energy.

The luck of one generation is the curse of the next. Like Pericles,
your parents inherited a dollar; they leave you a peso. They took over
the strongest, richest, most competitive nation in the world. And like
Pericles they minded everyone's business but their own. Now, not
only does the United States owe money all over town, its government puts out trillions more in IOUs every year—each one with
your name on it. You're not even out in the real world yet, and you're
getting the bill for 50 cents of every dollar the feds spend—almost
none of it earmarked for you. But that is the thing about the real
world your teachers probably forgot to tell you about. It is more
unreal and fantastical than anything you studied.

Here's what's real: You've been dealt a bad hand. From the bottom
of the deck . . . your parents have slipped you some nasty cards. Our
advice? Fold 'em. Get up from the table before they clean you out.

# NOTES

## INTRODUCTION: HELL IN A BUCKET

1. The Treasury department records show that since 1960, Congress has acted 78 separate times to permanently raise, temporarily extend, or revise the definition of the debt limit—49 times under Republican presidents and 29 times under Democratic presidents. https://home.treasury.gov/policy-issues/financial-markets-financial-institutions-and-fiscal-service/debt-limit#:~:text=Since%201960%2C%20Congress%20has%20acted,29%20times%20under%20Democratic%20presidents.

## CHAPTER 1: THE OLD "NEW ECONOMY"

1. We provide an in depth overview of the history and influence of the dollar on the global economy in our companion book, *Demise of the Dollar*.
2. "The Future of Fed Is Data-Driven," tylertech. Available from https://www.tylertech.com/resources/resource-downloads/the-future-of-fed-is-data-driven.

3. Moore passed away on March 24, 2023, while we were writing this edition of *Financial Reckoning Day*. We mean only to recognize and observe his contribution to the modern economy we inhabit and with which we must live.

4. It's worth pointing out, since becoming friends with George, even serving as his publisher for a number of years. During that time, we had one of our analysts "do price."

5. See article by George Gilder and Bret Swanson, "Metcalfe's Exaflood," *Shalom Equity Fund Newsletter* (June 26, 2001). Available from www.imak-enews.com/shalomequityfund/e_article000030389.cfm.

6. "Forbes.com: Forbes 400 Richest in America 2002." n.d. www.forbes.com. Accessed June 24, 2023; Twenty years later, Winnick had parlayed the sale of his Global Crossing stock into a $2 billion pile. https://labusinessjournal.com/special-editions/wealthiest-angelenos/wealthiest-2022/43-gary-winnick/].

7. Rodes Fishburne and Michael Malone, in an interview with Gordon Moore and Bob Metcalfe titled "Laying Down the Law," *Forbes ASAP* (February 21, 2000). Available from www.forbes.com/asap/2000/0221/096.html.

8. Ibid.

## CHAPTER 2: *HOMO DIGITALIS*, OR "IF YOU KNOW, YOU KNOW"

1. See article by Bill Bonner, "The Digital Man," *Daily Reckoning* (August 15, 2000). Available from www.dailyreckoning.com.

2. You'll recall George W. Bush called himself "the decider" of issues equally as important in those days. See article by Bill Bonner, "The Digital Man," *Daily Reckoning* (August 15, 2000). Available from www.dailyreckoning.com.

3. See article by David Denby, "The Quarter of Living Dangerously: How Greed Becomes a Way of Life," *New Yorker* (April 24, 2000/May 1, 2000).

4. Ibid.

5. See article by Mark Leibovich, "MicroStrategy's CEO Sped to the Brink," *Washington Post* (January 6, 2002): A01.

6. If you're the type to skip ahead to the end of the book, we'll save you some trouble. Saylor reappears later in the story as a champion of Bitcoin.

7. See article by Larissa MacFarquar, "A Beltway Billionaire and His Big Ideas," *New Yorker* (April 3, 2000): 34.

8. See article by Mark Leibovich, "MicroStrategy's CEO Sped to the Brink," *Washington Post* (January 6, 2002): A01.

# CHAPTER 3: DREAMERS AND SCHEMERS

1. "Playboy Interview: Jeff Bezos," *Playboy,* vol. 47, no. 2 (February 1, 2000): 59.
2. See article by Joshua Cooper Ramo, "Jeffrey Preston Bezos; 1999 Person of the Year. The Fast-Moving Internet Economy Has a Jungle of Competitors and Here's the King," *Time* (December 27, 1999): 50.
3. See article by Gretchen Morgenson, "A Year Underachievers Everywhere Can Be Proud Of," *New York Times,* sec. 3 (December 31, 2000): 1.
4. Cuofano, G. (2023). *Is Amazon profitable without AWS?* [online]. FourWeekMBA. Available at: https://fourweekmba.com/is-amazon-profitable-without-aws [Accessed 10 May 2023].
5. Rivera, E. (2022). *William Shatner experience profound grief in space. It was the "overview effect"* [online]. NPR. https://www.npr.org/2022/10/23/1130482740/william-shatner-jeff-bezos-space-travel-overview-effect#:~:text=Tama%2FGetty%20Images-,Star%20Trek%20actor%20William%20Shatner,space%20on%20October%2013%2C%202021.&text=William%20Shatner%20is%20probably%20the%20most%20famous%20astronaut%20in%20the%20world.
6. Eric Beech, "U.S. Government Says It Lost $11.2 Billion on GM Bailout," *Reuters.* Available from https://www.reuters.com/article/us-autos-gm-treasury/u-s-government-says-it-lost-11-2-billion-on-gm-bailout-idUSBREA3T0MR20140430.
7. See article by Bill Bonner, "End of the Gildered Age," *Daily Reckoning* (June 20, 2002). Available from www.dailyreckoning.com.
8. David Shenk, *Data Smog: Surviving the Information Glut* (San Francisco: Harper, 1998).

# CHAPTER 4: IN THE BATH BLOWING BUBBLES

1. See article by John Cassidy, "The Fountainhead," *New Yorker* (April 24, 2000/May 1, 2000): 162.
2. See article by Bob Woodward, "Behind the Boom," *Washington Post* (November 12, 2000): W08.
3. See article by Richard W. Stevenson, "Inside the Head of the Fed," *New York Times,* sec. 3 (November 15, 1998): 1.
4. See article by Joseph N. DiStefano, "Worst of Times for an Internet Apostle," *Philadelphia Inquirer* (December 6, 2000): A01.
5. In 2000, the French government bestowed their highest civilian recognition, the Legion of Honour. Two years later, in 2002, Queen Elizabeth II followed suit, making him an honorary Knight of the British Empire. https://www.britannica.com/biography/Alan-Greenspan.

6. See article by David Hendricks, "Economist Says Looming War with Iraq Has Slowed Rebound," *San Antonio Express-News* (December 12, 2002).

7. See article by Bob Woodward, "In '87 Crash, All Eyes on Greenspan," *Washington Post* (November 13, 2000): A01.

8. See article by Warren Vieth, "Consumer Spending Spree May Be Ending," *Los Angeles Times*, pt. 3 (September 10, 2001): 1.

9. See article by Sam Zuckerman, "People are Borrowing to Maintain Lifestyles," *San Francisco Chronicle* (June 3, 2001): E1.

10. Ibid.

## CHAPTER 5: "FREE MONEY" AND OTHER NEW ERA HALLUCINATIONS

1. See article by Bill Bonner, "End of an Era," *Daily Reckoning* (May 5, 2000). Available from www.dailyreckoning.com.

2. See article by Sharon Reier, "5 Years Later, Greenspan's 'Irrational Exuberance' Alert Rings True," *International Herald Tribune* (December 1, 2001): 13.

3. See article by Joseph N. DiStefano, "Worst of Times for an Internet Apostle," *Philadelphia Inquirer* (December 6, 2000): A01.

4. "S&P/Case-Shiller U.S. National Home Price Index," Stlouisfed.org. Available from https://fred.stlouisfed.org/series/CSUSHPINSA.

5. See article by Thom Calandra, "Defying Naysayers, Tiny Gold Stocks Thrive," *CBS MarketWatch* (March 1, 2002).

6. "Hearing of the Senate Banking, Housing and Urban Affairs Committee," Federal News Service, Inc., Senator Paul Sarbanes chaired (July 16, 2002).

7. See article by Mike Clowes, "Monday Morning: Bad Time for Rise in Personal-Saving Rate," *Investment News* (September 2, 2002): 2.

8. See article by Brendan Murray and Craig Torres, "Not So Green for Greenspan," *Pittsburgh Post-Gazette* (October 27, 2002): D10.

9. Countrywide Financial June 2007 operational data.

10. See article by Bill Bonner, "The Housing Market's Stray Puppy," *Daily Reckoning* (July 18, 2007). Available from http://dailyreckoning.com.

11. See article by Andrew Ross Sorkin, "Lehman Files for Bankruptcy; Merrill Is Sold," *New York Times* (September 14, 2008).

12. See article by Leah Nathans Spiro, "Dream Team," *BusinessWeek* (August 29, 1994): 50.

13. See article "Uncharted Waters," *Upside*, vol. 13, no. 1 (January, 2001): 178–184.

14. See article by Rob Norton, "In Greenspan We Trust," *Fortune* (March 18, 1996): 38.

15. "Hearing of the Senate Banking, Housing and Urban Affairs Committee," Federal News Service, Inc., Senator Paul Sarbanes chaired. (July 16, 2002).

16. See article by Mike Clowes, "Monday Morning: Bad Time for Rise in Personal-Saving Rate," *Investment News* (September 2, 2002): 2.

17. See article by Murray N. Rothbard, "Alan Greenspan: A Minority Report," *Free Market* (August 1987).

18. See article by Reed V. Landberg and Paul George, "Greenspan 'Mess' Risks US Recession, Stiglitz Says," *Bloomberg* (November 16, 2007).

19. For more information on Bernanke's speech, see Chapter 4.

20. See article by John Mauldin, "What the Fed Believes," *Daily Reckoning* (December 3, 2002). Available from www.dailyreckoning.com.

21. Vivien Lee and David Wessel, "Janet Yellen: 10 Quotes on Her Past and the Economy." *Brookings*, 5 Mar. 2018, www.brookings.edu/blog/up-front/2018/03/05/janet-yellen-10-quotes-on-her-past-and-the-economy/. Accessed 26 June 2023.

22. Wikipedia Contributors. "James Tobin." *Wikipedia*, Wikimedia Foundation, 25 Jan. 2019, en.wikipedia.org/wiki/James_Tobin.

23. Vivien Lee and David Wessel, "Janet Yellen: 10 Quotes on Her Past and the Economy." *Brookings*, 5 Mar. 2018, www.brookings.edu/blog/up-front/2018/03/05/janet-yellen-10-quotes-on-her-past-and-the-economy/. Accessed 26 June 2023.

24. Kathryn Watson, "Yellen Admits She Was 'Wrong' about Inflation in 2021 - CBS News." www.cbsnews.com, 1 June 2022, www.cbsnews.com/news/inflation-janet-yellen-wrong-treasury-secretary/. Accessed 26 June 2023. Note: for a more in-depth analysis of the inflationary period 2021–2023 please see our complimentary analysis, *The Demise of the Dollar*.

# CHAPTER 6: A THEORY OF MORAL HAZARDS

1. Paul Krugman, "The Hangover Theory," *Slate* (December 4, 1998). Available from http://slate.msn.com/?querytext=krugman+hangover+theory&id=3944&action=fulltext.

2. Paul Krugman, "Setting Sun," *Slate* (June 11, 1998).

3. Ibid.

4. Jeffrey Tucker, "Mr. Moral Hazard," *Free Market,* vol. 16, no. 12 (December 1998). Available from www.mises.org/freemarket_detail.asp?control=48.

5. See article by Bill Bonner, "The Perils of Success," *Daily Reckoning* (January 13, 2003). Available from www.dailyreckoning.com.

6. Alan Greenspan, "Remarks by Chairman Alan Greenspan," remarks before the Economic Club of New York on the Federal Reserve Board's website (December 19, 2002). Available from www.federalreserve.gov/boarddocs/speeches/2002/ 20021219/.

7. See article by Martin T. Sosnoff, "Blame Greenspan," *Forbes* (August 7, 2007).
8. See article by Greg Ip and Jon E. Hilsenrath, "How Credit Got So Easy and Why It's Tightening," *Wall Street Journal* (August 8, 2007).

## CHAPTER 7: FIRST IT GIVETH. . .

1. See article "Bush Signs Economic Stimulus Package," Associated Press (February 13, 2008).
2. See article by Brian Swint and Jennifer Ryan, "King, BOE Face 'Crisis of Confidence' After Rescue," *Bloomberg* (September 17, 2007).
3. Remarks by Governor Ben S. Bernanke at the Sandridge Lecture, Virginia Association of Economics, Richmond, Virginia. March 10, 2005. www .federalreserve.gov/boarddocs/speeches/2005/200503102/default.htm.
4. Global Financial Stability Report, April 2006, Chapter 2: The Influence on Credit Derivative and Structured Credit Markets on Financial Stability.
5. Henry Paulson, interview on CNBC Television, March 13, 2007.
6. Ben Bernanke, Semiannual Monetary Policy Report to .the Congress Before the Committee on Financial Services, U.S. House of Representatives. July 19, 2007.

## CHAPTER 8: JOHN LAW AND THE ORIGINS OF A BAD IDEA

1. Antoin E. Murphy, *John Law: Economic Theorist and Policymaker* (Oxford, UK: Clarendon Press, 1997).
2. Paul Strathern, *Dr. Strangelove's Game* (London: Penguin Books, 2001).
3. Charles Mackay, "The Mississippi Scheme," *Extraordinary Popular Delusions and the Madness of Crowds* (London: Wordsworth Editions, 1995).
4. Marc Faber, *Tomorrow's Gold* (CLSA, 2002).
5. See article by Bill Bonner, "A Freer Place?" *Daily Reckoning* (May 31, 2001). Available from www.dailyreckoning.com.
6. Quote from Ferdinand Lips' lecture "Why Gold-Backed Currencies Help Prevent Wars," delivered at the Humanitarianism at the Crossroads Congress in Feldkirch, Austria (August 30–September 1, 2002).
7. See article by Dan Denning, "Life After the Credit Depression," *Daily Reckoning—Australian Edition* (January 9, 2009). Available at http:// dailyreckoning.com/au.

# CHAPTER 9: THE DIGITAL AGE OF CROWDS

1. See article by Bill Bonner, "Traditional Values," *Daily Reckoning* (June 10, 2002). Available from www.dailyreckoning.com.
2. Ibid.
3. Alfred N. Whitehead and Bertrand Russell, *Principia Mathematica* (New York: Cambridge University Press, 1927).
4. The New Liberty Standard Exchange recorded the first exchange of Bitcoin for dollars in late 2009. Users on the BitcoinTalk forum traded 5,050 bitcoins for $5.02 via PayPal, making the first price mediated through an exchange a bargain basement price of $0.00099 per bitcoin.
5. "59 Inspirational Quotes on Bitcoin & Freedom (DIGITAL GOLD)." *Gracious Quotes,* 16 Apr. 2020, graciousquotes.com/bitcoin-quotes. Accessed 24 June 2023.
6. Christiaan Hetzner, "Musk Accused of Insider Trading (Again) to Rake in $124M from Dogecoin Sales." *Fortune,* fortune.com/2023/06/02/elon-musk-lawsuit-dogecoin-insider-trading-shiba-inu-twitter-logo. Accessed 24 June 2023.
7. Ari Redbord, "Tom Brady and Other A-Listers Sued for Fumbling FTX Endorsements." *Forbes,* www.forbes.com/sites/ariredbord/2023/02/01/tom-brady-and-other-a-listers-fumble-ftx-endorsements-but-will-they-be-held-liable/?sh=5f3569b87d8c. Accessed 24 June 2023.
8. Ava Benny-Morrison and Annie Massa, "From Math Camp to Handcuffs: FTX's Downfall Was an Arc of Brotherhood and Betrayal." Bloomberg.com, 16 Feb. 2023, www.bloomberg.com/news/features/2023-02-16/sam-bankman-fried-s-old-friend-co-founder-gary-wang-is-key-to-case-against-ftx. Accessed 24 June 2023.

# CHAPTER 10: THE CRACK-UP BOOM

1. See article by James K. Glassman, "Stocks Won't Fall Forever," *Washington Post* (January 6, 2002): H01.
2. See article by Bill Bonner, "Great Expectations," *Daily Reckoning* (January 9, 2003). Available from www.dailyreckoning.com.
3. Ludwig von Mises, *Human Action: A Treatise on Economics* (Laissez Faire Books; 4th Rev. Edition, January 9, 2008).
4. Ibid.
5. Gustave Le Bon, *The Crowd* (Mineola, NY: Dover Publications, 2002).
6. Robert A. Peterson, "A Tale of Two Revolutions," *Advocates for Self -Government's Freeman Archives* (August 1989). Available from www.self-gov.org/freeman/8908pete.html.
7. Ibid.

8. Ibid.

9. See article by Bill Bonner, "The Age of Chic," *Daily Reckoning* (June 27, 2002). Available from www.dailyreckoning.com.

10. See article "The Unfinished Recession," *The Economist* (September 28, 2002).

11. See article by Eric Wing, "Edelman Resigns GU Post over Students SEC Charges," *Washington Business Journal* (February 26, 2001). https://www .bizjournals.com/washington/stories/2001/02/26/newscolumn2.html.

12. *American Economic Review* (May 1978).

13. Lindsay McGuire, *The Problem with Paper: Statistics That Will Blow Your Mind*, formstack.com (January 13, 2022). https://www.formstack.com/ resources/blog-paper-statistics#:~:text=The%20Impact%20of%20 Paper%20in%20the%20U.S.&text=U.S%20offices%20use%2012.1%20 trillion,of%20office%20paper%20per%20year.

14. Martin Placek, "United States Postal Service's Total Mail Volume from 2004 to 2022." *Statista* (November 21, 2022). https://www.statista.com/ statistics/320234/mail-volume-of-the-usps/.

15. David Shenk, *Data Smog: Surviving the Information Glut* (San Francisco: Harper, 1998).

16. See article by Kurt Richebächer, "Bubble Aftermath," *Daily Reckoning* (November 13, 2002). Available from www.dailyreckoning.com.

17. See article "More Answers for Japan," *Investor's Business Daily* (September 11, 1998): A6.

18. See article by Paul Krugman, "Japan Heads for the Edge," *Financial Times* (January 20, 1999): 18.

19. See article by Justin Fox, "Saint Jack on the Attack," *Fortune* (January 20, 2003): 112.

20. See a research report by Richard Koo, "The Age of Balance Sheet Recessions: What Post-2008 U.S., Europe and China Can Learn from Japan 1990–2005," Nomura Research Institute (March 2009).

21. See article by Francesco Guerra and Aline van Duyn, "Wall Street Jobs Axe Threatens 70,000," *Financial Times* (November 9, 2008).

22. See article by Sam Mamudi, "Lehman Folds With Record $613 Debt," *MarketWatch* (September 15, 2008).

23. See AP article, "Bank of America to Acquire Countrywide," Associated Press (January 11, 2008).

24. See article by Tami Luhby, "Countrywide's Mozilo Accused of Fraud," CNNMoney.com (June 4, 2009).

25. See article by Vikas Bajaj, "Lax Lending Standards Led to IndyMa's Downfall," *New York Times* ( July 29, 2008).

26. See article by John Letzig, "WaMu Seized, Sold to JP Morgan Chase," MarketWatch (September 26, 2008).

27. See article by Neil King Jr. and Sharon Terlep, "GM Collapses into Government's Arms," *Wall Street Journal* (June 2, 2009).

28. See article by David E. Sanger, Jeff Zeleny, and Bill Vlasic, "G.M. to Seek Bankruptcy and a New Start," *New York Times* (May 31, 2009).
29. See article by Nick Sabloff, "Jim Cramer Declares the Depression 'Over,'" *Huffington Post* (April 4, 2009).
30. See article by Nouriel Roubini, "Light at the End of the Tunnel," *Forbes* (April 2, 2009).
31. See article by Edmund L. Andrews, "Bernanke Sees Hopeful Signs, but No Quick Recovery," *New York Times* (May 5, 2009).
32. Ibid.
33. See article by Sean Lengell, "Summers Sees End to Free Fall," *Washington Times* (April 27, 2009).
34. See article by Jack Willoughby, "Back in the Pool," *Barron's* (April 28, 2009).
35. See article by Takashi Nakamichi, "Japan Sets $100 Billion Stimulus Plan," *Wall Street Journal* (April 6, 2009).
36. Ibid.
37. See article by Michael Mackenzie, "Rising Treasury Yields Threaten to Stifle US Economic Recovery," *Financial Times* (May 28, 2009).
38. See article by Dexter Roberts, "China Worried After Lending 'Huge Amount' to US," *BusinessWeek* (March 13, 2009).
39. See article by Augusta Chronicle Editorial Staff, "No Laughing Matter," *Augusta Chronicle* (June 3, 2009).
40. See C-SPAN interview with Barack Obama (May 23, 2009).

# INDEX

Page numbers followed by *f* and *t* indicate figures and tables, respectively.